F R A M E W O R K S

International Marketing

Third Edition

L. S. Walsh
MA, MBA, FCIM, DipM, FIEx

D0994543

FINANCIAL TIMES
PITMAN PUBLISHING

FINANCIAL TIMES MANAGEMENT
128 Long Acre, London WC2E 9AN
Tel: +44 (0)171 447 2000
Fax: +44 (0)171 240 5771
Website: www.ftmanagement.com

A Division of Financial Times Professional Limited

First published in Great Britain in 1978
Second edition 1981
Third edition 1993

© Longman Group UK Limited 1993

ISBN 0 273 63417 8

British Library Cataloguing in Publication Data
A CIP catalogue record for this book can be obtained from the British Library.

10 9 8 7

Printed and bound in Great Britain by Bell and Bain Ltd, Glasgow

The Publishers' policy is to use paper manufactured from sustainable forests.

Contents

Preface

In 1978, when this book first appeared, it was possible to bemoan the comparative dearth of international marketing textbooks both in the UK and in the USA. No longer. The international marketer and the student are now well served by a whole range of textbooks, most of which have become available over the last fifteen years. This must surely reflect an upsurge in interest in the subject, but it is nevertheless with agreeable surprise that the author of this book has seen its sales forge ahead. Perhaps first of all, therefore, a word of thanks is due to the Chartered Institute of Marketing, the CAM Foundation and the Institute of Export, all of whom continue to recommend the book as an approved text, to those lecturers who include it in their reading lists, and to those international marketers and students who buy it.

In this edition the original text has been entirely revised and updated, and the number of illustrative examples has been considerably increased. Much greater attention has been paid to the international marketing environment, with additional chapters on the economic, cultural and social, political and legal, and financial background. International marketing planning and market selection have now been given chapters to themselves; a new chapter is devoted to the European Community, and the chapter on the former USSR now relates to Russia alone. Three new case studies have been included.

The objectives remain unchanged: the book is concerned with international marketing, and as far as possible only with international marketing; that is, with those aspects of marketing management that are of special importance in an international context, from indirect and direct export on the one hand to the marketing operations of the multinational company on the other. The more general aspects of marketing are avoided, except for a brief explanatory introduction to those chapters where otherwise readers unfamiliar with marketing theory might find themselves at a disadvantage. *International Marketing* is thus likely to be of greatest interest to the domestic marketing executive taking over international responsibilities for the first time or to the student who already has a grasp of basic marketing techniques.

Similarly, the aim is still to present the essential principles of international marketing condensed into the form of study notes for ease of comprehension and retention. With this in mind, examples have been kept separate from the main text, diagrams illustrate chapter content where this is thought helpful, and lengthy items such as agency or licensing agreements are presented in tabular format as separate checklists.

Paradoxically, any book concerned with international marketing must have a national orientation if it is to deal in much more than generalities; even the most globally minded of multinational companies has a home base somewhere in the world. This book is written quite deliberately from the viewpoint of the UK-based international marketer, to whom, it is hoped, it will be of real practical value in that most difficult of tasks, the identification of suitable international opportunities and their transformation into profitable results.

International Marketing draws extensively on the author's experience as an export manager and, subsequently, an international marketing consultant. But experience alone is never enough. A debt is owed, and is here gratefully acknowledged, to a variety of textbooks and journals (most of which are mentioned in the bibliography or acknowledgements) and, inevitably of course, to a whole range of the ever more valuable publications of the Overseas Trade Services of the Department of Trade and Industry.

May 1993

LSW

Acknowledgements

The author would like to record his grateful thanks to those who contributed to the preparation of all three editions of *International Marketing* or who so readily gave permission for the publication of extracts from their work.

The sources of the illustrative examples are given at the foot of each example. In this context particular mention must be made of:

- Mr Richard Hobbs of the Centre for International Briefing, who prepared Tables 3.1 and 29.1 specially for this third edition;
- Mr Robin Godfrey of the Association of British Chambers of Commerce, who checked through Table 8.6;
- Mr Ian McMeeking and Ms Fabienne Brazzill of Employment Conditions Abroad Ltd, who prepared the example in 23:8;
- Mr Carl David of the Export Credits Guarantee Department, who checked and improved upon the ECGD sections in Chapters 5 and 6.

Where so indicated, questions from past examination papers are reproduced by kind permission of the Chartered Institute of Marketing (CIM), the CAM Foundation and the Institute of Export (IEx).

Mr John Soper, formerly International Marketing Director of Letraset International, Mr Jerry Waters, Planning and Development Manager of Esselte Letraset, and Mr Norman Burden, formerly Director of Group Marketing at CompAir, all read through their relevant cases and made many valuable suggestions for improvement. To them, and to three directors of Kwikpak, the author is especially grateful.

Definitions of marketing terms are usually identified in the text with the name of the appropriate author, further details being given in the Bibliography. In those few cases where a definition is given in inverted commas but without further attribution the source is the American Marketing Association's *Glossary of Marketing Terms*.

Part one

What is international marketing?

1

The international marketing concept

1. Marketing

As marketing has developed as a technique, numerous definitions have been offered.

The UK Chartered Institute of Marketing defines marketing as 'the management process responsible for identifying, anticipating and satisfying customer requirements profitably.'

The American Marketing Association's definition, agreed in 1985, is 'the process of planning and executing the conception, pricing, promotion and distribution of ideas, goods and services to create exchanges that satisfy individual and organisational objectives.' In particular, this definition emphasises that marketing is of value to non-profit organisations such as governments, as well as to commercial companies.

Another useful definition suggests that marketing is a matching process, aimed at matching the skills and resources of an individual or organisation with those opportunities in the market-place that may realistically be exploited so as to achieve profit or other objectives.

Peter Drucker long ago suggested that marketing is so basic that it cannot be considered a separate function. 'It is the whole business seen ... from the customer's point of view.'

2. The essentials of marketing

Whatever the formal definition, it is generally accepted that marketing requires:

(a) a genuine understanding of and attention to customers' needs and wants (usually specific target segment(s) are selected);
(b) satisfaction of those needs and wants, while at the same time ensuring the achievement of profit or other objectives;
(c) orientation of the whole organisation towards the customer satisfaction process.

3. Marketing management and the marketing mix

Marketing management consists of the planning, organisation, implementation and control of marketing activities. To this end, marketing management is given decision-making authority over:

(a) the planning and development of products or services that customers require;

(b) the distribution of products through appropriate channels (wholesalers and retailers, for example);
(c) the establishment of prices that offer value to customers and a satisfactory margin to the supplier;
(d) promotion of the products or services, including advertising, sales promotion, public relations and personal selling.

These four groups of activities, often referred to as product, place, price and promotion, constitute the marketing mix. They include, in summary, all the elements of marketing decision-making under the control of the supplying organisation: the 'controllables' (Fig. 1.1).

The value of this marketing mix concept is that it helps to ensure that all aspects of marketing management, including those that may sometimes appear to be less than urgent, such as new product development, are given their due weight and consideration. In recent years, suggestions have been put forward that other aspects of marketing should be similarly highlighted: some, for instance, would single out 'people' and public relations. This book retains the traditional four aspects; people and public relations, for instance, are covered as appropriate under the four main headings.

4.   The marketing environment

The marketer must also take into account environmental factors which will significantly affect the degree of success achieved but over which there can be little or no control: the 'uncontrollables'. These include, for example, the economic, financial, cultural, social, political and legal environments, technological developments and competitor activity.

The challenge for marketing management is to devise a marketing mix that will enable the organisation to adapt to its environment in such a way that profit and other objectives are achieved.

5.   The international marketing environment

The task of international marketing management is, similarly, to tailor the marketing mix to the environment, but in this case the environment is vastly more diverse, with many more nations to be considered. Further, though environmental differences may be readily discerned *within* any one nation, the differences *between* nations are, as a rule, much more marked.

These more marked differences do not imply any fundamental change in marketing as a technique; there still remains a basic similarity of human motivation and economic practice throughout the world. The *principles* of marketing are of universal application.

International environmental differences, however, do require a change of emphasis. Certain aspects of marketing that are largely irrelevant in a purely national context, such as countertrade (6:6) achieve real significance. Other aspects require, in international trade, a far more detailed knowledge than might be necessary within any one nation. Examples are licensing (15:2), joint ventures (15) and the use of agents in the selling function (24). It is with

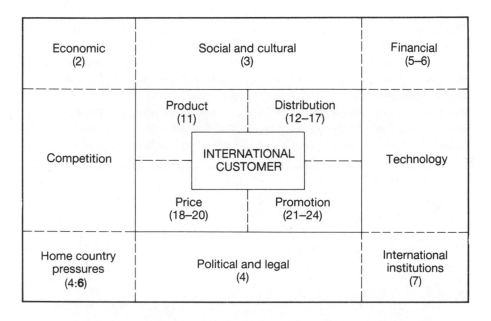

Figure 1.1 *The international marketing environment and the marketing mix.*

NOTES:

(a) The eight outer areas summarise the principal aspects of the international marketing environment, the 'uncontrollables' to which the organisation and its marketing mix must adapt.

(b) The four inner areas represent the four main categories of the marketing mix, the tools available to marketing management, the 'controllables'.

(c) The figures in brackets indicate the chapters in which the international environment and marketing mix are further discussed.

these special international aspects of marketing, and as far as possible only with these aspects, that this book is concerned.

The environmental background to international marketing decisions is shown diagrammatically in Fig. 1.1 and discussed in more detail in Part two of this book.

6.   Definition of international marketing

The term 'international marketing' may be regarded as a shorthand expression for the special international aspects of marketing.

A more formal definition of international marketing might be:

(a) the marketing of goods, services or ideas across national boundaries; and
(b) the marketing operations of an organisation that sells or produces within a given country when:

(*i*)   that organisation is part of, or associated with, an enterprise which also operates in other countries; and

(*ii*)   there is some degree of control of, or influence on, that organisation's marketing activities from outside the country in which it sells and/or produces.

It is in this sense that the expression 'international marketing' is used throughout this book. It covers the whole gamut of international marketing operations, from indirect export on the one hand to the marketing operations of multinational companies on the other.

7.   The multinational company

The term 'multinational company' (MNC) is loosely used and has been variously defined. One definition put forward by James C. Baker is:

a company which has a direct investment base in several countries; which generally derives from 20% to 50% or more of its net profits from foreign operations; and whose management makes policy decisions based on the alternatives available anywhere in the world.

A UN estimate suggests that, world-wide, more than 9,000 firms fall within this definition. Typically an MNC will be a large and powerful corporation with sales amounting to hundreds of millions of dollars, a technological lead and developed marketing and other special skills.

Multinational companies are further discussed in 26:**10**.

8.   The major international marketing decisions

When a company contemplates marketing abroad, or extending existing international marketing activities, management faces five major decisions:

(a) *the international marketing decision:* the initial and fundamental decision on whether or not to market or expand abroad;
(b) *the market selection decision:* the determination of which market(s) to enter;

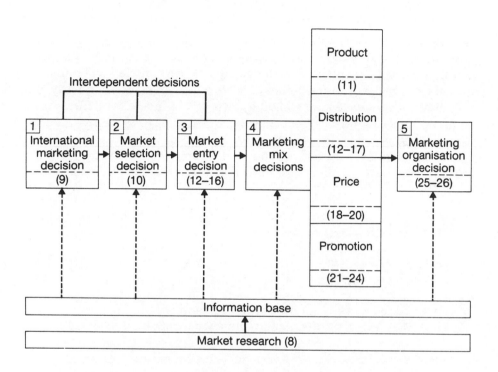

Figure 1.2 *International marketing: the five major decisions.*

NOTE: Numbers in brackets refer to chapters.

(c) *the market entry decision:* the determination of the most appropriate method of entry into those markets (for example, direct export, licensing or manufacture abroad);

(d) *the marketing mix decision:* planning a marketing mix appropriate to the market environment;

(e) *the organisation decision:* preparation of an overall marketing plan and determination of the organisation structure most appropriate to its implementation.

All these decisions must be taken on an informed basis and market research will often be required.

The first three decisions are, of course, interdependent. For instance, the various methods of market entry open to a company in respect of a given country, and the amount of investment and risk each implies, will influence the company's decision on whether or not to enter that market. Similarly, the possibility of entering a potentially highly profitable market will influence a company's decision on whether to market abroad at all. However, for the sake of simplicity, each decision is separately considered.

The five major decisions are shown diagrammatically in Fig. 1.2. They are covered, together with market research, in Part three of this book.

Progress test 1

1. 'There is no fundamental difference between international marketing and domestic marketing.' Discuss. *(CIM)*

2. What are the main environmental considerations in international marketing? How do they affect international marketing activity? *(CIM)*

3. 'International marketing is simply the latest OK phrase for export marketing, the export manager's latest bid for prestige.' Refute this suggestion.

4. It has recently been said that the term multinational is used to describe so many different organisations that it is virtually meaningless. Comment on this proposition. *(CIM)*

5. 'Our justification for a separate treatment (of international marketing) lies not in propounding any new principles. The steps, concepts and techniques for effective marketing management are the same. The justification lies in the fact that differences between nations are typically more striking than regional differences within one country' (Philip Kotler). Expand on this statement and give specific examples in its support.

6. What do you understand by the term 'marketing mix'? Describe how you would define the marketing mix for a product of your choice. *(IEx)*

7. **(a)** Explain the term 'marketing mix'.
(b) What criteria would determine your decision to change a 'winning' marketing mix when entering a new market? *(IEx)*

8. Why study international marketing?

9. What are the key decisions facing the management of a company that is planning to market its products abroad for the first time?

Part two

The international marketing environment

2

The economic environment

1. Free trade

Free trade between nations permits international specialisation; it also enables efficient firms to increase output to levels far greater than would be possible if sales were limited to their own domestic markets, thus permitting significant economies of scale. The result is a vast increase in goods and services of all kinds. Competition increases, prices of goods in importing countries fall, while profits increase in the exporting country.

The benefits of free trade are not, however, universal. Manufacturers in importing countries lose business; unemployment may rise as a result.

The beneficiaries in the importing country are individual consumers dispersed throughout the country; their gain from any particular imported good is usually only a small part of its total purchase price. In contrast, damage to the manufacturers of that good in the importing country tends to be concentrated on a few companies and is often serious in its effects. As a result, governments, though convinced in principle of the desirability of free trade, often resist suggestions of reductions in barriers to trade.

This chapter looks at some of the barriers to free trade that have been erected over the years by governments, and at major economic associations that have been established with a view to encouraging free trade within certain regions.

2. Tariffs

Tariffs are taxes imposed on goods moving across national boundaries. They may be imposed on imports, exports, or goods in transit through one country on the way to another. The import tariff, or duty, is of most concern to the international marketer.

Import duties include:

(a) *ad valorem duties*, payable as a percentage of the value of the goods;
(b) *specific duties*, payable according to weight, volume or other unit of measurement;
(c) *countervailing duties*, imposed on imports that benefit from a subsidy paid by the government of the exporting country;
(d) *anti-dumping duties* (19:5).

Import duties have a dual effect: they tend to raise the price of the imported good and, therefore, protect domestic manufacturers from competition; at the same time they generate revenue for the government that imposes them.

Table 2.1 Some non-tariff barriers

Non-tariff barrier	Definition or references to definitions in this or other chapters
Quotas	4
Embargoes	4:6
Voluntary export restrictions	5
Import licences	6
Exchange control	6
Differential exchange rates	6
Boycotts	4:6
Import deposits	Importers required to deposit a proportion of the value of the goods well before the date of importation.
Import classification	Arbitrary classification of an imported product into a high-duty category.
Import valuation	Arbitrary valuation of imported products in excess of invoice value.
Customs clearance delays	Deliberate delays in customs administration.
Documentation charges	Excessive charges for import-related documents such as consular invoices.
Technical standards, health and safety regulations, packaging and labelling regulations	Regulations that are necessary and legitimate in themselves but which can be applied in a discriminatory manner to imports.
Government monopoly of import trade	State trading as exemplified by centrally planned economies.
Government subsidies	Subsidies to domestic industries that compete with imported products.
Biased public purchasing	Procurement policies favouring domestic rather than imported goods, such as the US 'Buy American' Act.

Usually duties are imposed for the purpose of protecting domestic manufacturers, but the economic effect is not always what is intended. For instance, in the case of products that are expensive to store, such as agricultural commodities, foreign sellers may lower their prices to remain competitive. Domestic producers will then gain little or no protection, though the government gains greater revenue from import duty.

3. Non-tariff barriers

Apart from tariffs, a whole arsenal of barriers to trade has been devised over the years. Most of them are listed and defined in Table 2.1; the most important are commented on below.

4. Quotas

Quotas are physical limits on the quantity of goods that may be imported into a country. They are a much surer means of protecting domestic industries. The domestic consumers, however, find their product choices limited. Prices tend to increase, since the exporter can often fill his quota without competing on price; in any case the goods imported within the quota tend to be the more expensive models carrying the highest profit margins.

5. Voluntary export restrictions

Voluntary export restrictions are agreements made by exporters in one country to limit their sales to another. The agreements are usually subject to a time limit. The word 'voluntary' is something of a euphemism: there is often an implied threat from the importing country that, if a voluntary agreement is not entered into, stronger measures will be taken.

6. Exchange control and import licences

Exchange control implies a government monopoly of all dealings in foreign exchange. A national company earning foreign exchange is required to sell it to a control agency, usually the central bank. In turn, a company wishing to import goods must apply to buy its foreign exchange from the control agency; the application is decided in the light of government priorities, which generally favour the importation of capital goods and discriminate against most consumer goods. Successful applicants receive an import licence.

Another approach to exchange control is a system of differential exchange rates, by which importers are required to buy foreign currency at rates less favourable than those set for other purposes, such as tourism.

In some countries, foreign exchange is auctioned. In Nigeria, for instance, a fortnightly Dutch auction is conducted by the Central Bank. Authorised dealers (banks appointed by the Ministry of Finance) participating in these auctions base their bids on foreign exchange applications submitted by Nigerian businesses, who must show proof of a commercial or approved capital transaction. The auction system ensures that the rate of exchange is determined by market forces; the rate set by the bidding becomes the base rate for authorised dealers for the two weeks following each auction.

7.   International trade cooperation and tariff reduction

Systematic attempts at tariff reductions and the removal of trade barriers began after the Second World War when a number of major trading nations established the General Agreement on Tariffs and Trade (GATT), agreeing:

(a) to adopt as their objective continuing reductions in the barriers to international trade;
(b) not to impose tariffs that discriminated between GATT member nations;
(c) not to increase tariffs;
(d) not to provide export subsidies.

See also 7:**5.**

8.   Regional trade cooperation

Countries have also begun to group together on a regional basis with the aim of reducing tariffs and other protectionist systems and of encouraging economic integration.

Four main types of integration can be identified: the free trade area, the customs union, the common market and the economic and monetary union.

9.   The free trade area

Within a free trade area member nations remove all trade barriers between themselves, but each nation retains its own trade barriers with non-member countries. The best-known example is the European Free Trade Association (EFTA).

10. The customs union

A customs union is similar to a free trade area except that all member nations adopt a common external tariff against non-member countries. Individual member states thus lose their right to establish separate trade agreements with non-member states. The Benelux countries formed in the early 1920s a customs union that was subsequently incorporated within the European Community.

11. The common market

A common market has all the characteristics of a customs union, but in addition the free flow of resources (people and capital) between member states is encouraged. The European Community is the most successful example of a common market.

12. The economic union

A true economic union requires economic convergence: economic, fiscal

Table 2.2 Major regional economic associations

Associations	*Member countries*
ANCOM: Andean Common Market	Bolivia, Colombia, Ecuador, Peru, Venezuela
ASEAN: Association of South-East Asian Nations	Brunei, Indonesia, Malaysia, Philippines, Singapore, Thailand
CACM: Central American Common Market	Costa Rica, El Salvador, Guatemala, Honduras, Nicaragua
CARICOM: Caribbean Community	Antigua, Bahamas, Barbados, Belize, Guyana, Jamaica, Trinidad-Tobago and other Caribbean islands
ECOWAS: Economic Community of West African States	Benin, Burkina Faso, Cape Verde, Gambia, Ghana, Guinea, Guinea-Bissau, Ivory Coast, Liberia, Mali, Mauritania, Niger, Nigeria, Senegal, Sierra Leone, Togo
EC: European Community EU: European Union (*see* **28:21**)	Austria, Belgium, Denmark, Finland, France, Germany, Greece, Ireland, Italy, Luxembourg, Netherlands, Portugal, Spain, Sweden, United Kingdom
EEA: European Economic Area (remaining members - *see* **28:3**)	Iceland, Liechtenstein, Norway
EFTA: European Free Trade Association (remaining member – *see* **28:3**)	Switzerland
LAIA: Latin-American Integration Association	Argentina, Bolivia, Brazil, Chile, Colombia, Ecuador, Mexico, Paraguay, Peru, Uruguay, Venezuela
NAFTA: North American Free Trade Area	Canada, Mexico, USA

Notes:
1. In addition to the member countries shown, some regional associations permit associate membership.
2. The EC has special trading agreements with many former British and French colonial territories, the African, Caribbean and Pacific (ACP) countries.
3. The extent to which the Council for Mutual Economics Assistance (CMEA or Comecon) encouraged free trade has always been debatable, given that it consisted of centrally planned economies whose foreign trade was handled by state trading organisations. It is now omitted entirely from this table.

and monetary policies and government expenditure must be harmonised, and a system of fixed exchange rates or a common currency must be introduced. Clearly the formation of a full economic union requires the surrender of a large measure of national sovereignty to a supranational body. Such a union is only a short step away from political unification.

The Exchange Rate Mechanism and the Maastricht Treaty (28: 20) will take the EC a long way along the road to full economic union.

13. Principal regional economic associations

Table 2.2 lists the more important of the world's regional economic associations. The EC is discussed more fully in Chapter 28.

Progress test 2

1. Distinguish between a free trade area, a customs union, a common market and an economic union.

2. Whatever one's criticisms, the EC is undeniably the most successful of the regional economic associations that have come into being since the Second World War. Why do you think this is so? In your opinion, will NAFTA prove equally successful?

3. 'Economic integration among developing countries is not likely to yield big welfare gains.' Why not?

4. Why is free trade desirable?

5. Discuss the impact of tariffs on import levels and on government revenue.

6. As tariff barriers have fallen world-wide, non-tariff barriers have proliferated. Which kinds of non-tariff barrier are especially likely to be introduced between nations in regional economic associations?

7. Given that, under present GATT rules, the common external tariff of a regional economic association may be set at the average of the tariffs obtaining in member countries before the association was formed, does *regional* integration increase *global* economic welfare?

3

The cultural and social environment

1. Culture and society

At a superficial level practically everyone understands the concept of culture, though an agreed and succinct definition seems to have eluded anthropologists. It seems generally agreed, however, that culture consists of behavioural traits that are:

(a) learned and not innate, but are nevertheless transmitted from one generation to the next;
(b) shared by a group of people, a society.

2. Culture, society and marketing

Marketing is concerned with the satisfaction of human needs and wants (1:2). In order to satisfy these needs and wants and then to influence the customer, the marketer must first of all understand them. They are not, clearly, merely a function of income: two individuals with the same income may well manifest very different patterns of consumption. These differences can only be explained by factors other than income, including the cultural environment – hence the application of the behavioural sciences to marketing and the development of the techniques of consumer and industrial buyer behaviour.

Cultural and social factors are thus of relevance in any marketing context, domestic or international. In the domestic market, however, the marketer starts with an advantage: first-hand acquaintance with the local culture(s). In international marketing there are a whole range of complex cultures of which the marketer may have no prior knowledge whatever. The marketer must, in order to avoid serious error, investigate at least the salient aspects of the culture of the countries in which he or she intends to operate.

George P. Murdock listed more than 70 aspects of culture that are to be found in all societies; these he called 'cultural universals'. Most, if not all, of these universals are in some way of interest to marketers. This chapter, however, considers only those that might be regarded as being of special importance to international marketing: family and other aspects of social organisation, religion, education and language.

For consideration of another of Murdock's universals, law, as a manifestation of culture in the USA, see 32:**2**, **6** and **12**.

3.   Social organisation

The family is an important purchasing group in any society. In the UK, marketers are accustomed either to the so-called nuclear family, with father, mother and children all living together under one roof, or, increasingly as society changes, the single-parent family. In other countries the key unit is the extended family, with three or four generations all in the same house.

Socio-economic groupings are a tried and tested tool in marketing. In the UK the National Readership Surveys (NRS) groupings (A,B,C1,C2,D,E) are familiar to all followers of political polls. Neither these nor alternative UK groupings can be transplanted abroad.

For the USA, for instance, Warner put forward a six-category classification: upper upper class, lower upper, upper middle, lower middle, upper lower and lower lower. The categories bear no relation to the six UK NRS categories. Class A in the UK, for instance, approximately 3 per cent of the population, consists of the 'higher managerial, professional or administrative' class; the US equivalent, upper upper, also 3 per cent of the population, is defined as 'the social élite of society', with 'inherited wealth from socially prominent families the key to admission'. The US high-income professionals are relegated to the lower upper class, described by Warner as those 'who have earned their position rather than inherited it', the 'nouveaux riches'.

In contrast, in Soviet Russia it would have been hard to find useful socio-economic groupings beyond white-collar worker, blue-collar worker and collective farm worker.

Social organisation may also affect *industrial* purchase decisions, as, for example, in the case of the formal 'ringi' group decision-making process in Japanese companies (Fig. 3.1).

4.   Religion

Religious customs are a major factor in marketing. The most obvious example, perhaps, is the Christian tradition of present-giving at Christmas, yet even in this simple matter pitfalls lie in wait for the international marketer: in some Christian countries the traditional exchange of presents takes place not on Christmas Day but on other days in December or early January.

The impact of religion on marketing becomes most evident in the case of Islam. Islamic laws, based on the Koran, provide guidance for a whole range of human activities, including economic activity (Table 3.1).

5.   Education

Educational levels are of importance to the international marketer from two main standpoints: the economic potential of the youth market and, in developing countries, the level of literacy.

In most West European countries full-time schooling is compulsory to age 16. In the UK, most 16-year-olds then take a job in industry, receiving on-the-job training at the most, and their wages may be as high as 80 per cent of those of a trained adult in the same job. In Germany, in contrast, a school

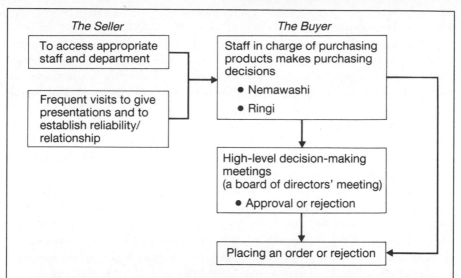

The purchasing decision-makers in Japanese companies are staff members in charge of purchasing products, or all staff members attending product selection meetings. Higher level managerial or senior staff in production, engineering and/or R&D departments are responsible for purchasing technologically advanced or new products. The purchasing department may be involved directly or indirectly from the early or later stages in the decision-making process. If the commitment is long term, large scale and/or crucial, then the company's final decisions concerning whether or not to purchase products are sometimes made at director meetings. This business practice stems from the fact that Japan is a consensus-oriented society.

It is extremely difficult to find out who is the key decision-maker concerning the purchase of products in companies, especially when they are large and have various divisions and departments. This is true even when Japanese suppliers begin selling their products to potential buyers with whom they have had no business relations in the past. Even if the potential buyers recognise the features and benefits of using the suppliers' products, the staff, regardless of their position in the company, will not be able to make final decisions at their own discretion. Prompt answers will always be avoided and the staff will probably say, 'We will discuss the matter within our company,' thereby not committing to when the company will make a final decision.

When the staff in charge of buying a product perceive it will be useful and beneficial to the company, they utilise **group decision- making(ringi)** in order to obtain approval from people at different levels within the company. The ringi system is often used in Japan, particularly in large companies. A document is circulated to managers in all departments relevant to the items to be purchased. An important decision is made when these managers place their stamp (**Banko**) of approval on the document. Thus, the responsibility for the decision is shared. The system is frequently used for critical purchasing decisions. If the purchase of the product is an important issue to the company's present and future business plans, a board of directors' meeting is convened.

Prior to group approval on purchasing decisions many buyers will have informal individual meetings to gain support for the product they wish to purchase (**nemawashi**). Nemawashi is an extremely important and frequently used tactic. If nemawashi is successful, the product in question is quickly and smoothly approved for purchasing in high-level decision-making meetings.

Figure 3.1 *Opening a new account with a Japanese company—the ringi system*
(Source: *Industrial Goods Distribution in Japan*, 2nd edn, Dodwell Marketing Consultants, Tokyo. Copies available in UK from Proplan, Amersham, Bucks.)

leaver will usually enter a formal apprenticeship, government-approved and supervised, which typically will continue for three years and involve continuing part-time education. These apprentices might earn in their first year a quarter as much as a fully-trained craftsman. In the USA the contrast is even more marked: although compulsory schooling ends at age 16, most students stay on at school until they are 18. About half then go on to four-year first-degree courses of some kind, though the drop-out rate during the four years is by UK standards very high.

In most industrialised countries, literacy levels are close to 100 per cent; the whole range of communications media is open to the marketer. In developing countries literacy rates can be as low as 25 per cent, and in one or two 15 per cent or less, though at such low levels the figures can be no more than estimates. In those same countries television sets and even radios are economically beyond the reach of most of the population, though communal television sets are sometimes available. The consumer marketer faces a real challenge in deciding on promotional policies.

6. Language

Language has been described as the mirror of culture. On one level, its implications for the international marketer are self-evident: advertising must be translated (21:**10**); brand names must be vetted for international acceptability; business negotiations must often be conducted through expensive interpreters or through the yet more expensive acquisition of a foreign tongue. In the latter case, genuine fluency is essential; persuasion and contract negotiation present enough difficulties even in a mother tongue. It is often said in the UK that foreigners much appreciate even an attempt to acquire a smattering of their language. This may well be so; or it may be a simple courtesy to pretend so. Certainly the Japanese are said not to appreciate botched efforts to speak their language (*see* Table 29.1).

Less obvious is the fact that a foreign language may imply different patterns of thought and different customer motivations. In such cases a knowledge – again, a good knowledge – of the language will do more than facilitate communication; it provides automatic insight into the relevant culture.

Sometimes, in countries where more than one language is spoken, the minority language can become a much-esteemed manifestation of a separate cultural identity, defended with a tenacity not always understood even by fellow, non-minority, nationals.

Example _____

In Quebec a Charter for the French Language enforces the right of every person to communicate with public bodies and business firms in French, now the province's only official language. With certain exceptions all children must be educated in French. All commercial signs outside premises must be in French; bilingual French and English signs are not permitted. Traffic signs reading 'Stop' are being altered to 'Arrêt'; the fact that there are thousands of

Table 3.1 Doing business in Saudi Arabia

Which is the more important in any business deal, your personal relationship with the individuals with whom you are doing business or the legal wording of the contract? Relationships take some time to build up and are between individuals; contracts can be interpreted by any competent lawyer. In Saudi Arabia it is the relationships that count and that may explain why it can take some time before you can really get down to business; but, once you have formed a good relationship with someone, then business can be done quickly and easily because you are trusted. Under these circumstances it does not make much sense to change the company representatives frequently or to send different people on every visit because they have different skills; there has to be continuity.

Saudi Arabian culture is based on the Koran, which, although it is a holy book revealed in the Seventh Century, is very much alive today. Relationships between people are defined very clearly in the Koran and particularly those between men and women, and however westernized you may think your opposite number is, his values and conventions will all be based on his religion. Hospitality is one of the great Islamic values and so social occasions are a major opportunity to forge good personal relationships, but any offences against the laws of hospitality, even if they are unintentional, can cause real problems for the businessman. As an example, it is not acceptable to bring a gift for your hostess if you are invited to a meal.

Because business is a matter of relationships, you may find that what you thought was going to be a simple deal, made between two people, may involve several others who happen to be related or who are close friends of the person you have come to visit. Because what is being negotiated is a relationship, it is not seen as anything strange that it involves others who are not related to the business in hand. A negotiation may, by Western standards, be an agonisingly slow process and be achieved in an indirect way, with matters directly involved in the business being discussed intermittently with breaks for socialising and maybe the introduction of new people in between. Any sign of anger or impatience can ruin the chances of a successful conclusion.

There are many taboos concerned with cleanliness in Saudi Arabia. It is not acceptable to show the soles of your feet or shoes to the person to whom you are talking, nor is it acceptable to use your left hand for anything that would involve your host, such as handing him something with your left hand; you should be particularly careful about matters concerning this on Friday, the day on which your friends will be attending the mosque.

Finally, what about presents and where do presents go over the line which defines generosity or corruption? Saudis are extremely generous and many are very rich, but presents are very much part of the Saudi culture and you are expected to give and to receive appropriate items while making certain that your gift is not perceived as an attempt to gain a commercial advantage.

Arab culture is very different from our own and it will be a real advantage if the businessman knows something about Saudi culture before starting to do business in that kingdom. Proper briefing and preparation is a very worthwhile expense because it may prevent your making mistakes – which your hosts will be far too polite to mention to you – which can damage your chances of doing business successfully. It is the mistakes which we don't realise we have made that do the damage, because we have no opportunity to correct them.

(Source: Richard Hobbs, Director of the Centre for International Briefing, Farnham Castle, Surrey GU9 0AG.)

'Stop' signs in France itself seems to make no difference. So-called language vigilantes ensure that language laws are observed. More than a quarter of a million anglophone Canadians are said to have left the city of Montreal on language grounds.

7.   The self-reference criterion

The international marketer must make constant efforts to avoid the trap of the 'self-reference criterion', the unwitting reference to one's own cultural values that comes instinctively to all of us. The successful international marketer is one who has abandoned or at least suspended his or her own cultural prejudices.

Paradoxically, this is sometimes easier of achievement in countries that are culturally very different from the UK, such as Japan or Saudi Arabia. Here, the cultural divide is obvious; the marketer is on guard, and may have read round the subject and attended courses. In markets nearer, in cultural terms, to home, the marketer may well not be so alert to subtle differences, remaining in blissful ignorance of cultural transgressions.

Example

But, of course, success in Germany is not just a matter of quality of product and service. There is also the very different business culture to take into account. Edward Barrientos, an international consultant with Management Partner GmbH, argues that, while personal relationships are the foundation for doing business in Germany, these can be hard to establish:

> Beginning with the language and its formal orientation and extending to the manner in which Germans perceive friendship, establishing relationships is a difficult task for the British as well as for the Americans ... Many non-Germans make the mistake of hurrying the friendship development process by trying to be too frank, too open or overly friendly and personal. This often backfires within the German cultural context because it is perceived as insincere or superficial. Allowing the Germans to determine the speed at which the relationship develops, as well as its personal depth, is often a more effective and less risky approach.
>
> (Source: *Export Today*, September/October, 1992)

8.   Bribery

Bribery is the cultural universal that George Murdock forgot to mention. It is endemic to every nation and every stratum of society, from the petty official exacting a few paltry dollars for oiling the workings of bureaucracy to the government minister demanding millions. In recent years princes, presidents and prime ministers have been found succumbing to its temptations.

Bribery is by its nature a furtive proceeding; reliable information is hardly likely to be available except perhaps on those rare occasions when it reaches the courtroom. Nevertheless, experienced international marketers would probably agree that bribery is much more frequently encountered in certain developing countries, especially in Latin America, Africa and the Middle East. In those countries, the attitude towards bribery is often relaxed: far from being regarded as unethical, it is simply accepted as a fact of business life.

Example

... the director of the London-based Committee for Middle East Trade, an advisory and lobby group, says: 'It is a region where you need friends and contacts.' Nobody denies that Middle Eastern palms are greased; it is normal in the third world. 'We have to face the fact: if baksheesh did not exist, there simply wouldn't be a word for it. It is a tricky and sophisticated business and I don't recommend inexperienced visitors to get involved ...'
When the matter of backhand payments is broached, there are the crucial questions of how much and to whom. Probably only a local would have the instinctive understanding of the system and that is where indigenous agents really come in useful. Indeed, in some countries payments to certain officials, which might be regarded as blatant corruption in Britain, are regarded as legitimate.

(© The Telegraph PLC, 15.8.91)

The advice to the inexperienced not to get involved might seem well-founded. The same *Telegraph* article reminds us that a British businessman accused of bribery was sentenced to life imprisonment in Iraq.

Most industrialised countries adopt, in their sacred quest for exports, an ambivalent approach: at home, they make bribery a serious criminal offence; abroad they turn the loftiest of Nelsonian blind eyes to bribery by their own nationals. One nation, at least, has taken a principled stand. The US Foreign Corrupt Practices Act of 1977 specifically forbids US companies, their subsidiaries or their representatives to make payments to foreign government officials, political parties or political candidates if the purpose is corruptly to assist in securing or retaining business. The Act is being enforced and heavy fines have been imposed for a breach of its provisions.

Predictably, US businessmen have been vociferous in their complaints, arguing, with good reason, that the Act places them at a serious disadvantage in relation to foreign competitors. In 1988 the Act was amended to provide that, for a US firm to commit an offence, it must have actual knowledge of, or show wilful blindness to, the illegal nature of the payment, thus at least removing concerns about inadvertent violations of the law; the amendment also specifically permits payments made to encourage routine governmental action, such as the prompt processing of documents. All quite reasonable, of course. Or has a crack opened up in the wall of rectitude?

There have been suggestions that bribery might be controlled by an international agreement introduced through GATT or OECD. Respected though these bodies are, it is difficult to imagine what they might achieve that the threat of life imprisonment fails to achieve.

Bribery negates much marketing effort, is economically damaging and morally repugnant. It must be stamped on and stamped out.

Or is this international marketer falling into the trap of the self-reference criterion?

Progress test 3

1. Discuss the view that culture lies at the heart of all the problems connected with international marketing. *(CIM)*

2. Other than language difference, why may an advertising message used successfully in one country be inappropriate in another, where economic conditions could be considered alike? *(CIM)*

3. Give specific illustrations of how cultural and social differences between nations have an impact on marketing policy.

4. As an export manager you are spearheading a major effort in Japan, a country about which neither you nor your company have previously had any knowledge. What steps will you take to familiarise yourself with Japanese culture?

5. How might a country's religion affect a company's marketing policies?

6. Contrast social organisation in any two countries with which you are familiar. How does it affect market research and media advertising in those same two countries?

4

The political and legal environment

1. Why consider the political and legal environment?

The *political* environment in a country includes attitudes towards business enterprise, both national and foreign. These attitudes give rise to a whole range of laws and regulations governing the conduct of business, the *legal* environment.

The international marketer will be principally concerned with the political and legal environment in *host* countries, those countries in which operational units, whether manufacturing, distribution or sales, have been established. Concern with host countries is not in itself sufficient, however: the political environment in the *home* country can influence international operations, while the international marketer must also have regard to what might be loosely described as international law, a whole range of regulations emanating from international institutions. The international marketer's purpose will in all cases be to avoid political and legal risk or reduce it to acceptable proportions.

A more detailed view of the international political and legal environment is given in Fig. 4.1. This chapter follows the format of Fig. 4.1, except that most of the legal aspects are separately considered in relevant later chapters.

2. Host country political environment

There are now more than 180 sovereign states. The task of assessing the political climate in all these different countries is so complex as to be almost impossible.

Fortunately, however, there is a uniformity of motivation behind government attitudes and actions; it is helpful to consider government policies in the light of these motivations. Most governments have three basic aims:

(a) the maintenance of national sovereignty and, consequently, the safeguarding of national security and survival as an independent state;
(b) continuing improvements in the standard of living of their citizens;
(c) the maintenance of a political ideology and its encouragement in other nations.

3. Host country sovereignty and security

An MNC may be regarded from one viewpoint as a threat to national sovereignty: by definition, a subsidiary or even a branch office in a host country, though subject to that country's laws, is controlled to some extent by

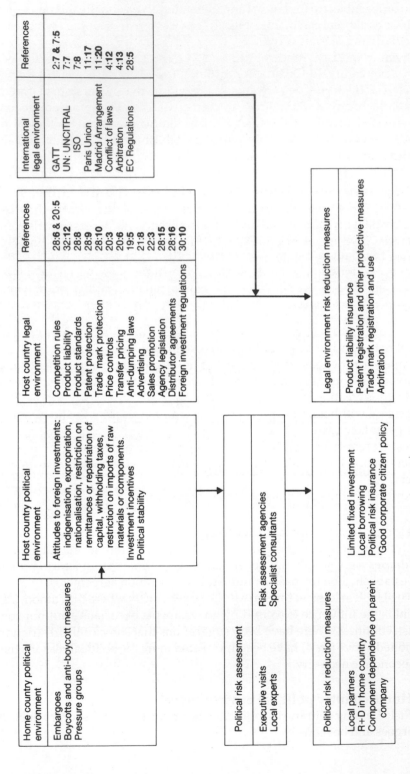

Figure 4.1 *The international political and legal environment.*

NOTE: The various aspects of the legal environment are further discussed under the chapter references given.

a head office subject to the laws of another nation. Occasionally this perception of MNCs as a threat can manifest itself, especially in developing countries, in particularly unpleasant ways.

Even in industrialised countries MNCs can be seen as a threat to economic sovereignty. In Canada, for instance, the Foreign Investment Review Agency (22:16) has a veto over any change in the ownership of foreign subsidiaries or any new foreign investment in Canada. The veto seems to have been directed mainly at the USA, which dominates certain sectors of the Canadian economy. Presumably, with the establishment of NAFTA (*see* Table 2.2), the veto will one day be ended.

4. Improvements in living standards of host country citizens

At the same time, almost all countries recognise the contribution that foreign capital investment can make to their economies. Most countries offer substantial investment incentives in the form of cash grants, tax holidays, low-rent land and buildings and the like.

Once an investment is made, however, and a subsidiary company is successfully established, the picture may change. In pursuit of their own economic interest, governments may:

(a) introduce indigenisation programmes, under which a certain proportion of local nationals must be employed in certain industries (30:10);
(b) impose restrictions on the import of raw materials or components in an endeavour to force the multinational subsidiary to seek local sources of supply, thus creating jobs for their nationals;
(c) increase withholding income taxes on remittances from the host country to the parent company;
(d) restrict remittances of dividends or repatriation of capital;
(e) nationalise the subsidiary, with appropriate compensation to shareholders;
(f) expropriate the subsidiary without compensation.

5. Host country political ideology

Under the communist regime in the former USSR, foreign manufacturing subsidiaries were simply not permitted, though some manufacturing plants were established on the basis of industrial cooperation agreements.

The USSR at least let foreign MNCs know exactly where they stood. Less evident is the influence exercised by governments of socialist, but not communist, countries. There have been suggestions that some of the restrictions mentioned above (*see* 4) have been motivated more for political reasons than from economic necessity.

6. Home country political environment

Risks arising within the home, rather than the host, country include embargoes and boycotts.

Embargoes are prohibitions on trade with a particular country, imposed for political reasons or on the grounds of national security. They may cover all exports or merely the export of certain specified products. Examples which come to mind are the British government's sanctions against Rhodesia and its ban on the supply of weapons to Iraq.

A boycott is a prohibition of *all* trade with certain selected *companies*, usually those that have traded with political enemies. The best-known boycott of recent times is probably the Arab League countries' boycott of companies said to have traded with Israel. The League listed several hundred companies, though not all member countries enforced the boycott fully.

International marketers must also take cognisance of pressure groups in their own home markets. These have on occasion achieved notable successes, as, for example, in the case of South Africa during the apartheid years, when a number of multinationals either withdrew from South Africa or significantly reduced their scale of operation. Recently environmentalists have had some success in discouraging the use of tropical hardwoods.

7.   Political risk assessment

It will now be clear that an MNC needs to make a careful political assessment of any country in which it intends to set up an operation. Unfortunately, the task does not end there; in many countries the political situation can be volatile and the assessment of political risk must be a continuing preoccupation even after a branch or subsidiary has been established. Many foreign companies, for example, were taken unawares at the time of the downfall of the Shah of Iran and lost significant sums of money as a result.

A first approach to risk assessment might be to send executives on market visits. This is almost an essential, but the results can only be superficial and are best regarded, perhaps, as a starting point.

The opinions of host-country experts can be sought on a continuing basis. The obvious problem is the selection of the right experts.

A number of research organisations offer specialised political risk assessment services. The best-known, perhaps, is the Business Environment Risk Index (BERI) of Delaware University.

8.   Political risk reduction

The most obvious means of limiting political risk is to minimise fixed investments in high-risk countries. An MNC may prefer to lease its premises rather than buy outright, and to buy components locally rather than manufacture them itself.

Similarly, when it is economic to do so, an MNC may prefer to borrow from host-country banks and financial institutions. Sometimes, however, host governments place restrictions on local borrowing by foreign companies, who might otherwise exhaust the often limited local credit resources.

High-technology companies may decide to retain R&D at head office. Without continuing access to such technology a manufacturing subsidiary may find it difficult to continue in business for any length of time. It becomes an unattractive candidate for expropriation or nationalisation.

For companies not in a high-technology business it is possible to arrange for a subsidiary to be dependent on the parent company, or on subsidiaries in other countries, for the supply of components. Again, nationalisation becomes difficult; in addition, each of the individual component suppliers benefits from economies of scale.

Overseas investment risks can in certain circumstances be insured with ECGD (5:3). For high-risk countries, however, the premium can prove a significant addition to investment costs, while for some countries the risk may be such that cover is not available at all.

Finally, it should be recognised that an overseas subsidiary is to some extent the master of its own fate. It should endeavour to be, and be perceived as being, a 'good corporate citizen' of the host country. The conduct demanded of a foreign subsidiary will naturally vary from one country to another, but the guiding principles laid down by the Canadian Foreign Investment Review Agency (22:16) indicate general standards that most countries would wish to see observed.

9. Host country legal environment

The international marketer does not need to be a lawyer. He must, however, be aware of those areas of the law that are likely to affect his marketing decisions and know when to call in specialist legal advice so that problems either do not arise or are at least minimised. The complexity of his task can be gauged from the list of relevant areas given in Fig. 4.1. The list includes only the more important areas of legislation.

Each of these areas is discussed in later chapters of this book. Figure 4.1 gives references.

10. The international legal environment

The international marketer must also take cognisance of laws which transcend national boundaries:

(a) EC 'Regulations', which do not have to be confirmed by national parliaments in order to have binding legal effect in member states (28:5);
(b) rules made by various international bodies which might possibly be described as international law, though they must be incorporated in national legislation to have effect.

11. International law

There is, of course, no international equivalent of the national legislatures of sovereign states with the power to introduce, pass and enforce legislation, but certain treaties or agreements between nations may be regarded as having to some extent the force of law. Those of special interest to the international marketer include:

(a) GATT, the General Agreement on Tariffs and Trade (7:5);
(b) various United Nations agencies, especially UNCITRAL (7:7);
(c) various conventions concerned with the protection of industrial property, such as the Paris Union (11:17) and the Arrangement of Madrid (11:20).

12. Conflict of laws

Given the absence of any significant body of international law, questions arise, once a transaction takes place across national boundaries, as to which national law is to apply.

The parties to a contract will often include a clause agreeing that in the event of a dispute the laws of one particular country are applicable.

In the absence of such a clause, the court to which the case is brought will decide which law is applicable. It may decide on:

(a) the law of the country where the contract was made; or
(b) the law of the country in which the contract was, or is to be, performed.

13. International arbitration

Arbitration is the process of settling disputes by reference to an independent and disinterested party who will deliver an unbiased decision. The decision may or may not be binding on the parties to the dispute.

Arbitrators are usually not judges, but people with practical experience of the business world. Their decisions are based not so much on points of law but rather on practical considerations of equity; in this way differences between one national legal system and another are minimised. Arbitration is therefore likely to prove quicker and cheaper than a resort to law.

Perhaps the most important international arbitration body is the International Chamber of Commerce (ICC) (7:10). The procedure is that the ICC endeavours to settle the dispute through mediation. If this fails, each party to the dispute selects one arbitrator from a panel of lawyers; an additional arbitrator is appointed by the ICC. The ICC Court of Arbitration receives more than 250 new cases every year, involving parties in around 80 countries.

A company wishing to settle disputes by arbitration should include a clause to that effect in its contracts. The clause should specify the arbitration authority.

UNCITRAL (7:7) has formulated a set of rules on arbitration which might one day lead to a consistent approach world-wide.

Progress test 4

1. Before your company tackles, for the first time, an overseas market, you have been asked to write a report on the legal factors that affect your UK marketing operation. Prepare this report so as to highlight potential

problems both in the EC and elsewhere, should your company proceed with an overseas marketing operation. *(CAM Foundation)*

2. International marketers are not employed as lawyers. Why should they concern themselves with the legal systems of countries overseas?

3. 'With regard to political risks, constant vigilance is required of the international marketer.' Outline the nature of political risk and indicate how such risks can be assessed on a regular basis.

4. What can multinational companies do to reduce exposure to political risk?

5. 'Competition is the ultimate factor which supersedes voluntary and legal controls in the market-place.' Please discuss in essay form. *(CAM Foundation)*

5

The financial environment I:
Avoiding risks

1. Nature of financial risk

The international marketer must confront three main types of financial risk: the commercial, or credit, risk; the political risk; and the foreign exchange risk.

This chapter discusses ways of avoiding or minimising these three types of risk. The chapter content is summarised in Fig. 5.1.

2. Commercial and political risks

The commercial risk is the risk of insolvency of, or a protracted payment default by, the buyer. This, of course, is a risk faced by most businesses. The difference in international marketing is that distance and, often, a lack of reliable financial information make the risk far more difficult to assess.

Example

In the experience of Dick Watt, senior underwriting manager with Trade Indemnity, relatively few export sales are clear when it comes to assessing credit risk. Accounts filed on time, established management, good track record and it is easy to say yes. Filed for Chapter 11 in the States and it is pretty obvious that the underwriter will say no.

But sixty to eighty per cent of all limits requested by Trade Indemnity's export customers fall into what Dick Watt describes as the 'grey area.' The most common problem is quite simply a lack of positive information. It may be a joke to talk about Italian companies running three different sets of accounts but he says that even in sophisticated northern Europe accounting standards are very different from those which operate in the UK. 'Even in the States there are large numbers of private companies which don't file accounts. In fact there are very few countries where accounts are filed centrally. And when you go to less developed countries, the problems are even greater. The most you can get for some Middle East countries is a three-line statement which is effectively saying that the company exists.'
(Source: Carol Debell, *Export Today*, November/December, 1992)

The political risk is completely beyond the control of buyer or seller. It includes exchange transfer delays imposed by an overseas government; cancellation or non-renewal of an import licence; war, revolution and civil disturbances; expropriation or confiscation of assets by an overseas government; and the introduction of new legislation, such as sanctions, that may prevent an exporter from fulfilling his contract.

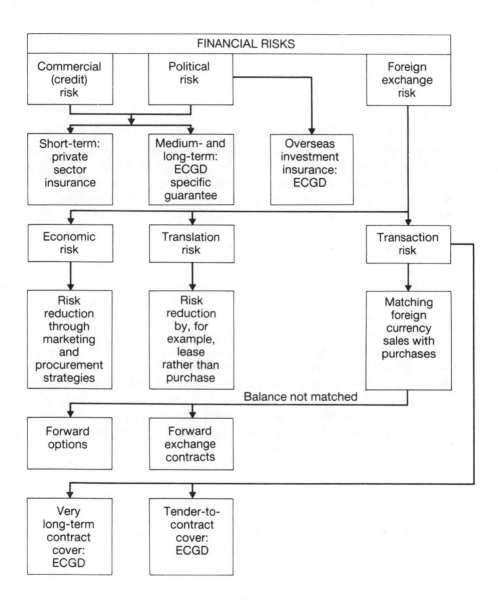

Figure 5.1 *Financial risks and their avoidance.*

3.   Managing commercial and political risks (short term)

Short-term commercial and political risks (up to 180 days) are insurable with private-sector insurance companies. The two major UK-based credit insurers are NCM in Cardiff and Trade Indemnity plc in London.

NCM, a Dutch company, is one of the largest credit insurers in Europe. In 1991 it purchased Insurance Services Group (ISG), the arm of the Export Credits Guarantee Department (ECGD) responsible for short-term credit insurance, taking on both the commercial and the political risks of the ISG portfolio. On the occasion of the sale the UK government provided NCM with some limited transitional reinsurance facilities and a separate national interest facility to enable it to maintain cover for a small number of high-risk markets for which private-sector cover is not available.

Trade Indemnity is the only major non-governmental British export credit insurer. Its policies insure an agreed proportion of a company's export sales against insolvency or protracted default; political risks may also be covered. Policies cover either a company's total export turnover, or its turnover in a group of markets or in one specific market. Premiums are calculated as a percentage of estimated export turnover; the exact figure depends on the company's credit history, its markets, its customers and its industry.

4.   Managing commercial and political risks (medium and long term)

ECGD continues as a government department with the main aim of providing medium-term (180 days to five years) and long-term (over five years) credit insurance facilities.

The ECGD Specific Guarantee insures an exporter against commercial and political risks encountered in relation to a project-related capital goods or services contract, to the extent of 90 per cent of the loss incurred. It may cover both the pre-credit risk (expenditure necessarily incurred by the exporter in, for example, the purchase of raw materials, manufacturing components, or the hiring of staff, etc.) and the credit risk (amounts due under the contract after delivery of goods), or simply the credit risk alone.

ECGD's Overseas Investment Insurance is designed to encourage investment in less developed countries. It provides companies with long-term cover (normally for 15 years) against political risks such as expropriation, war, and host government restrictions on repatriation of capital or profits. The scheme applies to *new* direct investments of at least three years' duration in overseas enterprises, whether in the form of an equity holding or a loan. It is not necessary for the insured to have a management role in the enterprise. Preliminary applications must be submitted before the investor becomes irrevocably committed to making the investment.

5.   Foreign exchange risks

Three types of exchange risk may be distinguished: the transaction risk, the translation risk and the economic risk.

Transaction risk arises out of a company's normal trading activities. In an export transaction, there is a danger, when a contract price is agreed in a foreign currency, that the exchange rate between that currency and the exporter's domestic currency may, between the date of the price agreement and the date of payment, move in a manner adverse to the exporter's interest. Suppose, for instance, that a British exporter sells goods that will be paid for in dollars six months later. If the dollar weakens against the pound, the exporter will receive less in sterling than had been expected.

Translation risk arises because a company's assets and liabilities abroad need to be given a value in the consolidated balance sheet in terms of the domestic reporting currency. Investments made in a country with a consistently declining currency will result in a decline in the reported value of total net assets. It might be argued that the effect in the short term is more apparent than real; the physical assets, after all, remain unchanged. The reality may be brought home when the assets are disposed of and the reduced proceeds of the disposal are repatriated, as was the case with several British companies in the late 1980s in Nigeria.

Economic risk arises from a company's choice of overseas raw materials supply and from its selection of export markets. For instance, if a company is dependent on two or three export markets and the currencies in those markets gradually and consistently depreciate in relation to the exporter's domestic currency, then, even if the exporter holds his prices steady, the price to the customer in the export market must consistently rise and the market may eventually be lost. The problem is exacerbated when the exporter has relied heavily on low price as part of his marketing strategy.

Even a company which buys, manufactures and sells exclusively in its domestic market can be vulnerable to economic risk from currency fluctuations, in that it may suffer increased competition from imports from a manufacturer based in a country with a constantly depreciating currency.

6. Managing the translation risk

There can rarely be a complete solution to the problem of translation risk. Translation exposure should, however, be taken into account whenever a decision is made to invest in assets overseas. For instance, leasing of premises, rather than outright purchase, will reduce foreign currency commitments.

A company investing in a country with a weak currency will seek a higher rate of return than usual to compensate for the additional risk and costs. Operating policies (in relation to pricing, for example) must also reflect this need.

7. Managing the economic risk

Limitation of the economic risk is a matter of procurement and marketing strategies. Again, the risk must be taken into account at the stage of strategy formulation. A narrow spread of markets might be taken as a danger signal.

8.   Managing the transaction risk

The international marketer may, of course, simply accept the transaction risk; in the days of almost fixed exchange rates he could do so without undue concern. With floating rates, however, acceptance of the risk is tantamount to gambling on the currency exchanges in opposition to professional speculators such as the international banks. The results could be disastrous.

Alternatively, an exporter could conceivably avoid the exchange risk entirely by quoting only in his domestic currency. The risk does not, of course, disappear; it is merely transferred to the buyer, who may be unable or unwilling to accept it, and who may, therefore, take his business elsewhere. For most serious exporters, quoting only in the domestic currency is not an option.

Many companies, especially multinationals, will be in a position to hedge their risks by *matching* their sales in a particular currency with their purchases in that currency. Few firms, however, can expect to hedge all, or even most, of their risk in this way. Many hedge actively in the financial markets, using mainly *forward exchange contracts* and *forward options*.

9.   Forward exchange contracts

A company can cover its exchange risks by selling in advance the currency it expects to receive. It will take out a forward exchange contract, fixing immediately a price (the forward rate of exchange) for the future sale of the foreign currency it will receive from the buyer.

The difference between the current, or spot, rate of exchange and the forward rate is determined by interest-rate differentials. While forward rates for some currencies will be at a premium to spot rates, others will be at a discount. The cost of forward exchange cover should be allowed for in the quoted price for the goods or services. It should be noted that the cost can be negative.

Forward exchange contracts are available from banks for the leading trade and investment currencies for periods from 30 days to several years ahead. Forward rates are published daily in the financial press.

10.   Forward options

An exporter who takes out a forward exchange contract has an obligation to complete the deal with his bank on the agreed date; he will make neither a profit nor a loss on the exchanges.

A forward *option* gives companies the *right*, but *not* the obligation, to take advantage of a particular forward contract. If the exchange rate moves against the company, it can take up its option and limit the damage; if the rate goes in its favour, it can let the option lapse and take a windfall profit.

Options are for those companies that do not want to hedge away all the firm's foreign exchange risk. They can speculate in the currency markets, and the option provides protection against serious loss if their speculation goes awry.

There is, of course, a price to be paid for this protection. The ordinary forward contract, after allowing for premiums or discounts, is no more expensive than a deal in the spot market. In contrast, an option has a lump-sum price that must be paid whether or not the option is eventually taken up. That price varies wildly according to market conditions, the currencies and the option period, but for a mere three-month option prices have approached 3 per cent of the total contract value.

11. Foreign exchange cover for very long-term contracts

Very long-term contracts such as, for example, major construction projects often envisage payment so far ahead that it may be difficult to secure from commercial sources forward exchange contracts to cover the whole period. This risk can be covered by ECGD's Forward Exchange Supplement (FES) scheme. If sterling appreciates, ECGD will compensate the exporter for any sterling shortfall in the foreign-currency proceeds of the contract.

12. Tender-to-contract foreign exchange cover

FES can be combined, if desired, with tender-to-contract (TTC) cover. With major projects, the buyer will often take a long time to make up his mind before placing an order. A company that has quoted in a foreign currency will be exposed to a foreign exchange risk: sterling may strengthen between the submission of the tender and the signing of the contract, so that the sterling value of the contract will be reduced.

Ideally, the tender should include a clause which allows the tender price to move in accordance with fluctuations in the exchange rate, but buyers are naturally unwilling to accept such a condition.

Alternatively, the tenderer could enter into a forward exchange contract with a bank at the time of tendering. If the tenderer does so and then fails to win the contract, the tenderer will still be committed to delivering to the bank large sums in foreign currency, which will have to be bought at the prevailing spot rate, possibly at a significant loss.

ECGD covers this tender-to-contract risk for contracts worth £5 million or more, provided the applicant intends to take out the basic ECGD insurance if and when a contract is placed.

13. Other means of avoiding the transaction exchange risk

Both without-recourse factoring and forfaiting offer the exporter a means of avoiding the foreign exchange transaction risk. See 6:**2** and **3**.

For the role of export merchants and *del credere* agents, see 13:**2** and 14:**7**.

Progress test 5

1. Explain fully the advantages and disadvantages to the exporter of quoting in the buyer's currency. *(IEx)*

2. You have quoted a prospective buyer in West Germany on a sterling basis for the supply of goods. He expresses an interest in the product but insists on quotations in ECUs and Deutschemarks. Prepare the memorandum required by your managing director indicating: **(a)** what an ECU is; **(b)** the risks involved in complying with the buyer's request; **(c)** your recommendations as to how those risks can be minimised. *(IEx)*

3. Why does the credit risk present so difficult a problem in international markets? What methods can you suggest for dealing with it?

4. 'Companies devote much time and effort to avoiding the foreign exchange transaction risk. But in the long term the more insidious translation and economic exchange risks present problems that are just as serious, if not more so.' Explain this point of view and suggest what can be done to counter the translation and economic risks.

6

The financial environment II: Creating opportunities

1. Financing international marketing operations

The international marketer may seek to create business opportunities by offering finance at competitive rates of interest. Many overseas buyers, especially those in developing countries, are short of foreign currency. Commercial banks, whether domestic or foreign, are usually willing to finance only first-rate credit risks; recent difficulties with certain debtor countries have, understandably, led to a further hardening of attitudes on the part of the banks. The offer of finance can, therefore, often influence the placing of a contract as much as, or more than, the basic price.

This chapter is concerned with the means by which the international marketer can assist in making finance available to potential customers at competitive interest rates. It also discusses various aspects of countertrade, by which the customer can pay for some or all of his purchases in goods rather than in scarce foreign currency.

2. International factoring

Factoring is essentially a method of exchanging book debts, as evidenced by invoices, for cash. It is mainly suitable for exporters selling on open-account terms, with credit periods up to 180 days.

Factoring is conducted by factoring houses, owned usually by the larger banks. These have overseas branches or correspondents for the provision of credit status information and for the collection of overdue accounts.

The full factoring service includes:

(a) total responsibility for and administration of the client's sales ledger;
(b) collection of outstanding accounts;
(c) investigation of the credit status of buyers;
(d) acceptance of 100 per cent of the credit risk, without recourse to the seller;
(e) cash advances of up to 85 per cent of invoice value immediately on receipt of invoices, the balance being paid when the buyer has paid.

Under these arrangements the overseas buyers are necessarily made aware of the factoring arrangement.

The advantage to the exporter of the full service is complete relief from certain administrative costs, the foreign exchange risk and the non-payment risks, whether commercial or political. The exporter also receives immediate cash, while the overseas customer has the benefit of an agreed credit period.

A more limited service may be agreed, depending on the client's requirements. In some cases, for instance, the client company maintains its own sales ledger and collects its own debts, without the benefit of bad debt cover, merely discounting selected invoices with the factoring house. In these cases the existence of the factor need not be disclosed to the buyer.

There are usually two charges for factoring, a service charge and a financing charge. The service charge might be between 1 per cent and 2.5 per cent of factored debts, depending on the workload and the bad debt risk. The financial charge, applicable only when the exporter requires an advance payment, is usually comparable with an overdraft rate.

3.   Forfaiting

Forfaiting is undertaken by banks. It was originally developed to facilitate the provision of medium-term credit for capital goods, mainly for export to Eastern bloc countries. In recent years, however, forfaiting banks have been prepared to consider a much wider range of goods, with credit periods as long as ten years. They normally look for a contract value of between £500,000 and £5 million, but will consider contracts of lower value.

The normal procedure is that the exporter obtains bills of exchange or promissory notes in return for his goods. These bills or notes must have been avalised (unconditionally guaranteed) by the central bank or other reputable bank in the importer's country. The forfaiting bank will then buy the documents at a discount from the exporter for immediate cash and without recourse. The discount will, of course, allow for exchange cover, non-payment risks and the forfaiting bank's charges.

The exporter thus receives an immediate and entirely risk-free cash payment, while the customer obtains medium- or long-term credit through the forfaiting bank at rates more competitive than a local bank could offer.

4.   ECGD Supplier Credit Finance

ECGD's Supplier Credit Finance facility applies to export contracts for capital goods or services. The buyer is allowed, depending on the contract value, at least two years' credit. The supplier, however, receives immediate payment on presentation to his bank of bills of exchange or promissory notes issued by the buyer; these must normally be endorsed by an acceptable bank in the buyer's country. The financing of the contract is undertaken by the bank at competitive rates which reflect the fact that payment against the bills or notes is guaranteed by ECGD.

5.   Buyer Credits, Project Lines of Credit and General Purpose Lines of Credit

ECGD provides export credit support through Buyer Credits, General Purpose Lines of Credit (GPLOCs) and Project Lines of Credit (PLOCs) for projects, capital goods and services sold overseas on credit terms of two years and above.

Buyer Credits, GPLOCs and PLOCs are all types of loan from a bank in

Britain to an overseas party (an importer or bank in the case of Buyer Credits and a bank in the case of the other two facilities) to finance up to 85 per cent of the value of projects undertaken by British exporters. ECGD guarantees the lending bank full repayment and a reasonable return on its funds.

An exporter can draw on a Buyer Credit as work on an export order proceeds; payment is thus, in effect, on cash terms. A GPLOC may be used to finance purchases by overseas buyers from a number of British exporters in connection with a specific project.

Under a supplementary arrangement, the Fixed Rate Export Finance (FREF) Scheme, the bank may lend to the buyer at a rate of interest which remains fixed throughout the life of the loan. The bank, however, will have to fund the loan through the short-term money markets, where its costs of borrowing will fluctuate. ECGD will compensate the bank when the bank's borrowing costs, plus a reasonable profit margin, exceed the fixed-rate payment by the buyer; conversely, if the fixed-rate payment should exceed the bank's costs plus profit margin, the bank will pay the surplus to ECGD.

6. Countertrade

Countertrade has been defined by the UN as 'those transactions which have as a basic characteristic a linkage, legal or otherwise, between exports and imports of goods or services in addition to, or in place of, financial settlements.'

Barter, the original form of countertrade, consists of a simple exchange of goods between two traders. Barter does not involve any currency payments whatever, and for that reason is very difficult to arrange; it is not easy to find two parties willing to make a simultaneous exchange of goods of equal value. In modern commerce, therefore, several variations on the original barter trading theme have been developed to meet special trading conditions or seize particular opportunities.

Five different variants of the barter or countertrade approach are discussed below. It should be noted, however, that there is no general consistency of nomenclature; most of the terms relating to countertrade are used loosely and alternative descriptions may be encountered.

7. Forms of countertrade

The *parallel deal* is an arrangement whereby the two parties sign two separate contracts that specify the goods that are to be exchanged. The contracts are often of unequal value and in such circumstances a compensating amount is paid in cash.

An *offset deal* is similar, except that the selling company, whilst not placing any immediate countertrade contract, guarantees to import components to an agreed value for incorporation in its final product. This kind of deal is becoming increasingly common, especially in the defence equipment field.

Example
_____

The Boeing Aircraft Company of Seattle, USA succeeded in securing the contract for the AWACS airborne early-warning radar system in spite of strong opposition from GEC, the UK company that had already made considerable progress with its rival system. To clinch the deal, Boeing had to guarantee to spend ultimately 30 per cent more than the total contract value on aircraft components manufactured in the UK.

Switch dealing, or *triangular compensation,* involves three contracting parties in three different countries. Goods are delivered from, for example, the UK to East Europe. The East European organisation in return provides goods which are transferred to the third country, from which the UK exporter will be reimbursed. The East European deliveries will almost by definition be goods that are not readily saleable on the open world market. Often the assistance of specialist traders with good contacts in appropriate industries is an essential part of a successful deal. Even then the goods may have to be sold at a heavy discount on world market prices.

Example
_____

Greece has accumulated the equivalent of $1 million of credit in Romania through its sales of cotton and fresh oranges, but has agreed to take Romanian canned goods, which it does not want, as payment. It asks a bank in Vienna to act as its switcher. The bank offers the equivalent of $700,000 in hard currency for the overvalued Romanian credit position. The Greeks accept the offer and purchase aircraft parts from Boeing in Seattle, something they wanted all along. The switcher finds a customer in Africa who is willing to accept the Romanian canned goods if the price is right. If the switcher has done his job properly the prices will be acceptable to the Africans, and everyone else will benefit too.

(Source: Robert E. Weigand, *Harvard Business Review*, November/December 1977)

Under a *buy-back arrangement,* one party agrees to supply manufacturing plant or a licence to use technology that will ultimately enable the other party to produce goods that are then used to repay the cost of the plant or licence.

Example
_____

Fiat assisted in the establishment of a car plant in the USSR. It was ultimately repaid by the delivery of components from that factory to Italy.

Clearing arrangements are *bilateral* agreements between two *governments* to exchange products not easily sold on the open market. Such arrangements define the goods to be exchanged, their respective values and the settlement date. At the expiry of the contract any deficit on either side is cancelled either by payment of a previously agreed financial penalty or by the acceptance of unwanted goods. For convenience a bank account is established in non-convertible'clearing account units'; either side may accumulate a limited surplus or deficit for a short period, but the units are not withdrawable in cash.

Example
_____

East Germany and a West African country agree that they will exchange machine tools for cocoa. The Germans ship machine tools whose open market value is 20,000 English pounds and agree to take cocoa beans in return. The beans will be shipped regularly during the year. The total value of the beans should come to £20,000 by settlement day a year later.

(Source: Robert E. Weigand, *Harvard Business Review*, November/December 1977)
_____

8. The rise of countertrade

Countertrade became popular as Eastern bloc countries endeavoured to overcome their shortage of convertible currency. Developing countries in a similar position soon adopted the idea; industrialised countries later became involved, mainly through offset deals in the defence industries. It has been estimated that by 1990 between ninety and one hundred countries had requested countertrade deals in one form or another. Estimates of the proportion of total world trade covered by such agreements are necessarily imprecise, but they vary from 10 per cent by value to as high as 30 per cent.

GATT (7:5) has expressed serious concern at the popularity of countertrade: bilateral agreements of any kind distort market forces and are a hindrance to free trade.

9. Advantages of countertrade

Few companies, of course, like to exchange their products for goods offered by the buyer; they prefer hard cash. Nevertheless, countertrade can offer significant advantages:

(a) it can provide access to many markets that would otherwise be quite out of reach;

(b) the typical countertrade contract is usually much larger than might be expected in the normal course of trade;

(c) in the case of the buy-back deal, lower wage rates in the manufacturing country may provide the plant supplier with what amounts to additional low-cost manufacturing capacity.

10. Handling a countertrade deal

A company engaged in countertrade faces more pitfalls than are usual even in the international field. The prudent company will, before signing any contract:

(a) ensure that countertrade really is essential if the export contract is to be secured;

(b) negotiate hard in an endeavour to obtain as high a part-payment as possible in cash;

(c) ensure that the goods to be received in countertrade are described as specifically as possible in the contract, in terms of origin, quantity, quality and price in local or international trading currency;

(d) check on the world market price of the goods and ensure *in advance* that it can dispose of them, either by its own efforts or through intermediaries such as a specialist merchant house or a bank;

(e) ensure that the sale of those goods is not likely to be impeded by any dumping duties (19:5) or import restrictions;

(f) check, where relevant, with its credit insurers to confirm that its own export sale and the part-payment in cash are insurable;

(g) check on the nature of countertrade regulations imposed by the countries concerned (more than 100 countries have introduced some form of regulation);

(h) estimate the overall profit on the transaction.

The profit calculation is by no means as simple as it may appear. It should be possible to estimate reliably in advance the profit on the export sale and to agree on discounts or commissions to intermediaries. The profit or loss on the sale of the countertrade goods is less certain: the world price of commodities such as crude oil (often the subject of countertrade) can fluctuate significantly over a short period; unforeseen delays can leave significant sums tied up in inventory and storage costs; and the marketing costs required for the disposal of the goods can sometimes be much higher than expected.

The difficulties are formidable. Most companies will be well advised to seek the services of countertrade specialists. A list of such specialists is available from the DTI.

Progress test 6

1. List five different ways in which export sales may be financed, making clear the source of such finance. For each type of financial support describe the advantages and disadvantages. *(IEx)*

2. An exporter has said to you 'All our exports are to Western Europe, the US and Canada, Australia and New Zealand, and all are on open account. So we don't need to bother about export finance.' Do you agree? Justify your answer. *(IEx)*

3. Contract terms and conditions offered to an overseas buyer often have greater influence than the price quoted. Why should this be so? *(CIM)*

4. Describe the role of the Export Credits Guarantee Department and give a brief description of the ways in which it can, directly or indirectly, assist UK exports. *(IEx)*

5. 'Countertrade? Just steer well clear of it.' Explain this attitude. Indicate how, with no previous experience in countertrade, you might be able to respond more positively to an enquiry suggesting that you might be paid at least in part in crude oil.

7

International institutions and the DTI

1. Introduction

This chapter describes briefly a number of international institutions of interest to the international marketer. It also outlines the Overseas Trade Services of the Department of Trade and Industry (DTI).

2. The International Monetary Fund

The International Monetary Fund (IMF) was conceived in 1944 at the Bretton Woods conference in the USA. Essentially, it aimed at achieving currency convertibility between member nations and at the same time producing a degree of stability in exchange rates. Member countries were required to establish a par value for their currency in terms of the US dollar and to maintain the currency within ± 1 per cent of that value.

Convertibility was achieved in 1958 and from then on a system of relatively stable exchange rates obtained. Devaluations did occur from time to time, but were to some extent avoided by the offer of additional credit, Special Drawing Rights (SDR), to member nations in difficulties. As a condition of granting credit the IMF would often insist on supervision of the debtor nation's economic policy.

By the early 1970s, however, multinational companies, banks and the like had at their disposal funds so extensive that it became difficult for central banks to defend the par value of their currencies. The holders of funds would move out of currencies they regarded as weak and likely to devalue, and into currencies they regarded as strong. This was no more than prudent money management from one viewpoint; from another it was currency speculation. But the result was that central banks finally gave up their attempts to maintain the par value of their currencies. From 1973, the currencies of the major industrialised countries were allowed to float, fluctuating according to supply and demand. This is the position today except for those currencies within the EC Exchange Rate Mechanism (28: **18**).

Thus the original *raison d'être* of the IMF no longer applies. The objectives of the IMF have now changed: in place of short-term balance-of-payments assistance in support of faltering currencies it offers long-term credits to developing nations. Before providing such assistance the IMF may require the country concerned to cut government expenditure, to take measures to curb inflation and to reduce tariff barriers.

3. The World Bank, IDA and IFC

Also conceived at Bretton Woods in 1944 was the International Bank for Reconstruction and Development (IBRD), better known as the World Bank. The Bank acts as an intermediary between the private capital markets and the developing nations. It makes long-term loans at interest rates that reflect market conditions. Because of its high credit rating, the Bank can borrow in the capital markets at low rates. These savings are passed on to the developing nation.

A subsidiary of the Bank, the International Development Association (IDA) makes loans to developing countries at especially low interest rates. This is only possible because it relies for its funds not on the capital markets but on donations from member nations.

Another subsidiary, the International Finance Corporation (IFC) provides risk capital by purchasing shares in newly established companies in developing nations. When the company achieves success the IFC will sell its shares on the local capital market and reinvest the proceeds in other fledgling companies around the world.

The activities of the World Bank are of special interest to international marketers. Its loans finance major construction and civil engineering projects which offer profitable contract opportunities.

4. The Organisation for Economic Cooperation and Development (OECD)

After the Second World War the Organisation for European Economic Cooperation (OEEC) was established in order to facilitate cooperation between European states and assist in their economic recovery.

Once that recovery had been achieved it was recognised that continuing cooperation between all the industrialised nations of the West was highly desirable. In 1960 twenty countries, including the USA and Canada, signed a convention establishing the OECD. Other countries have since joined, notably Japan.

The objectives of OECD are to promote the expansion of trade worldwide, to encourage economic growth in member states, and to assist the less developed nations.

5. The General Agreement on Tariffs and Trade (GATT)

GATT is a multilateral treaty signed by nations who between them account for more than 80 per cent of world trade. It has formulated a set of rules which member nations must observe in their trade with other members. (2:7).

The most important rule is perhaps the 'most favoured nation' clause, which lays down that a tariff concession granted to one member state must be extended to all other members. Other rules cover, for example, anti-dumping duties (19:5).

GATT also provides a framework within which member countries can negotiate tariff reductions in pursuit of continuing liberalisation of world trade. Since its establishment in 1947 GATT has sponsored eight major tariff negotiations, or 'rounds'. The first seven of these have been major and undoubted successes, resulting in reductions in tariffs for tens of thousands of products and a general easing of trade restrictions.

By definition, however, each success increases the difficulties of the next round. The eighth round, the Uruguay round, embarked upon in 1986, encountered problems, which were undoubtedly exacerbated by difficult world economic circumstances. At the same time some GATT member nations have devised new ways of circumventing GATT rules, such as voluntary export restrictions (2:5).

6.   United Nations Conference on Trade and Development (UNCTAD)

UNCTAD is a permanent organ of the United Nations. Its objective is the furtherance of the economic activities of developing nations, by trade as well as by other means.

Although, with the aid of GATT, trade in manufactured goods has expanded, tariffs are of less importance in the case of commodities, where tariff rates have traditionally been low. UNCTAD aims at increasing the prices of commodities through commodity agreements.

UNCTAD is also working to establish a tariff preference system favouring the export of manufactured goods from developing countries. Preferential treatment has been accorded to such exports by the EC, the USA and Japan.

7.   United Nations Commission on International Trade Law (UNCITRAL)

UNCITRAL aims to promote a uniform commercial code for the whole world, avoiding the present conflict between countries with different legal systems. It produced in 1983 a Convention on Contracts for the International Sale of Goods.

8.   International Standards Organisation (ISO)

Differing technical standards between nations are a major obstacle to international trade. The ISO, to which most industrialised countries belong, aims to develop uniform standards that will be internationally accepted. Progress is necessarily slow; changes in technical standards will usually involve expensive modifications to manufacturing processes and plant, to say nothing of a change of attitude on the part of customers who have relied for so long on their national specifications.

9.   The Berne Union

Most industrialised countries have established organisations equivalent to ECGD (5:3) which offer overseas buyers officially supported long-term credit at competitive rates of interest. A shrewd buyer, not unnaturally, may

Table 7.1 Overseas Trade Services of the DTI

1. Export Development Advisers

Expert advice from experienced export managers drawn from industry with the aim of increasing exports. Of special benefit to new exporters but may also be of value to experienced exporters.

2. Market Information Enquiry Service

On-the-spot market enquiries undertaken by the Posts overseas. Provides details of the specific market for the product, an assessment of market prospects, recommendations on future action, a list of agents, distributors and buyers, and information on tariffs and relevant legislation.

3. Export Marketing Research Scheme

Free professional advice on export market research, with financial support for research projects in certain circumstances (8:**14**).

4. Export Representative Service

Assistance in locating suitable representatives abroad, whether agents, distributors or potential partners for joint ventures or manufacture under licence (*24*:**5**).

5. Overseas Status Report Service

An impartial report on a prospective agent or distributor, covering its trading interests and capabilities, effective territorial coverage, warehousing and distribution facilities, technical know-how, after-sales service, and other agencies held (*24*:**5**).

6. New Products from Britain Service

Posts aim to place newsworthy reports of innovative products in suitable overseas media. Story written by experienced journalist and professionally translated in UK or overseas. Organised through the Central Office of Information (*see* 22.**15**).

7. Overseas Promotion

Organised group support at selected overseas exhibitions. In-store promotions overseas. Help with specialist seminars. Support for outward missions (group visits to overseas markets) and inward missions (groups of business people and journalists from overseas).

8. Information Services

Research and library facility in London, the Export Market Information Centre. Export intelligence (details of overseas enquiries and invitations to tender).

endeavour to obtain the best financing terms possible by playing off one national credit organisation against another. To counter such attempts a number of countries established the International Union of Credit and Investment Insurers, better known as the Berne Union. Membership now extends to 40 insurers in 32 countries.

Berne Union members arrive at a consensus on minimum interest rates, maximum credit periods, and the minimum percentage of order value to be paid on delivery. Actual figures vary according to the debtor country, with the poorer countries being offered the more generous terms.

10. The International Chamber of Commerce (ICC)

The ICC aims to promote the greater freedom of world trade, to harmonise and facilitate business and trade practices, and to represent the business community at international levels.

Activities of special value to international marketers include its role in arbitration (4:13), its standardisation of customs and practice in relation to documentary credits and international commercial terms, and its guides to commercial agency agreements.

11. The Department of Trade and Industry (DTI): Overseas Trade Services

The services formerly provided by the DTI, Foreign and Commonwealth Office and other government departments are now integrated as Overseas Trade Services. It now has in London alone some 2,000 staff, eleven regional offices across the UK and 185 diplomatic posts overseas, all dedicated to helping UK exporters. Table 7.1 summarises the services offered. Some of these services may attract a grant from public funds, others are free of charge, and for some a modest charge is made.

The DTI is an essential first port of call for a new exporter; experienced exporters will benefit substantially from regular contact.

Progress test 7

1. 'If you are interested in selling engineering or management consultancy services, you cannot afford to ignore the World Bank.' Why not?

2. Explain, with examples, how the Overseas Trade Services of the DTI can be of real value to large companies already exporting the major part of their production.

3. 'All international marketers should familiarise themselves with the services of the International Chamber of Commerce.' Why?

4. It has been suggested that the GATT rules on anti-dumping actions and

voluntary export restrictions should be strengthened. Some economists have suggested that merely rewriting the rules is not enough; powerful trading blocs have flouted GATT articles time and again, the EC Common Agricultural Policy being merely one of many instances. Enforcement of the rules is the problem. What methods of enforcement could they have in mind?

Part three

The principles of international marketing

8

International market research

1. Market research

Market research has been defined as 'the systematic gathering, recording, analysis and interpretation of data on problems relating to the market for, and the marketing of, goods and services.'

2. Secondary and primary research

Data-gathering may be considered under tw' ieadings: secondary research and primary research.

Secondary research (also known as desk, library or bibliographical research) involves the location and examination of available, usually published, data of relevance to the project.

Primary research (also known as original or field research) involves obtaining information from informants by observation, interview or mail questionnaire. It is inevitably many times more expensive than secondary research.

3. Market research projects

Most market research projects will follow a logical sequence:

(a) definition of the marketing problem or opportunity;
(b) decision on whether or not market research can usefully contribute;
(c) if so, careful definition of the objectives and scope of the research;
(d) preparation of detailed terms of reference;
(e) research design;
(f) information collection;
(g) information analysis and interpretation;
(h) research report and conclusions;
(i) marketing decision and its implementation.

Many of the above stages will require especially careful consideration in an international context. Of special importance, however, are the problems of information collection, in relation to both secondary research and primary research.

4. Secondary research

Data on specific products or product groups that one might normally expect to be available in the UK and other industrialised countries will often not be produced at all in developing countries. One or two countries, for instance, do not even produce population statistics.

Data are often so out of date as to be worthless. One country that does produce population statistics, for example, has not carried out a census for the last 25 years.

Data are often of suspect reliability. The last population census for Nigeria, for instance, was officially repudiated by the Nigerian government. Informants from whom data is collected may have some reason for falsifying the figures, especially where they originate from some tax-based function. Tax evasion in the UK is doubtless common enough, but in some countries it is said to have been elevated to the status of a national sport.

Often data are not directly comparable between different countries. In the case of import-export figures the position has much improved in recent years as nations adopted the Customs Cooperation Council Nomenclature (CCCN), a system of standardised classification of all imported and exported goods. Traps remain, however, for the unwary: the definition of 'urban', for instance, varies substantially from one set of national statistics to another. Douglas, for example, points out that in the UN Demographic Yearbook the definition of urban varies from one country to another: in Japan, the urban population is defined as those living in towns with at least 30,000 inhabitants; in India the equivalent figure is 5,000, and in Kenya 2,000; while in Nigeria 'urban' includes simply the forty largest towns.

5.   Use of secondary data

For these reasons the international researcher should approach secondary data with caution, enquiring as a matter of routine:

(a) exactly what is included in a statistical classification;
(b) who originally collected the data, for what purpose, and whether there might conceivably be a motive, on the part of the *collector*, for misrepresentation;
(c) from whom the data were collected and whether *informants* might have any motive for misrepresentation;
(d) how the data were collected and how reliable the methodology might have been;
(e) how consistent the data are with any other local or international statistics.

6.   Secondary data collection

It is a truism of all market research that secondary sources should be thoroughly investigated before expensive field research is commissioned. Such thoroughness is especially important in the international field, simply by reason of the sheer volume of data, let alone its relative unfamiliarity.

It is no part of the aim of this chapter to provide exhaustive lists of documents that may or may not prove of value in any particular case. Rather it is the intention to suggest a systematic approach to secondary data collection that will guide the researcher through what might otherwise appear to be an unending statistical morass. Such an approach is outlined in Table 8.1.

Desk research undertaken abroad should follow a similar system. A personal call on the national statistical office of the country will usually prove worthwhile. Addresses are given in the DTI booklet *National Statistical Offices of the World*.

7. Primary research

The problems of international field research stem largely from the linguistic, social and cultural differences between nations, and their differing levels of economic development. The nature and extent of these problems will vary significantly from one country to another, but will as a rule be far more pronounced in developing, rather than in industrialised, countries. In the USA, for instance, UK researchers may feel themselves very much at home, while in some developing countries they may require all their ingenuity to overcome local difficulties and produce a reasonably reliable report.

The problems and the suggested (necessarily generalised) solutions discussed below should be regarded as applying mainly to developing countries.

8. Sampling

Research results should reflect within acceptable limits the views of the entire population from which the sample is taken. Such results, however, are achievable only when the sample is randomly drawn (i.e. selected on the basis of a table of random numbers or by some other statistically acceptable method from a list of all members of the relevant population in such a way that each member has an equal chance of being selected for inclusion in the sample). In the UK the electoral roll provides such a list of individuals; it is by no means complete or entirely up to date, but it is acceptable for all practical purposes. In many countries no electoral rolls exist; even where they do exist they are not always made available for market research or other non-electoral purposes.

An alternative sampling method, heavily relied upon in the UK, is quota sampling. A quota sample is controlled according to certain known characteristics that are significant in marketing terms (such as age, sex, socio-economic class); it reflects those characteristics in the same proportions as exist in the total relevant population. Whilst in most countries (though not all) population figures are available by age and sex, socio-economic data are either not available or are very broadly based.

To overcome these problems, researchers sometimes adopt the 'random walk' approach: the interviewer is given a specific route to follow and is instructed to select every *n*th house for interview. Even this method is by no means as straightforward as it sounds; often street maps are not available or are well out of date, houses may not be numbered, and it is difficult to decide exactly what constitutes a household (a single dwelling may be occupied by several family units).

Sampling and research methods adopted in a number of countries are set

Table 8.1 A systematic approach to the collection of secondary data

---

1. Examine all information available from internal company records and company personnel.

2. Obtain competitors' catalogues, which will often provide not merely product but also market information.

3. Examine the publications catalogues of the major international organisations, which often produce information available from no other source (Table 8.2).

4. Examine the publications catalogues of commercial organisations such as banks, international accountancy firms and market research organisations that offer information over a range of countries (Table 8.3).

5. For each country, consult the various guides to information sources (directories which, though offering no market information themselves, are intended to act as signposts to other reference works or organisations which may provide such information). In industrialised countries these guides will usually be found to cover:

(a) government or other official statistics;
(b) trade directories;
(c) trade associations;
(d) trade and technical magazines;
(e) previously published market research surveys;
(f) specialist libraries.

Table 8.4 gives as an example a list of such guides relevant to the USA.

6. Check, if a UK international marketer, on how much of the required information is available in the Export Market Information Centre, the British Library Science Reference and Business Information Service, and the City Business Library (all in London).

Table 8.2 Information sources (international organisations)

Organisation	Selected examples of publications of interest to the international marketer
United Nations, New York, NY	Statistical Yearbook, World Trade Annual, Yearbook of Industrial Statistics, Yearbook of International Trade and Statistics
UN Conference on Trade and Development and General Agreement on Tariffs and Trade	A Bibliography of Market Surveys by Products and Countries
UN Food and Agriculture Organisation	Production Yearbook, Trade Yearbook
International Labour Office, Geneva	Yearbook of Labour Statistics
International Monetary Fund, Washington DC	Balance of Payments Yearbook, International Financial Statistics
International Bank for Reconstruction and Development (World Bank), Washington DC	The World Bank Atlas (covers, briefly, economic and social matters)
Organisation for Economic Cooperation and Development, Paris	Economic Survey (of the 24 member countries), Statistics of Foreign Trade
Eurostat: Statistical Office of the European Communities, Luxembourg	EC statistics

Table 8.3 Information sources (commercial organisations offering information on a range of countries)

Organisations	Selected examples of publications of interest to the international marketer
Business International Corporation, New York, NY	*Market Size in 117 countries; Investing, Licensing and Trading Conditions Abroad; Executive Living Costs in Major Cities Worldwide*
Croner Publications Ltd, Kingston-upon-Thames, Surrey	*Reference Book·for Exporters; Reference Book for Importers*
Dun and Bradstreet Ltd, High Wycombe	*DunsMarketing Database* (information on individual companies)
Economist Intelligence Unit, London	*Economic Reviews* (by country); *Global Forecasting Service* (55 countries); *European Trends; Multinational Business*
Euromonitor Publications Ltd, London	*European Marketing Data and Statistics; International Marketing Data and Statistics*
Hong Kong & Shanghai Bank/Midland Bank, London	*Business Profile Series* (29 countries). Most international banks publish similar guides
Market Research Society, London	*Country Notes* (on market research methods); *International Directory of Market Research Organisations*
Predicasts Inc., Cleveland, Ohio	*Predicasts F+S Index* (United States, Europe and International); *Worldcasts*
Price Waterhouse, London	Information guides: *Doing Business in....* (a number of countries). Several of the major international accountancy firms publish similar guides
Business Environment Risk Index (BERI), Newark, Delaware	Political and other risk assessments

Table 8.4 Systematic secondary research: examples of guides to information sources in the USA

Information	Guides to information sources	Publishers
US government statistics	*Statistical Abstract of the US*	Bureau of the Census, Washington DC
	Bureau of the Census Catalog	Bureau of the Census, Washington DC
	Statistical Services of the US Government	Bureau of the Budget, Washington DC
	American Statistics Index	Congressional Information Service, Washington DC
Directories	*Directory of Directories*	Gale Research Co., Detroit, Mich.
	Guide to American Directories	B. Klein Publications, Coral Springs, Fla.
Trade associations	*Directory of National Trade and Professional Associations*	Columbia Books, Washington DC
	Encyclopedia of Associations	Gale Research Co., Detroit, Mich.
Trade and technical magazines	*Business Periodicals Index*	H. W. Wilson Co., New York, NY
	Standard Rate and Data	Standard Rate and Data, Skokie, Ill.
Published market research surveys	*Marketsearch*	Arlington Management Publications, London
	Directory of US and Canadian Surveys and Services	C.H. Klein & Co., Fairfield, NJ
	Findex	Find/SVP, New York, NY
Specialist libraries	*American Library Directory*	R.R. Bowker, New Providence, NJ

Note: Many of the above directories are available in the DTI's Export Market Information Centre.

out in *Country Notes*, published by the Market Research Society. Table 8.5 gives extracts from the sections on Spain and Indonesia.

9. Questionnaires

Every questionnaire demands the most careful phrasing if unintentionally misleading answers are to be avoided. In international research, translation of the questionnaire is often essential, providing yet more scope for misunderstanding.

Ideally, the questionnaire will be drawn up by a trained researcher who is both a native of the country in which the research is to be undertaken and fluent in the language of the research sponsor, though this ideal cannot always be achieved. In any case, translation alone is not adequate; in order to achieve cross-cultural comparability, substantial changes may be required in the original wording of the questionnaire.

10. Telephone interviewing

In the major industrialised countries the telephone penetration rate per household is such that telephone surveys are feasible, even for consumer research. The UK researcher can now commission relatively cheap research in Europe, in the consumer or industrial field, from specialist research agencies in London employing nationals of the countries to be researched.

In contrast, in developing countries, the number of telephones is so limited, delays in installation are so long, and the cost of calls is so high, that even in industrial research reliance on the telephone may be called into question.

11. Personal interviews

It will be clear that in developing countries the face-to-face interview is essential if reliable data are to be obtained. Unfortunately, however, it is precisely in those countries that the most serious difficulties arise, for two main reasons: interviewer recruitment and refusal rate.

In some cultures it is impossible to recruit female interviewers. Thus housewives can be interviewed only in the presence of the husband (or, perhaps, an acquaintance), and sometimes not at all.

Example
_____

Interviewers include many men, unemployed graduates and moonlighters. The Indian mother is not yet emancipated from the kitchen or deference to the male. Housewife interviewing, therefore, is frequently possible only between 07.30 and 09.30 and between 18.00 and 19.30, when the husband is at home.

(Source: G. Cranch, *International Marketing Research Supplement*, Market Research Society Newsletter No. 120, March 1976)

Table 8.5 Sampling methods in Spain and Indonesia

(a) Spain
Probability sampling
No reliable, up-to-date address lists of either households or individuals are available in usable form so that the closest probability sampling that can be achieved (for face-to-face or telephone, samples can, of course, be 'randomised') is strictly controlled random route. There are premium charges for this, and a detailed specification must be agreed before costing, since price will depend on the degree of rigour imposed.

Quota sampling
Quota sampling is the most commonly used sample selection method in Spain.
Quotas can be set regionally, interlocking in terms of sex and age. Occupation or approximate social grade controls can be applied, but there is insufficient official statistical information to allow for grossing up and weighting on these dimensions (individual institutes may have their own matrices based on accumulated back data).
Again, the quality of the sample depends on the quality and precision of the procedures and controls used. It is important, therefore, to specify whether you are looking for 'cheap and cheerful' or rigorously reliable results since there can be important cost implications.
Key points to check are: sampling point definition and selection; sample point control in the field (how far interviewers may travel, overlap problems in large cities, etc.); recruitment procedures (number of visits to a household, number of households visited in each apartment building, etc.).

(b) Indonesia
Probability sampling
Indonesian civil administration is based on a hierarchical structure. At the lowest level is the 'RT' or 'Rukun Tetangga', which comprises between 15 and 150 households, depending on the particular locale.
Each head of an RT is expected to maintain lists of households under his control and the name of the head of the household. Whilst record-keeping is improving, lists can be out of date both in terms of occupants and existence of dwelling units.
Nevertheless, as records are not centralised and there is no electoral roll, the RT is used as a basis of sampling.
The government can provide details of the number of RTs by geographical locale. Once a random selection of these is made, an interviewer visits the head of an RT and seeks permission to 'map' dwelling units. A sampling interval is then applied as required.

Quota sampling
As random surveys are often extremely expensive and, unless very heavily controlled, unreliable, quota sampling is often utilised.
Quotas can be applied by age, sex, social status, etc.
However, as government population statistics are grossly inadequate and limited, quotas tend to be applied by value judgement rather than an adequate knowledge and awareness of the 'universe'.

(Source: *Country Notes*, The Market Research Society, 15 Northburgh Street, London EC1V 0AH.)

Table 8.6 DTI Overseas Trade Services: Export Marketing Research Scheme

1. *Purpose*
To help and encourage UK firms to undertake overseas marketing research by providing financial assistance.
To ensure that users undertake or commission research based on sound methods.
To provide independent professional export marketing research advice.

2. *Eligibility*
The scheme is open to any company (but not divisions within companies) with fewer than 200 employees and whose products/services are mainly of UK origin and are exportable.
Trade associations are also eligible.

3. *Benefits*
Free advice from professional market researchers.
Payment of half the cost of professional research consultants.
Half of the essential travel costs and interpreter's fees, plus a daily allowance for one researcher, where the research is undertaken 'in house' by staff with appropriate ability and experience and is carried out outside the European Community.
One third of the cost of purchasing published market research (but not directories, market research, or subscription fees for studies updated on a subscription basis).

4. *Limitations on support*

Number of studies
Maximum of three studies, counting from 1.1.86.
No more than two studies in any one year.
Only one study per country (but two for the USA).
In addition, the purchase of the two *published* market research studies per firm per annum can be supported.

Amount of support
No more than £20,000 per study.
No more than £40,000 per firm per annum.

Areas not eligible for support
General background research.
Overseas visits where market research is not the primary objective.
Sales or promotional trips.
Research conducted wholly or mainly on a group visit or trade mission.

Table 8.6 Continued

Research carried out wholly in the UK.
Market development.
Omnibus studies.
Market research projects already commissioned, under way or completed.
Published market research already purchased.

5. *Trade associations*
First study supported at 75%, subject to maximum grant of £60,000.
Second study 66⅔%, maximum grant £53,000.
Subsequent studies 50%, maximum grant £40,000.
No limitations on the number of studies, but reports must be made available to all association members.

6. *Confidentiality*
Report contents are regarded as completely confidential. Except in the case of trade association research, no other organisations are ever informed of research projects, nor do they see the research reports.

7. *Application forms*
Available from the Association of British Chambers of Commerce,
Coventry.

Refusal rate is high for a number of reasons. In some cultures there is a general mistrust of strangers; in others, respondents may feel embarrassed at discussing even food products with a stranger.

Example

[In India] there is currently a government drive against tax evasion. Matters of salary or expenditure or possession of more expensive items therefore present problems. It puts an increased burden on confidentiality and willingness to be interviewed. A random sample may have a 30% or more refusal rate.

(Source: G. Cranch, *International Marketing Research Supplement*, Market Research Society, Newsletter No. 120, March 1976)

In industrial research, businessmen are often accustomed to keeping to an absolute minimum any disclosure of information to government, employees and shareholders, let alone market researchers. Sometimes suspicions may arise of a political motivation on the part of the research sponsor.

Example

In a survey in the Middle East, one male respondent who fell within the sample turned out to be a government official who was highly suspicious of the survey, particularly so when he heard it had American sponsorship. However, he did not complain about the interview until it was completed and the interviewer was about to leave. He then threatened to have her arrested. She reported this to the supervisor who telephoned the respondent immediately to assure him the survey had government approval and he (the supervisor) offered to come to the respondent's house to discuss the survey in person. This pacified the irate respondent.

(Source: S. Watson Dunn, *Handbook of Marketing Research* (ed. R. Ferber), McGraw-Hill, 1974)

12. Successful research in developing countries

As mentioned, adaptability and ingenuity are essential for research in developing countries, but it is possible to lay down general guidelines. It will usually pay to:

(a) rely entirely on the personal interview;

(b) in consumer research, rely heavily on the group interview;

(c) ensure good communications with respondents by an even greater than usual reliance on display cards, illustrations and samples;

(d) provide more than usually thorough training and briefing for interviewing staff;

(e) arrange for the sponsoring company research staff to participate in experimental interviews;

(f) give closer and more direct interviewer supervision;

(g) place greater emphasis on the issuing of credentials to interviewing staff, including photographs;

(h) anticipate any politically sensitive questions, rewording or deleting whenever possible;

(i) where there is any possibility of the imputation of political motives, however unjustified, clear the research programme in advance with the appropriate authorities.

13. Research infrastructure

In many smaller or less developed markets the research and support services taken for granted in industrialised countries, such as retail audits, consumer panels, fieldwork agencies and the like, will simply not be available. The international marketer should refer to the Market Research Society's *International Directory of Market Research Organisations,* so as to be fully aware in advance of the resources at his disposal. The directory has almost world-wide coverage and gives details of more than 1,700 market research organisations.

14. The Export Marketing Research Scheme

In certain circumstances, companies with fewer than 200 employees and trade associations may be eligible for government financial support for export market research (Table 8.6).

Progress test 8

1. Analyse the reasons for using a marketing information system in international markets. What are the main information sources you would expect to use? *(CIM)*

2. When carrying out market research in a foreign country, why would it usually be necessary to collect both quantitative and qualitative data? *(CIM)*

3. Describe what steps you would take to identify a suitable export market for a product of your choice. Explain what market research you would undertake, and say what you understand by primary data and secondary data. *(IEx)*

4. Explain fully the roles of field and desk research in the development of an export market. *(IEx)*

5. In the field of market research, explain what you understand by the term secondary data. Explain how you would obtain such data and detail eight possible sources of information which you might use. *(IEx)*

6. Give reasons why it is important for companies to undertake desk research before embarking on an overseas marketing campaign. *(IEx)*

7. 'Secondary data in many overseas markets suffers from a number of serious shortcomings.' What specifically are these shortcomings? And what precautions would you take in using such data?

8. Outline the main problems faced by organisations attempting to conduct consumer market research in a developing country. What are the implications of such problems to any organisation? *(CIM)*

9

The international marketing decision

1. Introduction

This chapter considers more fully the first of the five major decisions set out in Fig. 1.2, the decision on whether or not to become involved in international marketing at all.

The essential justification for a decision to move into international markets is that, in the long run at least, profit opportunities will be greater than those in the domestic market. These opportunities may come about in a number of ways.

2. Domestic market saturation

The domestic market may be approaching saturation or be otherwise unattractive. This may, for instance, be the case with cigarettes in industrialised countries, where relentless government health warnings, restrictions on advertising and anti-smoking pressure groups have taken their toll of sales. Cigarette manufacturers may prefer to concentrate their efforts on markets where restrictions are less severe.

3. Recession

An international operation may provide a safety net in times of recession. A business downturn will not usually affect all countries equally at the same time.

4. Economies of scale

Sometimes the domestic market is not large enough to permit the realisation of all possible economies of scale. Additional turnover in new markets can then reduce costs for all markets. Research and development costs, in particular, can be spread over a much higher turnover.

5. Product life cycle

A product nearing the end of its life cycle in the home market may find a new lease of life in a developing market (11:11).

Similarly, an innovative product with doubtful patent protection may be introduced as quickly as possible in a number of markets so as to gain maximum advantage before competitors can develop comparable products of their own.

6.   Lead markets

A lead market is one in which the level of development and innovation in product technology, manufacturing processes or marketing methods is ahead of that in all other countries. For many industries the USA is the lead market, though in consumer electronics and photography, for instance, the lead market might be Japan.

Companies may feel that they must maintain a presence in what is the lead market for their industry, so as to keep in immediate and first-hand touch with new ideas and their development.

7.   Attack on competition

A company may move into a competitor's home market with the aim of sharpening its own competitive edge, thus weakening the competitor firm at home and perhaps at the same time distracting its attention from other markets.

8.   Absence of strong competition

New markets are emerging in the more rapidly developing countries. In these, competition may be less intense and less well established.

9.   Customers

Sometimes companies have little choice but to follow their major customers in investing overseas or lose a considerable amount of business. Component suppliers, for instance, often follow car manufacturers. Service companies, such as accountancy firms, advertising agencies and management consultancies, have taken the same route to expansion abroad.

10. Lower production costs

Many companies have found it possible to secure low-cost production facilities where labour costs are low and government investment incentives are significant.

11. Aid programmes

In developing countries international aid programmes offer opportunities amounting in total to £30 billion p.a. This offers a clear inducement to overseas development for certain industries, mainly construction and consultancy.

12. National interest

Exporting and the earning of foreign currency is undoubtedly in the national interest. Patriotism, however, is not in itself a good reason to engage in international marketing. Exporting at a loss, for instance, is in the long term in no one's interest.

Progress test 9

1. What general arguments can you adduce for and against a company's involvement in *exporting*? *(IEx)*

2. Competition can in various ways influence a company towards international marketing. In what ways precisely?

3. A number of companies have established a presence in what they consider to be the lead market for their industry, with the objectives of keeping in immediate touch with innovation in product or process technology and marketing techniques. But a mere presence alone will not achieve these objectives. What do you think these companies must do to ensure that the anticipated benefits are in practice achieved?

4. 'We export or die. We must all put our shoulders to the wheel.' Must we? Suggest some types of company that might be excused.

10

International market selection: Screening and segmentation

1. What is a market?

A country does not necessarily equate with a market. A market, in an international context, may perhaps be a country, but it may also be a region within a country, or a group of several countries. Equally, it may be a defined segment of consumers or industrial users within one particular country or several similar segments across a number of countries.

However, much of available international data is produced by national governments or based on national boundaries. It is convenient, therefore, to take countries as a starting point in the process of market selection.

2. The need for market selection

There are more than 180 sovereign states. No one company is likely to have the resources to develop profitable business in all of them; few of even the largest multinationals operate in more than 100 countries. All companies must make a choice.

Clearly, companies will wish to select those countries that offer the greatest profit opportunities.

3. The need for a screening process

The selection of these countries should not be arbitrary or haphazard; it must result logically from a factual appraisal of all markets open to the company. Such an appraisal will necessarily rely heavily on market research.

A full programme of research in all countries of the world would, however, prove hopelessly uneconomic. What is required is some systematic procedure which:

(a) is based principally on the relatively inexpensive desk research (most of which can be satisfactorily undertaken in the UK);
(b) initially covers all markets worthy of consideration;
(c) then eliminates markets in successive stages as soon as the desk research indicates they do not have significant potential;
(d) arranges for limited original research to be undertaken in the small number of markets still under consideration;
(e) then ranks the countries still regarded as possible target markets in some reasonable order of priority for the undertaking of the vastly more expensive field research, before a decision is taken on whether or not to enter one or more of these markets.

This approach permits the international marketer to select on a factual basis those countries that offer the highest profit potential, while at the same time avoiding excessive unnecessary expenditure on market research.

4.   A market selection model

Such a screening process is shown diagrammatically in Fig. 10.1 with an indication of the screening criteria applicable at each stage. The stages are discussed in greater detail below, and some indication is given, by way of example, of the kind of information sources likely to be of value.

The process is of special relevance to a company moving into international markets for the first time. It is also appropriate when a company is contemplating expansion of its international operations or undertaking a periodic review of its existing markets.

Stage 1
The initial screening criteria amount to no more than a broad assessment of each country's economy, the political risk, and financial risks and regulations.

For this economic assessment the sources listed in Tables 8.2 and 8.3 will prove useful, especially Business International's annual assessment of market size and growth for 117 countries. For the political risk the BERI or similar reports should be consulted. Financial regulations are set out in the Price Waterhouse publications, while any country for which ECGD or other credit insurers have suspended cover would automatically be rejected or referred for later consideration.

A country rejected on economic grounds could well offer prospects as a result of development aid provided by United Nations agencies, the World Bank, or other development banks or development funds. The World Aid Section of the Projects and Policy Division of the DTI provides a central point for information about projects funded by these agencies.

Stage 2
The screening criteria now become accessibility (tariffs and non-tariff barriers) and market size.

The DTI can help with rates of duty, local taxes, exchange control regulations and legislation affecting British exporters. Market size assessment is sometimes a very simple matter in that the product may be specifically mentioned in official or trade statistics or in syndicated surveys. Details of the latter can be found in *Marketsearch, Findex* and the like (Table 8.4). More usually at this stage the researcher will need to use some ingenuity to establish some proxy variable: for instance, the number of hospital beds may well prove a useful, if crude, indicator of the demand for other hospital equipment. Again, a large number of countries will be rejected or referred at this stage.

A country rejected on the grounds of tariff or similar barriers may, of course, still be considered for licensing or local manufacture.

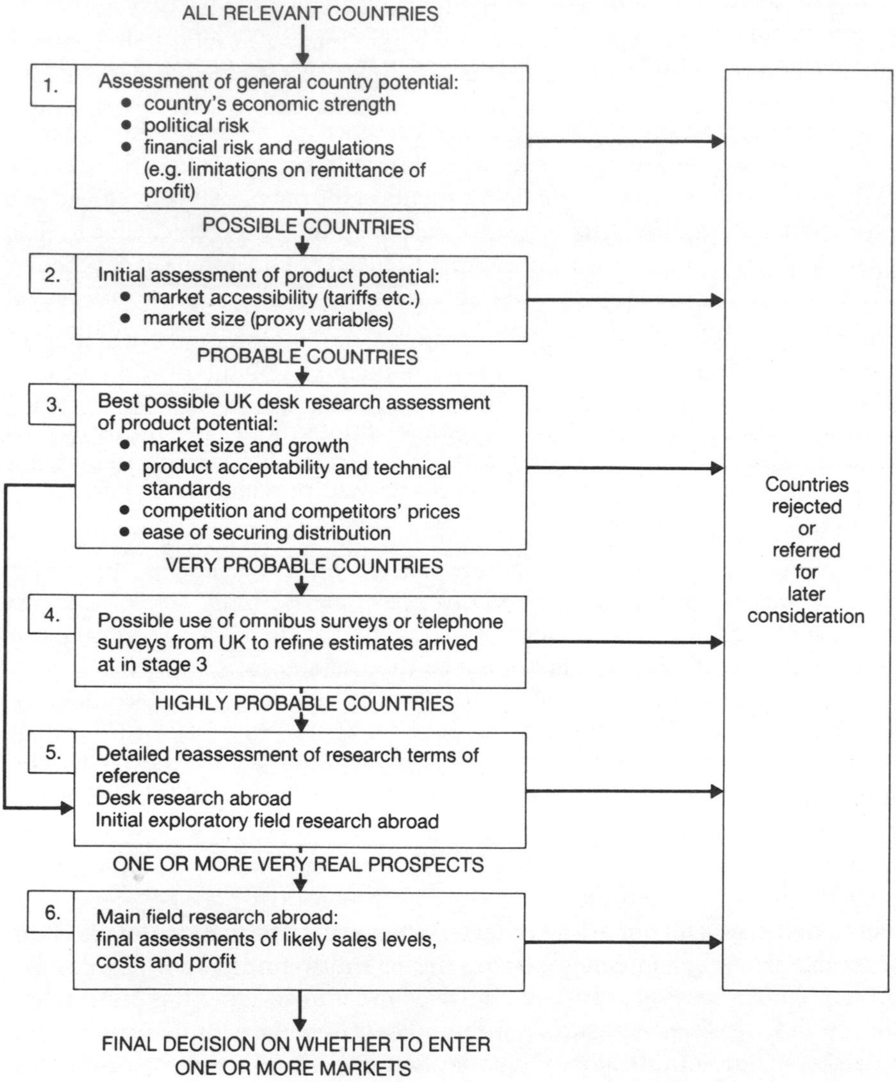

ALL RELEVANT COUNTRIES

1.	Assessment of general country potential: • country's economic strength • political risk • financial risk and regulations (e.g. limitations on remittance of profit)

POSSIBLE COUNTRIES

2.	Initial assessment of product potential: • market accessibility (tariffs etc.) • market size (proxy variables)

PROBABLE COUNTRIES

3.	Best possible UK desk research assessment of product potential: • market size and growth • product acceptability and technical standards • competition and competitors' prices • ease of securing distribution

VERY PROBABLE COUNTRIES

4.	Possible use of omnibus surveys or telephone surveys from UK to refine estimates arrived at in stage 3

HIGHLY PROBABLE COUNTRIES

5.	Detailed reassessment of research terms of reference Desk research abroad Initial exploratory field research abroad

ONE OR MORE VERY REAL PROSPECTS

6.	Main field research abroad: final assessments of likely sales levels, costs and profit

Countries
rejected
or
referred
for
later
consideration

FINAL DECISION ON WHETHER TO ENTER
ONE OR MORE MARKETS

Figure 10.1 *A market selection model.*

Stage 3

For the by now much reduced list of countries, the screening criteria are extended to cover a more careful assessment of market size and growth, general product acceptability, technical standards, strength of competition, competitors' prices and the often thorny problem of securing distribution.

Product acceptability for consumer goods can often be gauged from mail order catalogues held by the Export Market Information Centre. Details of technical standards can be obtained from Technical Help to Exporters (THE) at Milton Keynes. Information on distribution channels can prove a difficult problem, but in some countries syndicated reports are available (e.g. Dodwell Marketing Consultants' *Retail Distribution in Japan* and *Industrial Goods Distribution in Japan*).

For the remaining information some presence within the overseas market is desirable, if not essential. The DTI's Market Information Enquiry Service (MIE), through the commercial departments of the overseas Posts, can advise on product suitability and test local response to the product. It can also provide information on the local competition and obtain details of competing prices where a published price list is available or when the product is on general retail sale. Commercial product pick-up services are also available.

Example
_____

IIS Ltd, part of the London-based Mintel International Group, offers an international product pick-up service in 128 countries. It has organised a team of 400 shoppers, all resident overseas, who will purchase and send to the customer any product that is in retail distribution.

Clients may specify an *ad hoc* service, covering one or just a few products, or a 'product trawl', which covers a whole category of product. IIS also offers store checks under which products on sale are listed under the name and address of the retail stores visited, with details of manufacturer, brand name, product description, shelf allocation, pack type and size, and price.

IIS clients use the service for initial market reconnaissance, competitor evaluation and product comparison, generation of new product ideas, independent monitoring of the quality of products manufactured by licensees, checking on patent or trade mark infringements, and discovery of parallel imports.

_____

Stage 4

Very often there will remain from stage 3 a few critical gaps in the information obtained. If so, consumer goods researchers may find it will pay to take advantage of an omnibus survey (a survey undertaken at regular intervals on behalf of several clients, each of whom commissions a limited number of questions). Such surveys, with details of countries and fieldwork dates, are advertised regularly in the Market Research Society's newsletter. Telephone surveys from a UK base, with interviewing undertaken by nationals of the relevant countries, are now economic and practicable, at least for Western Europe.

Stage 5

Original (field) research is now about to begin in earnest; from now on research costs are likely to be substantial. The precise nature of the information required must be re-thought in terms of the specific questions to be asked and the action that will or will not be taken on the answers. The inexperienced researcher will find the DTI's *'Industrial Marketing Researcher's Checklist'* of help.

Even now an initial and limited programme of field research may prove advisable; there is no point in spending a great deal of time and money on research if it becomes clear at an early stage that a negative is the likely outcome. Any such research should include a visit to the country's national statistical office. In addition, industrial research interviewers should make a point of asking all informants for sources of published information. A major syndicated survey, for instance, may have just been published and may not appear in *Marketsearch* or *Findex*.

Stage 6

The objective of this, the main fieldwork stage, will be to produce final estimates of sales levels, costs and profit. It should also provide the information input to the marketing plan.

5.   Market segmentation

Kotler defines *market segmentation* as the process of 'dividing a market into distinct groups of buyers (segments) who might require separate product offerings and/or marketing mixes'.

A *market segment* may be more fully defined as a group of customers or potential customers who:

(a) are different from the rest of the market in terms of certain characteristics (variables) that are significant in marketing terms;
(b) but are, in terms of those same characteristics, relatively homogeneous within the group.

The ideal market segment is one which:

(a) is identifiable and accessible, at least to the extent that it can be reached and served through appropriate media and distribution channels;
(b) is measurable, at least approximately;
(c) is substantial (large enough and profitable enough to be of interest to the seller);
(d) shows needs that the seller is particularly well placed to satisfy, so that a competitive advantage might be gained;
(e) is responsive to promotion.

There is no one right way to segment a market. Different segmentation variables may be tried either singly, sequentially or in combination, with a view to identifying useful segments. Imagination and creativity have a part to play in the selection of variables that can offer a competitive advantage.

6. Within-country segmentation

These days most companies of any size will have had to address seriously the problems and opportunities of segmentation in their own home market. It has been suggested that researchers do not always pay the same attention to segmentation within overseas markets, in effect regarding each individual country as a homogeneous whole.

The concept of segmentation is relevant to *any* market, domestic or overseas. Segmentation within one country, however, is beyond the scope of this book. Readers wishing to consider segmentation techniques further may like to consult, for consumer marketing, Frank, Massy and Wind and, for industrial marketing, Bonoma and Shapiro (*see* Bibliography).

7. Cross-border segmentation

Segments identified in one country will often differ significantly from those in another. Occasionally, however, there can be found a real similarity between groups of consumers that cuts across national boundaries and forms, in effect, a regional (in the sense of including several countries) or even a global segment.

Regional or global segments offer opportunities for standardisation, with significant economies of scale in production, R & D and marketing costs. The international marketer will be alert to the possibility of identifying and exploiting them.

Examples of such segments, often quoted, are the youth market (for jeans, pop records and cola drinks) and the business market (business suits, business magazines).

8. Country groupings

Segmentation techniques have been applied not merely to the identification of segments within or between countries but also to the grouping of complete countries into segments. The objective, again, is usually standardisation, with consequent economies of scale.

Some such groupings have been based on a single variable, the most obvious being stages of economic development or geographical proximity. The approach offers some advantages (in terms of convenience of management, for instance, in the case of geographical proximity) but it ignores social, cultural and political differences. Grouping whole countries by a single variable is unlikely to offer a real cost or marketing advantage.

At the other extreme, Jain lists a number of studies aimed at the grouping of countries that are based on several variables, in some cases more than fifty. At this level the use of multivariate statistical techniques such as cluster analysis is essential in order to reduce the information to meaningful dimensions. Jain points out that such approaches have yet to demonstrate that they offer in practice an advantage over the outcome that might be expected to result from a purely judgemental approach.

The conclusion must be that multivariate techniques applied to the grouping of whole countries offer as yet little practical benefit. It is at the product-market level that the real value of such techniques can be demonstrated.

Progress test 10

1. Suggest and justify ways in which international segmentation might be achieved in the case of a company exporting to more than fifty countries. *(CIM)*

2. Successful exporting depends heavily on taking adequate steps to select appropriate markets for products and services. What steps would you take to identify a suitable market for a product or service of your choice? *(IEx)*

3. Antique Sticks Ltd has been manufacturing and marketing reproduction furniture for the past three years and is now interested in entering the export market. They have now approached your company, Specialist Export Consultants Ltd, to seek your professional advice on marketing their products to markets outside the UK. How would you advise them to proceed with the selection and assessment of export markets? *IEx)*

4. Describe how outside sources of information can help the exporter to expand into new markets. *(IEx)*

5. As the market research manager of a firm making industrial fasteners for use in the building and engineering trades you have been asked by the export manager to assist him in selecting new export markets. Describe **(a)** the basis for selecting markets which you would propose, and **(b)** how the necessary information could be obtained. *(IEx)*

11

International product policy

1. Product

Kotler defines a product as 'anything that can be offered to a market for attention, acquisition, use or consumption that might satisfy a want or need.' It may include physical goods, services, persons, places, organisations or ideas.

The product planner must consider the product on three levels: the customer needs and wants that have to be satisfied; the tangible product itself and its associated quality, style and features; and the augmented product, items such as prompt delivery, credit terms, after-sales service and warranty that help to make up the total benefit package.

2. Product policy

Product policy is concerned with:

(a) modification of existing products with a view to improving product performance in current markets or extending into new markets;
(b) the planned development and introduction of new products;
(c) the planned elimination of failing products;
(d) packaging, after-sales service, warranties, patent protection and trade mark registration, and product liability.

All these are wide-ranging topics. Only the international aspects of product policy can be considered here.

3. Standardisation or product modification

International marketers must decide which is the more appropriate of two product design strategies: standardisation, or modification to suit each market's tastes and conditions. Standardisation means offering a common product on a regional or world-wide basis, with the immense cost savings that will usually result; modification to suit each market should offer improvements in sales turnover and price levels. The decision between the two extremes is clearly of fundamental importance but it is not an easy one to make; much depends on the organisation's objectives, the nature of its products, and the markets in which it operates or intends to operate. However, some of the facts which the international marketer will need to take into account are discussed below.

4.   Mandatory product modifications

A degree of product modification is sometimes unavoidable. For instance:
(a) minimum or special product standards are sometimes imposed by law, especially in relation to product safety;
(b) tariff levels may be so high that local manufacture, or at least local purchase of components, is essential, in which case standardisation may become impossible;
(c) governments may require that a proportion of components should be of local manufacture;
(d) certain technical changes (in, for example, voltage or calibration of measuring instruments) are obviously essential, though they are often of minor importance;
(e) government taxation policy may leave the international marketer with little choice (in France, for example, car tax is related to engine size and the age of the car, thus seriously discouraging the use of luxury cars);
(f) climatic conditions may require a product modification (the composition of car tyres, for instance, varies according to extremes of climate).

5.   Factors encouraging modification

The following factors will tend to influence the international marketer towards product modification:

(a) consumer tastes, especially in foodstuffs;
(b) inadequate consumer purchasing power, which may require a lower price and a corresponding reduction in quality;
(c) the general level of technical skills, which may require product simplification;
(d) poor maintenance standards (often a problem in developing countries) which may suggest either improvements in product quality or a simpler design;
(e) local labour costs, which may suggest a need for a higher, or lower, degree of automation.

6.   Factors encouraging standardisation

Factors encouraging product standardisation include:

(a) production economies of scale, which can be very significant;
(b) amortisation of product development costs over a larger turnover;
(c) reduction in inventory costs (each product must be carried at a level that reflects normal demand plus a safety margin to cover unexpected upsurges; as a result the minimum safe stock level for several different products exceeds that applicable to one standard product);
(d) interchangeable components, in that, in multinational production, plants can rely on components from the parent plant;
(e) the nature of the product (industrial products, for instance, are more likely to be standardised, given that most industrial processes are similar, whatever the country);

(f) tourist and similar products, which require instant recognition by travellers (for example, Kodak film and Hilton hotels);

(g) the existence of cross-border market segments such as the youth market (10:7);

(h) economies of scale in marketing, especially in relation to television advertising film production costs, which can be very significant;

(i) home country image, as, for example, with French perfume, whose consumer appeal lies in its national origin.

7. The global product

There are very few opportunities for producing products that are completely standardised world-wide; jeans require differing size ranges according to the market, and even cola drinks may demand adjustment of sugar content.

However, in response to the pressure for cost savings, some multinational companies now endeavour to create what they describe as a global product, though modularised product might be a better term. For this global product, major components are standardised to the maximum possible extent, while the remainder are tailored to meet the needs of individual markets. Such a product is particularly relevant, for instance, to car production. The production of new and entirely different models in each country, or even region of the world, is no longer economically possible; on the other hand, local market adaptation is essential for reasons of geography, climate, and national safety and other regulations. Ford's 'global car', the Mondeo, for example, was designed by engineers in the USA, the UK and Germany. It is assembled in Belgium and North America from components manufactured in several other countries.

8. New product development

New product development is a continuing preoccupation of the marketing-oriented company. Most of the procedures are of general application and are not considered here.

The international marketer, however, has potentially an immense advantage in the important first stage of the innovation process, idea generation. New product ideas originate from many sources, such as R&D, customer requests and employee suggestions, but one highly important source is ideas already generated, and perhaps already successfully developed, in other parts of the world.

It is not enough to accept that this advantage exists. International marketers must ensure that a system is in place to harvest and collate all ideas from wherever they have a presence. The investment in management time is likely to pay off handsomely. Product pick-up services (10:4) may be of value here.

This is not to say, of course, that a product successful in one market will necessarily be successful in another. Normal screening, testing and business analysis are still essential in each market.

9.   New inventions for specific overseas markets

One strategy open to the international marketer is the development of entirely new products to open up new markets. This is an approach which, it has been suggested, is relevant to developing nations, which have tended to adopt products of industrialised nations which are by no means always suitable to the local scene. As a general rule, market potential in most developing nations is unlikely to justify the commercial development of entirely new products, though instances can be found.

Example
_____

Emcol International has developed a product called Instant Road Repair, which repairs any size of pothole in tarmacadam, asphalt or concrete with a minimum of equipment. The material is a special formula of liquids and graded aggregate which is tipped from a container into the pothole, then banged flat with a shovel; traffic can proceed over the repair immediately. Thus a lorry loaded with containers of the product and some men with shovels can repair a broken road in around three minutes. This is particularly useful for road repairs in Nigeria, where access may be a problem and the labour is unskilled.

(Source: Julia Piper, *Marketing*, January 1978)

10.   Product elimination

Often, obsolescent or marginal products linger on in the range until their lack of profitability becomes too obvious to ignore. Long before this they become a costly burden which cannot be adequately disclosed by any financial accounting system. Such products, for instance, involve expensive short-run production as demand declines, take up an excessive amount of management time, give an image of a technologically backward company, and, most damaging of all, delay the search for new products.

For these reasons companies should establish some form of product elimination procedure (often a product review committee) to review the range and regularly phase out unwanted products. Before abandonment, of course, such a committee would consider not merely current product profitability but also such factors as future market potential, the likely effect on sales and profits of product rejuvenation, possible changes in marketing strategy, alternative product opportunities and the extent to which the product may assist the sale of other products in the range.

11.   International product elimination

In essence, the review and elimination procedures remain much the same in an international context, though the scale of the problem is often much greater, simply because both exporters and multinationals must take into account market potential in all their markets. In particular, although a product may not be over-profitable in the domestic market, it could well be in the growth stage of its life cycle in other markets with different per capita incomes or purchase influences.

Example _____

The Volkswagen Beetle, long forgotten in industrialised countries, is still successfully manufactured in Mexico, and is as ubiquitous as ever. The Enfield Bullet motorcycle, production of which ceased in the UK in the early 1950s, is still manufactured in large numbers in India. In recent years Bullets have been imported into the UK from the Indian factory.

_____

12. International alternatives to product elimination

The international marketer is fortunate in that rather more alternatives are open, as a rule, than to a domestic counterpart. The international marketer is sometimes in a position to derive some profit from the sale of services associated with the product, by licensing, franchising, contract manufacture or management contracting (15:**2, 8, 11, 14**). Such a course is possible, for instance, when it is production costs or small-scale production, rather than market potential, that are the cause of the product's decline.

13. Packaging

In the case of packaging, as with the product, a decision has to be made between standardisation and adaptation to specific market needs, though the decision is rarely so critical in profit terms. In arriving at the decision both the protectional and promotional aspects of packaging should be considered.

14. Protectional aspects of packaging

Protectional aspects include:

(a) climatic conditions, both in the market-place and in transit to the market-place;
(b) the handling the product is likely to receive;
(c) the length of time the product is likely to spend within the distribution chain, bearing in mind that the chain may include many more intermediaries than at home;
(d) consumer usage rate and consequent storage time.

15. Promotional aspects of packaging

Promotional aspects include:

(a) package size (for instance, a high level of car ownership and a developed supermarket retail system will indicate large packs, while in developing countries a very low per capita income may suggest small packs or, as with razor blades, even individual packs);
(b) the cost of the package (the standard package may be over-elaborate in some markets, adding unnecessarily to the price of the contents);
(c) local preferences in terms of colour (white is associated with mourning in some Far Eastern countries);
(d) legal requirements (Venezuela does not permit on-pack promotional gifts);

(e) recognition (tourist products, such as Kodak film, should be immediately recognisable to all nationalities, and therefore require an internationally standard package);

(f) literacy (a low level of literacy will require greater emphasis on pictorial design).

16. Servicing

For those goods that require service facilities, servicing is of special importance internationally; customers tend to give preference to national products if they have the least reason to fear inadequate after-sales service from a remote and foreign company.

Servicing may be looked at from two angles: organising the necessary facilities, and modifying the product design.

Ideally, a company might appoint a reliable distributor with an established servicing network compatible with the product. In practice, such distributors are rare and involvement by the manufacturer in the distributor's service function is often essential. This may require the training of distributor personnel at company headquarters, the establishment of teams of trainers, or the secondment of the manufacturer's own maintenance staff to the distributor. Direct servicing is possible in the case of major items of capital equipment, when it is economic to fly out maintenance and repair staff from company headquarters.

In some countries where technical skills are limited and maintenance standards are low, servicing requirements may entail product modification, with the aim of producing a simpler or sturdier design. Such modification is particularly appropriate to agricultural products in relatively isolated areas in developing countries.

Example

The African government had been buying from ... an American firm hand-operated dusters for use in distributing pesticides in the cotton fields. The dusters were loaned to individual farmers. The duster supplied by the corporation was a finely-machined device requiring regular oiling and good care, but the fact that this duster turned more easily than any other duster on the market was relatively unimportant to the farmers. Furthermore, the requirement for careful oiling and care simply meant that in a relatively short time the machines froze up and broke. The result? The government went back to an older-type French duster which was heavy, turned with difficulty, and gave a poorer distribution of dust, but which lasted longer in that it required less care and lubrication.

(Source: R. D. Robinson, *Journal of Marketing*, October 1961)

17. Protection of industrial property: patents

A patent is an exclusive right granted by government to the owner of an invention (a new product or process) which prevents anyone else from using that invention for a fixed period of time. The duration of a patent varies from one country to another but is usually between 15 and 17 years.

Application for registration of a patent must be filed in each separate country. This process is slow and expensive, especially since standards for patentability vary from one country to another.

The problems of registration are alleviated to some extent by international patent conventions. Under the Paris Convention, now subscribed to by over ninety countries, once a company has filed for a patent in one member country, it has priority in all other member countries. The convention also requires each member country to extend to the nationals of other member countries the same rights as it provides to its own nationals. The Inter-American Convention, subscribed to by the USA and most Latin American countries, offers protection similar to that provided by the Paris Convention.

Governments have a legitimate interest in licensing agreements and often require their formal registration. Developing nations, ever mindful of their usually limited foreign currency reserves, may lay down maximum percentage royalties and ban any clause prohibiting the export of products manufactured under licence. Industrialised nations are concerned that a licensing agreement should not allocate markets or impose other restrictions on the licensee that might hinder free competition. For specific examples, *see* the chapters on Brazil (27:6), Japan (29:12), Nigeria (30:8), the USA (32:6 and 7) and the EC (28:9).

18. Protection of industrial property: trade marks

A trade mark is 'a brand or part of a brand that is given legal protection because it is capable of exclusive appropriation'.

A brand is 'a name, term, sign, symbol or design, or combination of them, which is intended to identify the goods of one seller or group of sellers and to differentiate them from competitors'.

A trade mark is the customer's assurance of quality; it enables the manufacturer to promote his product without unduly benefiting his competitors. Its protection from imitation is often vital; sometimes the very survival of the company may be at stake.

19. National trade mark protection

Protection of trade marks is available at two levels, national and international.

Most countries offer a system of trade mark registration and protection for foreign, as well as domestic, suppliers. Two basic systems exist:

(a) in code law countries, such as France and Italy, priority of registration ensures protection;
(b) in common law countries, such as the UK and the USA, protection is established by priority of use.

A number of variants are to be found on these two basic themes. Some countries, for instance, insist on use within a certain period after registration;

and registration in most countries must be periodically renewed.

20. International trade mark protection

The Arrangement of Madrid covers the international registration of trade marks. A trade mark registered in any one member country in the name of a locally domiciled establishment is forwarded to a central bureau, giving priority for registration in all other member states, provided the mark is qualified for registration under the national registration rules of those countries. Unfortunately, only 26 countries are currently members of the Madrid Arrangement.

For details of trade mark legislation in specific countries, *see* again 27:**6**, 29:**13**, 30:**8**, 32:**8** and 28:**10**.

21. Trade mark imitation

Trade mark imitation aims to take advantage of the promotional expenditure and reputation of a major supplier by offering similar but inferior products under the same or very similar brand names, with similar packaging and labelling.

Examples
_____
(1) Johnnie Walker Red Label is the world's largest-selling Scotch whisky. In recent years the proprietors of the brand have had to bring proceedings to prevent the use of the name and its famous striding-figure device in relation to products as diverse as cigarettes (in the USA), blue jeans (in Colombia) and sewing thread (in India). For whisky itself, imitation of the packaging and labelling styles, for both Johnnie Walker and other brands, is more usual and the brand owners must be constantly on the alert, ready to take legal action.
(2) Gordon's Dry Gin devotes much time and money to protecting its name and packaging style against interlopers such as Cordón, London's, Garden's and so on.
_____

22. Trade mark piracy

Piracy in this context is the registration of trade marks in code law countries with the aim of selling the right to the marks back to the originating firm if and when such firms wish to enter the market. The firm must either pay the price asked, attempt to register and popularise another brand at significant expense, or abandon the idea of market entry.

Example
_____
Two leading French chemical companies, Péchiney and Ugine Kuhlmann, merged and filed an application for registration of the trade mark 'PUK', only to find that 'PUK' had been registered, immediately after the merger, by a third party not in any way involved in the actual use of such a brand. Péchiney Ugine Kuhlmann were forced to resort to litigation in order to establish their right to use the brand.
_____

23. Trade mark protection policy

At first sight it may seem desirable to register a trade mark in all countries. In practice, however, some compromise will have to be reached, simply because in some countries registration is expensive in terms of initial fees, renewal fees, legal fees and the cost of establishing trade mark use by gaining the necessary sales.

Registration is, of course, essential in those countries where the company is already operating or where it intends to start operations in the near future. For other countries the following factors should be considered:

(a) present and probable future market potential;
(b) ease and *total* cost of registration;
(c) the expense and inconvenience of selecting a new brand, should that eventually prove necessary;
(d) the importance of the brand name in terms of sales of the product;
(e) the importance of establishing one standard brand name world-wide.

For products bought by travellers, the establishment of a world-wide brand name is critical. In many other cases, sentiment apart, there is often no real need to insist on the use of the same name in all countries unless it offers significant promotional economies of scale. Such economies might arise, for instance, from:

(a) standardisation of advertising campaigns over several countries (21:**4**);
(b) the use of international media (21:**12**);
(c) the opportunities offered by media spillover (21:**12**).

24. Product liability

A person injured by a defective product may have the right to sue for damages. Product liability is the general term given to laws affecting that right.

As recently as ten or fifteen years ago a reputable manufacturer supplying a quality product outside the category of inherently dangerous goods such as fireworks was probably not seriously concerned with the question of product liability. With the rise of consumerism, however, and the introduction in many countries of more stringent legislation, it is now a subject that no marketer, and certainly no international marketer, can afford to ignore.

There are three generally recognised bases for a product liability action. The most stringent is based on 'strict' or 'absolute' liability: the manufacturer *or importer* of the product is always liable and has no defence provided the plaintiff can prove that the damage was caused by the product. This is the system adopted in certain states of the USA and by the EC Product Liability Directive.

The second system is similar to strict liability except that it permits a 'development risks defence'. For this defence the manufacturer must show that the product complied with the state of technical and scientific knowledge at the time it was put on sale. This defence is an optional provision of the EC

Directive; it has been incorporated in UK law in the Consumer Protection Act 1987.

The third system permits an action only on the basis of negligence on the part of manufacturer or importer. Under this system a good defence might be that the manufacturer designed and manufactured a safe product, that quality control and inspection were adequate, that all safety regulations relating to the product were complied with, and that the consumer was warned of any inherent dangers.

In general, the international marketer should be aware of current product liability legislation in any country in which he or she operates, should take all appropriate safety measures, and should regularly review relevant product liability insurance.

In certain markets, this will still not be sufficient. *See* the chapter on the USA (32:**12**).

Progress test 11

1. Is any product ever the same in every country in which it is sold? *(IEx)*

2. In a review of Japanese marketing practices you identify that the typical approach taken is to have a standardised product in each international market but an adapted advertising approach. Examine the justification for such an approach. *(CIM)*

3. Some products tend to be required in a standardised form in several countries while others emphasise local variations. What particular conditions could lead to **(a)** greater standardisation, and **(b)** greater variation? *(CIM)*

4. Give examples of three factors which could make it necessary to make modifications to a product in order for the product to be acceptable in an overseas market. *(IEx)*

5. What in your view is the future for global products?

6. 'As a multinational company we have a real advantage in the search for new-product ideas.' Why is this so, and what in practice might an MNC do to capitalise on these advantages?

7. A manufacturer of domestic electrical appliances decides to extend operations from his home market into a number of other countries. What demands is this likely to make on his product development facilities? *(CIM)*

8. 'Product elimination procedures are especially difficult, but especially important, in a multinational company.' Why?

9. You sell confectionery in the form of sweets and chocolates. You find there is a market for them in the main West African markets. What factors would you take into account when repackaging them for these markets? *(IEx)*

10. Detail and comment on six factors which you would take into consideration when deciding on the type of packaging you would adopt for a product of your choice in an overseas market. *(IEx)*

11. You are the marketing manager of a whisky manufacturer selling in some fifty countries. After a recent unfortunate experience in one market you have been asked to establish a clear brand protection policy for the future. Set out that policy in summary form.

12. Under what circumstances might a company regard the establishment of one single brand name world-wide as being of key importance?

13. Under what circumstances might it be desirable for a company to adopt different brand names in different countries?

14. One of your US distributors, appointed a year ago, has achieved a remarkable increase in turnover on your behalf. He has now suggested an amendment to his distributor agreement by which you would indemnify him against any possible actions for damages under product liability legislation. You, as a marketing manager, understand his viewpoint, but your managing director is on his high horse. Explain the position to him.

12

International distribution decisions I: Alternative channels

1. Definition

Some manufacturers sell and deliver their products direct to the user (e.g. many industrial goods manufacturers). Many companies, however, sell through middlemen, who perform a variety of functions connected with the marketing of the product. Such companies seek to link together the set of marketing intermediaries most appropriate to their profit and other objectives. Such a set of marketing intermediaries is known as the marketing channel or the channel of distribution. The most obvious example of such a channel is the producer-wholesaler-retailer distribution system adopted for many consumer goods.

2. Functions of middlemen

The functions of middlemen include some or all of the following:

(a) the assembly of products from many different producers into an assortment of interest to buyers;
(b) breaking bulk to meet the scale of need of the customer;
(c) adapting goods to market requirements;
(d) physical distribution (transport and storage);
(e) price setting;
(f) sales promotion and advertising;
(g) seeking out buyers and selling to them;
(h) extending credit to buyers.

All these are essential functions that must be undertaken by the manufacturer or by middlemen. The manufacturer will decide whether he can himself perform some or all of these functions more efficiently or whether it is desirable to hand the responsibility over to middlemen.

3. Importance of channel decisions

In any country, channel decisions are among the most important policy decisions facing management, for the four main reasons discussed below.

The channels selected will fundamentally affect almost every other marketing decision. For example, prices must reflect the mark-up allowed to an intermediary, and the size of the sales force must depend on whether sales are made direct to the retailers or only to wholesalers.

The channel decision involves the company in long-term commitments to other independent organisations, and these commitments are often extremely difficult to change.

Although these independent organisations work with the producer to their mutual advantage, there is an inherent conflict of interest between them, in that the producer wishes the middleman to sell at the lowest possible margin, thus maximising sales and the producer's profit, while the middleman wishes to sell at the price which will maximise his own profit.

The producer using middlemen necessarily loses a significant degree of control over his own market.

4. Channel design and management

Even in domestic marketing, therefore, a manufacturer must pay special attention both to the initial strategic decision as to design of channel and to subsequent channel management (i.e. the selection of individual intermediaries, their motivation, control and evaluation). The fundamental aim of channel management is to supply the product to the end customer at the right time and in the manner most profitable to the manufacturer.

5. Channel design and management and the international marketer

Compared with domestic marketing, the task of channel design and management internationally is one of infinitely greater complexity. The international marketer must take into account:

(a) channels between nations (market-entry channels);
(b) channels within nations (foreign-market channels).

Channels between nations

6. Definition

Channels between nations include:

(a) *indirect export*: sales to intermediaries within the UK who in turn re-sell to a customer abroad;
(b) *direct export*: sales to a customer abroad, who may be the end user of the goods or an intermediary, the latter being perhaps the exporter's own local office;

(c) *manufacture abroad*: on either a joint venture or an independent basis.

The principal alternatives open to the international marketer under each of the above headings are shown, with references to the chapters in which they are further discussed, in Fig. 12.1 (direct and indirect export) and Fig. 12.2 (manufacture abroad).

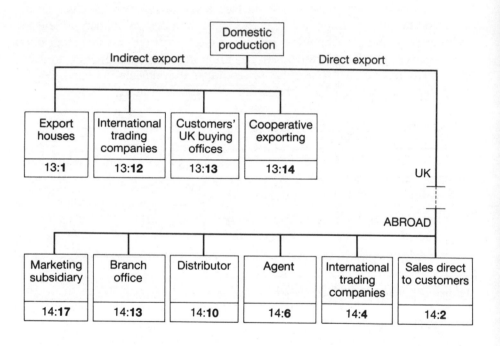

Figure 12.1 *Distribution channels between nations (direct and indirect export): principal alternatives.*
NOTE: Numbers refer to chapters and sections in the text.

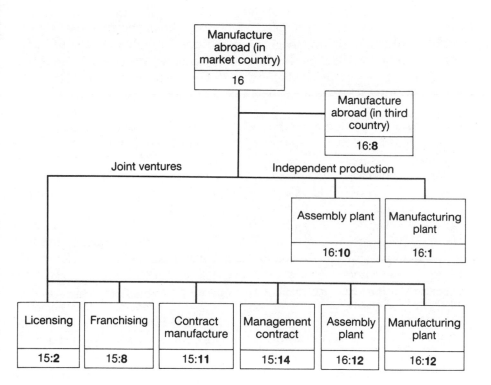

Figure 12.2 *Distribution channels between nations (manufacture abroad): principal alternatives.*
NOTE: Numbers refer to chapters and sections in the text.

7.   Selection criteria for channels between nations

Selection of the appropriate market-entry channels will depend in every case on company objectives, company size and product range. There are, however, more general criteria, largely independent of the company or its products, which should be borne in mind.

(a) *Channel availability*. Different markets require different approaches. Licensing, for example, may not be possible because no suitably qualified licensees can be found; in some small markets the only agent of value may already represent the competition.

(b) *Sales volume*. Sales volume depends not merely on market potential but also on the channel selected.

(c) *Operating costs*. Sales volume figures are not in themselves particularly meaningful; they must be related to the costs involved in achieving the volume. Both the initial and the recurring costs of entry should be considered.

(d) *Investment required*. Investment requirements are clearly highest in wholly-owned overseas production operations, but capital may also be required, for instance, to finance local stocks or extend credit to local distributors.

(e) *Personnel*. The alternative channels described vary greatly in terms of the requirement for skilled managerial and other personnel. Lack of suitably qualified staff may prove a bar to the adoption of certain of the market-entry methods outlined.

(f) *Risk*. The degree of risk is not only a function of the market but also of the company's method of involvement in that market.

(g) *Control*. The degree of control a company can exercise over its distribution channels will usually have a significant bearing on its success. Control will vary widely according to the channel selected. For instance, in the case of sales to export merchants the company will have no control whatsoever, while it is possible to exercise firm control through an overseas marketing or manufacturing subsidiary.

(h) *Flexibility*. A channel which is optimal at the time of market entry may cease to be so as market conditions change, or as sales develop. A company should, therefore, retain flexibility, the ability to change its degree of involvement to meet new conditions. Such flexibility is not easy to achieve under any circumstances (even agencies require a degree of commitment on the part of the principal), but a greater degree of flexibility is likely to be retained if it is planned for in advance.

All the above criteria should be considered in relation to all practicable alternative channels whenever entry into a new market or a change of established channels is contemplated.

Channels within nations

8. The whole channel concept

Many manufacturers, especially manufacturers of industrial goods, need consider only the problem of distribution channels between nations, as their products are sold direct to the end user (often another company or a government organisation).

Other manufacturers, however, face the additional problem of distribution within the foreign market, through local wholesale-retail or other channels. In such cases the task of the international marketer is not complete when the goods arrive (or are manufactured) in the overseas market. The international marketer should be concerned with the entire channel of distribution, from producer to the final buyer (i.e. industrial end user or consumer) even if it is not always possible to exercise a direct influence on the actions and policies of all intermediaries. This, the *whole channel concept*, is fundamental to good marketing. It implies, for each market, involvement in channel design and channel management.

9. The whole channel concept and the exporter

The overseas manufacturing subsidiary, often heavily dependent on the market in which it is located, will usually be closely concerned with channel design and management.

The exporter, however, frequently trading with a large number of markets, is all too often content to sell to a foreign importer, ignoring the subsequent distribution channels that link the importer with the final purchaser. In any market of importance, such an approach will usually prove less than optimal in profit terms; a channel is only as effective as its weakest member, and sales may be blocked at any point within the channel. The whole channel concept is just as relevant to the exporter as to the overseas manufacturing subsidiary.

Example _____

For an example, *see* the Letraset case study.
_____

Channels within nations (design and management) are considered further in Chapter 17.

Progress test 12

1. When considering the launch of a product overseas, the nature of the product will influence the choice of channels of distribution. Give examples of four types of product and indicate the most appropriate channels of distribution for each. *(IEx)*

2. Outline the main types of selling arrangement a company can use in its foreign markets. Briefly evaluate them in relation to:
(a) marketing automobiles in developing countries;
and
(b) marketing fashion clothing in highly developed countries. *(CIM)*

3. You export electronic components used by a wide range of industries. You find your sole distributors are not, in Norway, Sweden and Denmark, obtaining the business you think they should. What other methods of distribution would you consider and why? *(IEx)*

4. 'The international marketer's interest in a channel of distribution normally ceases when he transfers his title to a buyer.' In your experience, is this so? And should it be so?

13

International distribution decisions II: Indirect export

Export houses

1. Definition

The *Directory of the British Exporters Association* defines an export house as 'any company or firm, not being a manufacturer, whose main activity is the handling or financing of British export trade and/or international trade not connected with the UK.' There are around 750 export houses in the UK.

The operations of these export houses are difficult to define in view of the flexibility which is their most marked characteristic. However, from a distribution channel viewpoint, and ignoring those houses specialising mainly in finance, it is possible to distinguish three major categories:

(a) export merchants, who act as principals in the export transaction, buying and selling on their own account;

(b) confirming houses and buying/indent houses, who represent the buyer abroad;

(c) manufacturers' export agents and specialist export managers, who represent the UK manufacturer.

The characteristics of these different types of export house are compared in Table 13.1. They are explained in greater detail below, though it should be realised that many export houses manage to combine several of the functions discussed.

2. Export merchants

In essence, export merchants are domestic wholesalers operating in foreign markets through their own salesmen, agents, stockists and, very often, local branch offices. Their remuneration derives from the difference between the buying price and the selling price. They tend to specialise in certain territories, and sometimes in certain classes of goods.

3. Advantages of trade through merchants

The advantages to a manufacturer of using the services of merchants are:

(a) the manufacturer takes immediate advantage of the merchants' knowledge of foreign markets and their established contacts within those markets, this being particularly important in the case of the more difficult export markets such as Japan;

Table 13.1 Comparison of typical characteristics of UK export houses

Category of export house	Representation arrangement	Seeks	Accepts financing and credit risk (short-term)	Shipping, insurance and documentation	Remuneration	Manufacturer's degree of control over market	Handles competing lines	Continuing relationship
Export merchant	Acts as principal	Customers abroad and suppliers in UK	Yes	Undertaken	Difference between purchase and resale prices	Nil	Yes	No
Confirming house	Confirms, as principal, order placed by foreign buyer	Suppliers in UK	Yes	Undertaken	Commission from foreign buyer	Nil	Yes	No
Buying/indent house	Acts on behalf of foreign buyer, either buying with wide discretion on orders received or placing indents on suppliers specified by buyer	Suppliers in UK	Yes if required	Undertaken	Commission from foreign buyer	Nil	Yes	No
Manufacturers' export agent	Represents UK manufacturers	Customers abroad	Not usually	Not normally undertaken	Commission from UK manufacturer	Fair	No	Yes
Specialist export manager	Represents UK manufacturers	Customers abroad	Sometimes	Undertaken	Commission from UK manufacturer plus retainer	Good	No	Yes

(b) the manufacturer is relieved entirely of the need to finance the export transaction and of the credit risk;

(c) the manufacturer is, usually, similarly relieved of the problems of documentation, shipping and insurance;

(d) the manufacturer is able to export without any investment of money or of executive time, as there is no overhead load;

(e) many merchants have developed expertise in specialist fields such as countertrade where, for many companies, their services are essential;

(f) in certain circumstances, merchants carry greater weight in selling than individual manufacturers.

Many of the above advantages are clearly of particular value to the small exporter. It would be a mistake to assume, however, that export merchants have little to offer to the larger company. Such larger exporters may well find it more profitable to concentrate on direct sales in markets of major importance, while dealing through merchants in the less important markets, in the more difficult markets (for example, Japan), and on those occasions when specialist expertise, as in countertrade, is required.

4.   Disadvantages of trading with merchants

There are, of course, certain disadvantages in trading through export merchants:

(a) most serious, the manufacturer has little or no control over the market, and the product may be dropped at any time if a more profitable line appears;

(b) the manufacturer is not building up goodwill in the market as a basis for expansion;

(c) the export merchant needs volume to survive and may take on so many lines that the product of an individual manufacturer receives little attention;

(d) similarly, the merchant must secure an early return and therefore merchants are not a suitable channel where a long-term investment of time or money is essential for maximum exploitation of the market;

(e) if sales in a market expand very significantly, the manufacturer will often find it more profitable to deal direct.

5.   Confirming houses

The confirming house confirms as a principal an order which a foreign buyer has placed with a UK manufacturer who is unwilling to extend credit overseas. It finances the transaction, accepting the short-term credit risk, and receives a commission in return from the buyer.

As far as the UK exporter is concerned, trading through a confirming house is little different from trading with a merchant – the advantages and disadvantages are much the same.

6.   The buying/indent house

The buying/indent house acts on behalf of the overseas buyer, either buying with wide discretion against orders received, or placing indents on manufacturers specified by the buyer. It may act as a principal in the same manner as a confirming house. For the exporter the advantages and disadvantages are again much the same as for a merchant house.

7. Manufacturers' export agent

The manufacturers' export agent sells abroad on behalf of UK manufacturers, either in its own name or, more usually, in the name of the manufacturer. It will usually cover a particular sector of industry, representing to that sector a number of UK manufacturers of non-competing products.

Remuneration takes the form of a commission from the UK manufacturers.

8. Trading through a manufacturers' export agent

The advantages and disadvantages of trading through a manufacturers' export agent are similar to those of trading through an export merchant, except that:

(a) export finance, the credit risk, shipping, insurance , and export documentation are usually the concern of the manufacturer;
(b) the manufacturer, since the sale is usually in his name, retains much greater control over the market.

9. The specialist export manager

The specialist export manager, or combination export manager as he or she is known in the USA, offers a complete export management service, becoming in effect the export department of the manufacturer, acting in the manufacturer's name and normally using the manufacturer's letterhead. Such a manager will normally undertake finance and documentation and will sometimes accept the credit risk.

Remuneration is usually by way of a commission on sales, though in addition a small annual retainer is required.

10. Advantages of the specialist export manager

The specialist export manager offers all the advantages of the export merchant. In addition, the manufacturing company:

(a) immediately gains its own export department, at negligible overhead cost;
(b) secures the maximum possible degree of control over its market, short of establishing its own export organisation;
(c) is building up goodwill in the market under its own name;
(d) may expect, as a rule, a continuing and long-term relationship.

11. Disadvantages of the specialist export manager

On the other hand:

(a) the specialist export manager is subject to the same pressures as any other export house, and must drop or ignore products that do not offer a reasonably prompt return;

(b) as sales develop, the manufacturer may well wish to change to direct export, but will not have built up the necessary in-house experience and capability;

(c) the specialist export manager will normally expect a world-wide brief – naturally so, if the exporting company is not developing its own export department – yet is unlikely to be able to offer world-wide coverage.

The latter point is perhaps the key issue in the selection of a specialist export manager. The exporter must ensure that the target markets coincide with those in which the specialist export manager has genuine contacts and experience.

12. International trading companies

The international trading companies are highly diversified and large-scale manufacturers and merchants, often operating at both the wholesale and retail levels of distribution. They are of particular importance in South East Asia and in the former African colonial territories. For a British exporter, dealing with the UK trading companies is broadly the equivalent of dealing with UK merchant houses, although the size and market coverage of many such companies makes them also attractive as potential distributors. In some countries trading companies alone can provide adequate coverage, market access and political acceptability, though a growing nationalism means that in the long term their influence is likely to decline.

UK buying offices

13. Department stores

Many of the major department stores in industrialised countries maintain buying offices in the UK; others appoint UK export houses as their buying agents.

Buyers from many department stores, whether or not they have a London office, make regular visits to the UK. Notice of many of these visits is given through the DTI's Export Intelligence Service or is published in appropriate trade journals.

Cooperative export marketing

14. Complementary marketing

Complementary export marketing (often termed 'piggyback exporting') occurs when one manufacturer, the 'carrier', uses its established overseas distribution facilities to market the goods of another manufacturer, the 'rider', alongside its own.

Two alternative arrangements are possible:

(a) the carrier sells the rider's products on a commission basis, effectively acting as its agent;
(b) the carrier buys the products outright and re-sells at the best price it can obtain, thus acting as a merchant.

15. Advantages for the rider

It is important, if any such arrangements are entered into, that both parties should derive some significant advantage. The advantage to the rider is clear: complementary exporting provides a simple and low-risk method of beginning export operations – particularly important for a small company lacking the resources to engage in direct export.

16. Advantages for the carrier

The arrangement should result in increased profit for the carrier. Such profit is most likely to accrue if the rider's products:

(a) broaden an otherwise over-limited product range, offering economies of scale in distribution, compensation for seasonal down-turns in the basic product line, or generating distributor enthusiasm;
(b) or are related to the carrier's product lines in such a way that they assist in their sale.

Example

The Singer Sewing Machine Co. would piggyback products closely allied to its own, such as fabrics, patterns, thread and other sewing accessories.

17. Export consortia

An export consortium is a group of companies that join in an *ad hoc* working relationship which stops short of the formation of a new corporate identity but which tenders for and fulfils as a single entity a specified major export contract. On completion of the contract the consortium is usually dissolved and members are free to seek similar associations elsewhere. Export consortia seem to have become increasingly popular in recent years, especially for contracts for defence equipment and major construction projects such as the building of a complete factory.

The customer has the advantage of dealing with only one supplying or contracting organisation and can be reasonably sure that all the necessary technical skills are available to him.

Consortium members may expect to have a much greater chance of securing the contract and will in any case find that their marketing and tendering costs will be significantly reduced.

Progress test 13

1. Often the view is expressed that, because of the increasing tendency for exporters to either supply customers direct or appoint agents or distributors in a market, the role of export channels of distribution within the UK has become unimportant and such channels can, therefore, be ignored. As an exporter of hand and power tools, what would be your opinion of such a view? *(IEx)*

2. 'Export houses offer such a variety of services that their functions can be identified only in the context of their relationship with a given client company.' How far is this statement true? What general categories of export houses can you describe?

3. 'The real disadvantage to an exporter of using an export house is the loss of control over the market.' Discuss.

4. It has been said that you can export without going outside your own country. How can this be done and what advantages has it for small companies? *(IEx)*

5. Piggyback exporting has not proved an unqualified success. Can you suggest why this is so? What advice would you give to a small fabric company contemplating a piggyback arrangement with a large and successful international company producing sewing machines?

14

International distribution decisions III: Direct export

Sales direct to customer

1. Possibilities for direct sales

In many instances sales may, of course, be made direct to customers abroad without the assistance of any kind of agent or intermediary. This applies, for instance, in the case of:

(a) many types of industrial goods;

(b) goods sold to national governments, local authorities, and other official or quasi-governmental organisations;

(c) consumer goods sold to the final consumer by direct mail, or to retail stores, especially the major department store groups, or to mail order houses.

2. Retail stores

Reference has already been made to the London buying offices of the major international retail store groups (13:**13**).

3. Mail order houses

Mail order houses, similarly, may be regarded as important outlets worth a direct approach, though abroad, as in the UK, they tend to be demanding customers: delivery must be strictly guaranteed, and prices must remain unchanged for the period of validity of the catalogue (which could lead to difficulties at a time of varying exchange rates). The larger mail order houses often insist that offers should be sent to them on an exclusive basis and should not be offered to competitors, which limits the value of this channel in any one country.

International trading companies abroad

4. Japanese trading companies

A striking feature of the Japanese commercial scene is the many thousands of trading companies. These range from tiny import companies to immense organisations such as Mitsui, Mitsubishi, Sumitomo, Marubeni, and C. Itoh, the 'sogo-shosha'.

The sogo-shosha are closely linked with the major industrial groups which constitute the core of Japanese industry. They act as trading arms for these groups and have close connections with major banks. Their world-wide interests include multinational trading in industrial and consumer goods and commodities, exploitation of natural resources, construction projects, finance and investment, shipping and countertrade. With product lines numbered in thousands, they have offices in almost all the world's major cities.

5. Other international trading companies

Other international trading companies are to be found in Denmark, France, Germany, the Netherlands and Switzerland. The French trading companies are of special importance to any exporter wishing to trade with the former French colonies.

Example
The East Asiatic Co. (EAC), of Copenhagen, was founded in 1897 with shipping and commodity trading as its main activities and Asia as its main sphere of interest. Over the years its emphasis has shifted to more specialised products, with concentration on technical know-how and involvement in the actual production stage. Its interests now include graphics, informatics, a range of consumer goods, energy, property and transport, as well as international trading in timber, wool and machinery. It has offices and manufacturing plants in more than 40 countries and employs 15,000 people world-wide.

Agencies

6. Definition

Agency may be defined as the legal relationship that exists when one person or company (the agent) is employed by another person or company (the principal) to bring that principal into a contractual relationship with third parties. Thus a sales agent is employed to bring about a sales contract between his principal and a third party, the customer.

Strictly speaking, the legal title to goods never passes to the agent; it passes, as a result of the agent's efforts, directly from principal to customer, the agent receiving a commission by way of remuneration. In marketing practice, however, the expression is loosely used to include distributors.

7. Types of agent

Agents may be classified in many different ways. Some of the types of agent more important in international marketing are described below.

A *commission agent* fits most nearly the definition given above. Such an agent sells with the aid of, for example, catalogues or samples, and does not hold stocks of the product, merely passing orders on to the principal, who in turn delivers the goods direct to the customer. Such an agency, of course, is particularly appropriate to industrial goods.

A *stocking agent* stocks the product, providing storage and handling facilities, but does not take title to the goods. Such agents will usually receive a commission on sales plus a fixed sum to cover storage and handling.

A *del credere agent* is not so much a type of agent as a contractual arrangement that could apply to any agency agreement. In selling through agents, principals may find that they have large numbers of customers on their books with whose credit ratings they are entirely unfamiliar. The del credere agent accepts the credit risk, agreeing to pay the principal in the event of default by the customer.

8.   The appointment of agents: advantages

Agents are heavily relied on in the export trade, since at first sight, as a method of market entry, they offer significant advantages:

(a) the exporter obtains the services of (usually) an experienced local national, fully conversant with local business practices and perhaps also with the exporter's industry;

(b) the agent's existing product lines and contacts facilitate the introduction of the exporter's product;

(c) the exporter gains market experience and is able to test potential;

(d) the investment cost (to the exporter) is nil or negligible;

(e) results in terms of sales can often be immediate.

9.   The appointment of agents: disadvantages

It is to be feared that these very obvious advantages have tempted far too many UK companies into the over-hasty appointment of an agent (for one example, see the Letraset case study). The disadvantages of agencies are often, it seems, overlooked:

(a) a lack of commitment of time or money on the part of the exporter is likely to result in a similar lack of commitment on the part of the agent;

(b) the agent, in any case, must offer a number of lines – full attention cannot be given to the exporter's product;

(c) few agents can afford to take a long-term view – if sales are not readily forthcoming, even the most conscientious agent is likely to leave the product in the range, but make no active efforts to promote it;

(d) if the market proves to have real potential, the agent may not have the resources to exploit it fully;

(e) as with any other intermediary, as sales develop agency commission costs are likely to become disproportionately high in relation to alternatives such as a branch office.

For further discussion of agents *see* Chapter 24.

Distributors and stockists

10. Distributors

Distributors have been defined as customers who have been granted exclusive or preferential rights to purchase and re-sell a specific range of products or services in specified geographical areas or markets.

Essentially, therefore, a distributor is a wholesaler, whose remuneration arises from the difference between the purchase price and the re-sale price (and not from any commission granted by the suppliers). A distributor differs from a normal wholesaler by virtue of the 'exclusive or preferential rights' granted, but nevertheless the contractual relationship with the supplier is one of principal and principal, and not one of agent and principal.

11. Stockists

Stockists are distributors who receive a special price, discount, purchase terms or credit terms in return for undertaking to hold specified minimum levels of stock of a specified range of products.

12. The appointment of distributors and stockists

Although the relationship between supplier and distributor is one between principals, the granting of exclusivity or preferential terms usually implies the formal appointment of a distributor and the preparation of a distributorship agreement.

Further, most distributors will expect advice and assistance from their suppliers in the marketing of their products, and it will be in the interest of the supplier to provide such assistance.

In these respects, therefore, the appointment of a distributor offers much the same advantages and disadvantages as that of an agent.

Branch offices

13. Functions

A branch office abroad is simply an extension of the company into another country. There is no clear international definition of what constitutes a branch, and branch functions may vary significantly. In a distribution channel context, however, their responsibilities may include marketing and selling, physical distribution (transport and storage), servicing, repairs and the provision of spare parts.

14. Establishment of a branch

Some countries permit branch offices merely by implication; in other countries, branch offices are specifically prohibited. Where branches are permitted, the rules for their establishment vary, but they usually call for:

(a) registration of the name of the owning company, usually by submission to the appropriate registration authority of a certified copy (and sometimes an official translation) of the company's memorandum, articles of association and certificate of incorporation;
(b) a statement of the proposed activities of the branch;
(c) a declaration to the local tax authorities of the existence of the branch.

15. Legal considerations

A branch office of a UK company will usually be subject to UK law as regards its management and operation; it will normally, however, be subject to the laws of the host country for other purposes, including exchange control, employment regulations, and the law of contract.

Before establishing a branch abroad, therefore, a UK company should check the legal position on at least the following points:

(a) regulations concerning the number of local staff that the branch must employ (many countries lay down a minimum number);
(b) the difficulty and expense of dismissal of such staff;
(c) staff social security and pension entitlements;
(d) mandatory trade union membership;
(e) the capacity and authority necessarily delegated to local staff and their power to bind the owning company;
(f) the general implications of local contract law, where it applies.

16. Taxation considerations

Establishment of a branch normally exposes the owning company to taxation in the country in which the branch is situated. Assessments to local tax may be considerably in excess of the benefit the owning company considers it has derived from the branch. Enquiries as to methods of tax assessment should be made before the branch is established.

Marketing subsidiary abroad

17. Functions

A marketing subsidiary abroad performs much the same functions and offers much the same advantages and disadvantages as a branch office. The difference is simply that the subsidiary is incorporated as a local company. As such it has a local identity which:

(a) may assist in sales, especially to government and official bodies;
(b) isolates the parent company for legal and tax purposes.

Progress test 14

1. 'For capital goods, agencies are a last resort. Selling direct is the only way.' How far would you agree with this statement?

2. Some French retail stores have expressed a preference for direct dealing with UK exporters. Others have indicated an equally strong preference for dealing with a local French agent. Can you explain the likely motivations of the buyers in these stores?

3. You are a manufacturer of car accessories already exporting with great success. You intend to start exporting to a number of West African countries. What might be the advantages and disadvantages of using the services of British and French international trading companies?

4. How would you define a branch office overseas? Under what circumstances would you feel justified in establishing a branch in preference to an overseas sales subsidiary? What enquiries would you make before establishing the branch?

15

International distribution decisions IV: Joint ventures

1. Introduction
This chapter considers joint ventures entered into with a partner abroad:

(a) licensing;
(b) franchising;
(c) contract manufacture; and
(d) management contracts.

Assembly and manufacturing operations may, of course, be undertaken as joint ventures. These are discussed, however, in Chapter 16.

Licensing

2. Definition
The term 'licensing' covers a wide range of agreements relating to the sale or leasing of industrial or commercial expertise by one party to another in return for valuable consideration.

3. Saleable expertise
The industrial or commercial expertise which is the subject of the licence may include:

(a) a patent covering a product or process;
(b) manufacturing know-how not the subject of a patent;
(c) technical advice and assistance, including, occasionally, the supply of components, materials or plant essential to the manufacturing process;
(d) marketing advice and assistance;
(e) the use of a trade mark or trade name.

4. Payment for a licence
The valuable consideration may take the form of:

(a) an initial payment, payable as soon as the licence agreement is signed and often paid to cover the initial transfer of machinery, components or designs, but sometimes simply for know-how;
(b) an annual minimum payment;
(c) an annual percentage fee, which may be based on sales or profits;

(d) cross-licensing, a mutual exchange of knowledge and/or patents;
(e) any combination of the above.

5. Advantages of licensing

The advantages to the licensor of entering into a licensing agreement are:

(a) licensing permits entry into markets that are otherwise closed on account of high rates of duty, import quotas and the like;
(b) it requires little capital investment and should provide a higher rate of return on capital employed;
(c) similarly, the penalties of failure are low;
(d) the licensor is not exposed to the danger of nationalisation or expropriation of assets;
(e) because of the limited capital requirements, new products can be rapidly exploited, on a world-wide basis, before competition develops;
(f) the licensor can take immediate advantage of the licensee's local marketing and distribution organisation and of existing customer contacts;
(g) local manufacture may also be an advantage in securing government contracts, especially defence contracts.

6. Disadvantages of licensing

The disadvantages of licensing, again from the licensor's viewpoint, are:

(a) when the licensing agreement finally expires, the licensor may find he or she has established a competitor in the former licensee;
(b) the licensee, even if he or she reaches an agreed minimum turnover, may not fully exploit the market, leaving it open to the entry of competitors, so that the licensor loses control of the marketing operation;
(c) licence fees are normally a small percentage of turnover, and will often compare unfavourably with what might be obtained from a company's own manufacturing operation;
(d) quality control of the product is difficult – and the product will often be sold under the licensor's brand name;
(e) governments often impose conditions on remittances of royalties or on component supply (*see* 27:6).

7. Licensing agreement

A licensing agreement is simply a statement, in legally enforceable form, of the details of a commercial contract. It is properly the subject of detailed negotiation and hard bargaining between the parties, and there can be no such thing as a standard form of contract. A checklist is given in Table 15.1 of the major points that should be considered in drafting a licensing agreement. It is emphasised, however, that this list is necessarily over-simplified and that in all cases competent legal advice should be sought.

Table 15.1 Checklist of major points to be considered in a licensing agreement

---

1. Parties to the contract
Identification of licensor and licensee.
Extension of licence to licensee's subsidiaries and affiliates, if desired.
Reversion of licence in event of takeover or bankruptcy of licensee.
Licensee's right to assign benefits of licence.

2. Subject of the contract
Definition of the technical expertise.
Licensee's acknowledgement of the validity of all patents and trade marks.
Licensor's right, if any, to subsequent technical developments originating with the licensee and vice versa.
Capital investment required of the licensor, if any.

3. Territory
Definition of territory for manufacturing rights and sales rights, including exports.
Degree of exclusivity for licensee.
If exclusive, licensee's obligation to meet full market demand and licensor's rights if licensee fails in this obligation.

4. Financial
Licensee's royalty payments, including level of minimum royalty.
Currency of payment, exchange rate, action in event of devaluation.
Basis of royalty calculation and dates of payment.
Liability for payment of local taxes, such as withholding taxes, on royalty payments.
Action in the event of government restrictions on remittances or other payment difficulties.
Licensor's right to audit relevant records.

5. Contract performance
Quality standards required of licensee.
Licensor's right to check quality standards.
Extent of technical assistance from licensor.
Training by licensor of licensee's staff, secondment by licensor of technical staff, and provision for their expense.
Licensee's undertaking of confidentiality.
Licensee's undertaking not to sell competing products.
Licensee's obligation to protect patent in event of infringement by third parties.
Conditions as to licensee's use of trade marks and their protection in case of infringement.
Conditions of sale of any components, materials, plant, etc., to be supplied by licensor.

6. Legal
National law applying to the contract.
Place of jurisdiction.
Stipulation that disputes shall be referred to arbitration.
Situation if performance of the contract prevented by *force majeure*.
Duration of the contract and provision for termination.
Responsibility for official registration of the agreement and for obtaining any necessary government approvals.
Provision that the contract comes into effect only when such government approvals have been obtained.

Franchising

8. Definition
Franchising is a form of licensing by which:

(a) the franchiser provides a standard package of components or ingredients together with management and marketing services or advice;
(b) the franchisee provides capital, market knowledge and personal involvement.

Franchising is particularly suitable for products which are not patentable.

Example
Pepsi-Cola relies heavily on franchising. Their franchise holders own the bottling plants, employ local staff, and control their own advertising and sales promotion budgets. Pepsi-Cola International sells its concentrate to the bottlers and provides promotional support and general advice on management of the operation.

9. Advantages of franchising
The advantages of franchising are broadly similar to those of a licensing operation (*see* **5**), except that franchising, with its greater degree of control resulting from the supply of ingredients or components, offers the possibility of revenue from a product that is not patentable.

10. Disadvantages of franchising
Again, these are similar to those of licensing, except that franchising often tends to be a smaller operation. Many more franchisees are required, as a rule, and the search for competent franchisees can be expensive and time-consuming.

Contract manufacture

11. Definition
International contract manufacture involves merely a formal long-term contract, between parties in two different countries, for the manufacture or assembly of a product. The company placing the contract retains full control over distribution and marketing.
Contract manufacture is thus a half-way house between mere licensing and direct investment in manufacturing facilities.

12. Advantages of contract manufacture
Advantages of contract manufacture, to the company placing the contract, include:

(a) limited local investment, with no risk of nationalisation or expropriation;
(b) retention of market control;
(c) avoidance of currency risks;
(d) a locally-made image, which may assist in sales, especially to government or official bodies;
(e) possible cost advantages, if local costs are lower;
(f) entry into markets otherwise protected by tariffs or other barriers.

Contract manufacture is perhaps most likely to be of interest where a product has no patent protection, and where the market is too small to justify investment in manufacturing facilities.

13. Disadvantages of contract manufacture
On the other hand:

(a) contract manufacture is only possible when a satisfactory and reliable manufacturer can be found – not always an easy task;
(b) often, extensive technical training will have to be given to the local manufacturer's staff;
(c) as a result, at the end of the contract, the subcontractor could become a formidable competitor;
(d) control over manufacturing quality is difficult to achieve despite the ultimate sanction of refusal to accept substandard goods.

Management contract

14. Definition
A management contract is an agreement by which one company, the management company, manages some or all of the operations of another company in return for management fees and, sometimes, a share of the profits. Hilton Hotels, for instance, have management contracts with hotels abroad, earning fees for consulting and management services with little or no equity participation.

15. Advantages of the management contract
The management contract:

(a) permits low-risk market entry, with no capital investment and no expropriation risk;
(b) capitalises on management skills;
(c) provides a guaranteed minimum income and a quick return.

16. Disadvantages of the management contract
On the other hand:

(a) the local investor may seek to interfere with the way his or her investment is being managed;

(b) training and initial staffing requirements can be a serious drain on the other activities of the managing company – skilled personnel are always a scarce resource.

Progress test 15

1. Explain what you understand by the term 'franchising'. Give a detailed example of a company operating under a franchise agreement. *(IEx)*

2. Your company is about to license manufacture of a technically advanced photocopying machine in the USA and you have been asked to prepare the agenda for a meeting at which the draft of the licensing agreement is to be prepared. Jot down the main items for discussion.

3. You have been approached by a large Mexican company who wish to manufacture and sell your specialised chemicals in Mexico, where at present you do no business. Under what circumstances would you agree and how would you negotiate with the Mexican company? *(IEx)*

4. Your company is looking to commence marketing into other countries in Europe. Describe three methods of international marketing available to you, together with their main advantages and disadvantages. *(CAM Foundation)*

16

International distribution decisions V: Manufacture abroad

1. Introduction

Manufacturing abroad involves a tangible investment in production plant in a country other than that in which the investing company is established. Such an investment may be merely an extension of existing manufacturing facilities, or it may involve the initial establishment or acquisition of assembly or manufacturing facilities with the aim of gaining entry into, or retaining existing sales in, a market. This chapter considers manufacture abroad from the point of view of market entry, or retention, only.

2. Policy decisions

A company contemplating manufacturing abroad faces a number of policy decisions:

(a) whether to manufacture abroad at all (the initial investment decision);
(b) if so, in which country to locate the plant;
(c) whether to establish a full manufacturing operation or merely an assembly plant;
(d) whether to establish an independent operation or seek a joint venture with a local partner;
(e) whether to establish a new plant or acquire an existing company.

These decisions clearly have far-reaching implications in terms of company strategy, marketing and financial policy. In this chapter they can be discussed only briefly, with the emphasis, of course, on marketing. For simplicity, each of the decisions is considered separately in turn, though in practice, of course, they are interdependent.

The initial investment decision

3. The investment decision process

In considering a possible investment a company will normally calculate its anticipated rate of return. It will:

(a) estimate the current and future market potential;

(b) estimate the share of the market it is likely to achieve and, consequently, company sales;
(c) estimate production costs, both present and future;
(d) relate sales to costs to provide an anticipated profit (rate of return) on the investment.

There is clearly scope for error in these estimates in any market – an investment decision is among the most difficult faced by management.

An international investment decision, however, involves a yet greater degree of uncertainty and risk. Not only are errors in the initial estimates perhaps more likely, given a relative unfamiliarity with the marketing environment, but also political and exchange risks must be taken into account (4:**2** and 5:**5**).

4. Rate of return

Before making any investment decision, whether at home or abroad, a company will satisfy itself that its anticipated rate of return is at least equal to:

(a) its normal target rate of return;
(b) the return it might expect from any alternative investment under consideration.

For an investment abroad the company should adopt one additional criterion: that the rate of return should be high enough to compensate for the additional uncertainty and risk. The risk premium, of course, will vary from country to country.

5. Investment strategy

Investment decisions will usually result from a rational search for additional profit opportunities. International investment, however, may sometimes be a defensive measure, resulting, for instance, from a desire to retain an established export market which the company is in danger of losing, perhaps as a result of a change in currency values. In these circumstances, the company is tempted to depart from its investment strategy and make an isolated and urgent decision, without fully considering alternative investment possibilities.

It is important, however, that the company should still apply the same objective criteria as for any other international investment, including the required rate of return. The present or future loss of profit resulting from the loss of the export market is simply one factor, even if an important one, to take into account.

6. Factors influencing the investment decision

A full discussion of all the factors to be considered in arriving at a decision to invest abroad is beyond the scope of this book. Table 16.1 lists the more important items that typically require consideration, other than market potential (it is assumed that research has already selected the appropriate markets).

For details of ECGD insurance of overseas investments, *see* 5:**4**.

Location of investment

7.   The location decision
The investing company must decide:

(a) in which country to invest;
(b) exactly where in that country its plant should be located.

The second decision is outside the scope of this book and is not considered further. It will also be realised that the decision as to the country of investment is closely linked with the initial decision to invest at all. The factors listed in Table 16.1, therefore, are again relevant.

An investing company, however, should consider two additional location possibilities: third-country manufacture and free-trade zones.

8.   Third-country manufacture
The obvious site for a production plant would seem to be within one of the markets it supplies. Sometimes, however, it will pay to site the plant in a third country which enjoys free access to the markets served but offers additional advantages, such as lower tax rates or inducements for foreign investors.

Example
_____
A rum manufacturer set up a distillery in Puerto Rico in order to serve the United States market. Puerto Rico is a commonwealth of the USA, with free access to the US market as a whole. It offers significant inducements to investors, and a supply of not over-expensive labour, skilled in this trade. The raw material for rum, sugar cane, is grown locally. To supply the UK market, a distillery was established in the Bahamas, where a particular advantage was the right to supply the UK and other EC countries up to a permitted quota. As the quota was inadequate to supply the whole of the company's requirements within the EC, supplies for France were drawn from a distillery on the island of Martinique, which is legally part of metropolitan France and has, therefore, unrestricted access to the French market. It was decided to supply the Australian market from an existing distillery in Brazil, largely because of the highly attractive export incentives paid by the Brazilian government.

9.   Free-trade zones
For an example of the advantages of free-trade zones, *see* 32: **9**.

Table 16.1 Checklist of major factors to be considered before investing abroad

1. Political
Political stability or uncertainty.
Attitude of host government to private enterprise and, in particular, to foreign private investment.
Special inducement for foreign investors, such as tax holidays, grants, loans at favourable rates, tariff protection for newly-established industries.
Membership of a free-trade area, or trade agreements with other countries that might offer export opportunities.
Extent of import duty or non-tariff protection for the products to be manufactured.

2. Legal
Legal discrimination against foreign companies or their expatriate employees.
Percentage of company that may be foreign-owned.
Patent protection laws and ease of enforcement.
Trade mark protection.
Price control legislation.
Restrictive trade practice legislation.

3. Costs
Cost increases resulting from smaller scale of production, product modification to meet market needs, etc.
Wage costs, related to productivity.
Additional labour costs, such as company share of social security payments.
Availability and costs of local raw materials and components.
Availability and cost of transport services.
Freight, packing and insurance savings, if product previously exported to the country.

4. Taxation
Existence of a double-taxation agreement between host country and parent-company country.
Withholding tax payable on remittances to parent company.
Level of company taxation.
Method of calculation of depreciation allowances, stock valuation, etc.

5. Exchange control
Restrictions on remittances to parent company (for example, maximum percentage of foreign capital invested).
Restrictions on repatriation of capital.
Convertibility of local currency.

6. Finance
Local sources of capital, and interest rates payable.
Availability of debt–equity swaps.
Local accounting requirements and conventions.
Rate of inflation.

7. Personnel
Availability of labour.
Availability of local managerial talent.
Percentage of employees that must be local nationals.
Availability of work permits to expatriates.
Living conditions for expatriates (housing, education, medical, etc.).
Labour laws and regulations, especially regarding appointment and dismissal of staff.
Industrial relations, trade unions, worker participation in management.
Existence of compulsory profit-sharing schemes for employees.

Assembly operations

10. Advantages of assembly operations

An assembly operation is a half-way house between exporting and a complete manufacturing operation abroad. It offers many advantages:

(a) lower freight costs;

(b) lower import duties (lower in any case if duty is charged *ad valorem* but sometimes the rate of duty is lower as well);

(c) easier modification of the product to suit local market requirements;

(d) possible cost advantages from, for example, lower wage rates for the assembly operation or from local purchase of cheaper components;

(e) creation of a national image which may help in marketing;

(f) initial experience of the market which will be of value if a full manufacturing operation is to be established.

11. Disadvantages of assembly operations

Apart from the fact that some capital investment is required, a disadvantage of an assembly operation is that the host country may eventually apply pressure to bring about extension into full manufacture.

Joint ventures

12. Definition

An international joint venture involves some degree of association with an organisation in another country. Licensing and contract manufacture, for instance, are two examples of joint venture.

In the context of assembly or manufacture, however, an international joint venture is an operation in which:

(a) two or more companies in different countries join forces, not merely for manufacturing purposes but also (usually) for marketing, financial and management advantages; and

(b) all participants have both a share in the equity and a voice in management.

The proportion of shares held by each of the participants may vary widely, but, for the purposes of the present discussion, the essential feature of a joint venture is that no one participant holds a sufficient shareholding to exercise effective managerial control. (If this latter case does arise, the venture takes on many of the characteristics of an independent operation for the dominant partner , and becomes largely an investment in shares, though an important one, for other partners.)

13. Circumstances favouring joint ventures

Joint ventures are usually contemplated as an alternative to wholly-owned manufacturing operations abroad. In such a case a joint venture will often be preferred when:

(a) 100 per cent foreign equity ownership is not permitted by local laws;

(b) local government attitudes towards foreign investment are such that an independent operation, though legally possible, is not an attractive alternative;

(c) it is important to acquire quickly local marketing expertise or an established distribution network;

(d) there is inadequate capital to exploit fully all markets offering potential;

(e) managerial and other personnel resources are limited;

(f) political and other uncertainties call for some limitation of investment risks;

(g) a manufacturing company wishes to safeguard its sources of supply of raw material (for example, a steel works may enter into a foreign venture for the exploitation of iron ore deposits).

14. Conflict of interest

In any joint venture there is an inherent conflict of interest; each partner will inevitably wonder whether their reward is proportionate to the share of the profits their efforts have earned.

Disagreements are yet more likely to arise, however, in the case of an international joint venture, simply as a result of:

(a) national differences in culture, business practices and management styles;

(b) inadequate communications, arising from both distance and language problems.

15. Minimising conflict

It is therefore essential to minimise the possibility of conflict by:

(a) undertaking the most careful and detailed evaluation of joint venture partners;

(b) negotiating a joint venture agreement of benefit to both sides;

(c) covering in that agreement all eventualities that might reasonably be expected to give rise to differences of opinion, especially dividend policy (the amount to be distributed to the partners, and the amount to be retained in the business for further investment), the basis of transfer prices for components supplied to the venture by any of the partners, and export sales by the joint venture to countries in which either of the partners is operating, or to which they are exporting;

(d) arranging in advance some mechanism by which any unforeseen disagreements can be resolved, e.g. arbitration.

16. Achieving control

Companies are often unwilling, as a matter of policy, to accept a minority (or 50/50) interest in any venture, being unwilling to lose control. It is possible, however, to arrange to retain effective control over at least the key decisions, even with a minority shareholding. Subject to local regulations, a UK partner may, for example:

(a) arrange a management contract;

(b) retain ownership of key patents and trade marks;

(c) retain the right to appoint the directors, or the key managers;

(d) arrange for the issue of voting and non-voting shares, retaining a majority of voting shares;

(e) encourage equity participation by banks or insurance companies that have no interest in management;

(f) spread the majority shareholding over a multitude of small investors.

Acquisition of a company abroad

17. Definition

Acquisition of a company abroad involves the purchase of all or a majority of the shares of the company; otherwise the operation becomes at most a joint venture.

Often, of course, the acquisition question will simply not arise since:

(a) local government regulations and attitudes may make acquisition by a foreign company difficult, if not impossible;

(b) there may be, in the relevant country, no suitable candidate for acquisition;

(c) the suitable companies may not be interested in a takeover and a direct appeal to shareholders may be impracticable.

18. Advantages of acquisition

In comparison with an independent operation, acquisition offers three immensely important advantages:

(a) market entry, and revenue earning, are immediate;

(b) the purchase price includes not merely the production facilities but an established marketing and distribution organisation, market knowledge and contacts, and trained and experienced local staff;

(c) the cash requirement for the purchase may be minimal, since it may be possible to issue shares in payment.

19. Disadvantages of acquisition

Two principal disadvantages must be considered:

(a) the grants of capital, low-interest loans, tax holidays, and tariff protection for infant industries so often offered to foreign investors in new plant will not normally be available in the case of an acquisition;

(b) integrating any newly-acquired company is a difficult, expensive and time-consuming task that is not invariably successful, and it is a yet more difficult task in the case of a foreign company.

Progress test 16

1. Many companies have a policy of retaining control of a manufacturing operation overseas, despite the difficulties involved. Why do you think they take this attitude? In those countries where a foreign majority shareholding is not permitted how might they achieve their objective of effective control?

2. 'Financing overseas production is always more expensive than financing home production.' Comment.

3. Your company is considering a major investment in manufacturing facilities in a developing country. You are more than satisfied with market prospects, but your managing director has asked you to broaden the scope of your enquiries. What major factors would you investigate further?

4. What factors make joint ventures especially attractive in international operations?

5. A high proportion of joint manufacturing ventures end in break-up or in the takeover of the business by one of the partners. Why do you think this is so? And what can be done at the planning stage to endeavour, at least, to avoid such an eventual outcome?

17

International distribution decisions VI: Foreign market channel design and management

Channel design

1. Foreign market channel structures

For the reasons mentioned (*see* 12:3) channel decisions in any market are among the most important facing management. For any given product, several alternative channels may be practicable and it is often difficult to make the right choice between them.

The task facing the international marketer is infinitely more complex, simply because distribution systems vary so significantly between nations. Within each nation distribution systems have evolved over many years and they inevitably reflect not merely differences in economic development but social and cultural diversity. Figure 17.1 shows typical wholesale-retail distribution patterns for four different countries by way of example. Even with these necessarily generalised analyses of the distribution systems, fundamental differences become obvious (*see* also Fig. 29.1).

Under these circumstances, every product and every country presents the international marketer with a unique problem to which no general solution can be propounded. Unless, therefore, he or she is already well acquainted with the market, the international marketer will need to undertake careful research into the established distribution systems relevant to the product. Only on the basis of reliable information can the international marketer hope to design the most effective marketing channel.

Such research is likely to cover the market characteristics discussed below.

2. Examination of market characteristics

Channel design will involve consideration of such factors as:

(a) customer characteristics, such as number, geographical location, purchasing pattern, purchasing preferences;
(b) product characteristics, such as bulk, weight, perishability, unit value and servicing requirements;

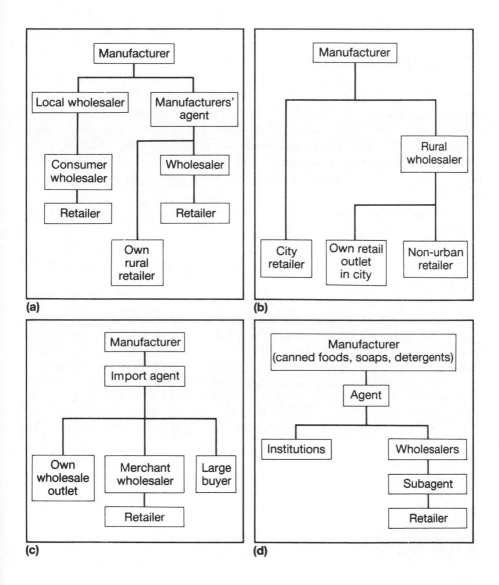

Figure 17.1 *Typical wholesale-retail distribution patterns in* (a) *India;* (b) *Turkey;* (c) *Venezuela;* (d) *Egypt.*

(Source: G. Wadinambiaratchi, *The Marketing Channel* (ed. B. Mallen), John Wiley and Sons, 1975).

(c) existing intermediaries and their activities, such as physical distribution, storage, advertising, selling and customer credit;

(d) competitor characteristics, such as the need to avoid, or to take advantage of, competitors' channels, or the degree of exclusivity offered to competitors;

(e) legal restrictions imposed by certain governments (e.g. Norway lays down specific licensing requirements for middlemen);

(f) company characteristics, such as size, financial resources, product mix, previous channel experience and overall marketing strategy.

3.   Consideration of alternative channels

It is at this stage that the international marketer will encounter some of the special problems of foreign market distribution. Often the channels adopted elsewhere will simply not exist. In other cases the obvious channel will not be available: the number of middlemen available in many developing markets is small and these may already have been attracted on an exclusive basis to competitors, or associations of middlemen may have joined in an agreement to restrict distribution to a limited number of suppliers (usually domestic).

Under these circumstances, a foreign company has a number of alternatives:

(a) to take over local distributors;

(b) to 'buy distribution' by offering extra high margins or other financial inducements;

(c) to build up its own parallel outlets from scratch;

(d) to develop a completely different type of channel from scratch (door-to-door selling of soap, for instance, is economically possible in some developing countries);

(e) to use its ingenuity in developing original methods of distribution, or transferring such methods from other countries.

Example _____

Tupperware Home Products Inc. sold in the USA through its 'party plan'. Housewives organised parties in their own homes, at which the products were on display, and received commission on sales. This system was transferred unchanged to Japan where, despite all the social and cultural differences, it was highly successful.

It should be borne in mind, however, that building up new channels is one of the most difficult tasks in international business.

4.   Evaluation of alternative channels

The final choice between the various alternative channels, existing or new, will depend on the balance between anticipated distribution costs on the one hand and, on the other, coverage, control and continuity (which in turn will affect likely sales volume).

Cost
Two kinds of channel cost may again be distinguished: the capital or investment cost of building or developing the channel, and the continuing cost of maintaining it (the cost of the company's own salespeople, or in the commission, mark-ups, etc., taken by intermediaries).

Coverage
Market coverage may be on an *intensive* basis, with product available in as many outlets as economically possible. Intensive coverage is not easy to develop in many markets and the international marketer will often have to be satisfied with intensive coverage of urban areas only.

Alternatively, coverage may be on a *selective* basis, with a limited number of outlets committed to the product, often with an exclusivity agreement.

A further consideration is coverage of *all* product lines: middlemen may take on the lucrative parts of a line but reject or ignore others. Occasionally, separate channels of distribution must be developed in foreign markets for products which would in other markets be regarded as a homogeneous line.

Control
A manufacturer enjoying intensive coverage can achieve control, just as in the domestic market, by heavy advertising to the ultimate consumer (the 'pull' strategy, by which customer demand, generated by advertising, draws the products through the distribution chain). This policy is, however, expensive and open only to the larger companies.

Continuity
Channels of distribution pose problems of continuity which should be considered at the evaluation stage. Many distributors in developing countries are small organisations – retirement of one or two partners can mean closure of the business. In many countries, too, distributors dependent on imports have learnt that political changes, exchange control or exchange rate variations can radically affect their competitive position. They may tend, therefore, to be less than loyal to their principals.

Channel Management

5. Selection of individual channel members

Selection of middlemen is particularly difficult in foreign markets. Many distributors, for instance, will suffer from low sales volume or under-financing; not all will prove reliable. Often the ideal will have to be rejected in favour of the expedient, especially in developing countries.

6. Motivation

Once the channel has been established, a motivational programme must be instituted to maintain a high level of middleman interest in the manufacturer's product. The manufacturer faces much the same problems of motivation as in the domestic market and any motivational programme assumes as a prerequisite that the middleman is achieving an adequate volume at an adequate margin. Additional motivational factors often of particular importance in foreign markets, however, are:

(a) training of dealer staff;
(b) credit terms;
(c) local advertising support;
(d) company communications, such as letters, newsletters, promotional conferences (often at company headquarters), publicity in company media, personal visits by company staff.

7.   Control

Direct influence down the whole channel is not always possible, but the indirect approach can often be successful.

Example

A spirits manufacturer introduced its product into West Germany. Initially the product was regarded as a luxury item and distributor margins were necessarily high. As sales developed the manufacturer persuaded its main agents to reduce their prices. The large retail groups and grocery chains responded by reducing their own prices accordingly, but most smaller retailers maintained their original prices and margins. Retail margins soon became a bar to further market penetration. The manufacturer offered special discounts to the retail groups and grocery chains, provided most of the discount was used to advertise the price reductions. The smaller retailers were forced to quote lower prices in order to compete. Sales (and profits for the manufacturer) showed a marked increase.

8.   Performance evaluation

As with any managed and controlled distribution channel, the performance of channel members should be regularly evaluated, preferably, in the case of exclusive dealerships, against standards agreed in writing. Where these standards are not met the causes should be investigated.

9.   Separation

Occasionally, it will be necessary to dispense with the services of a distributor whose performance is not up to the required standard. Where some form of agreement has been entered into between the distributor and the manufacturer this is, in some countries, by no means an easy matter:

(a) in many countries the business community is very small, and mishandling of the separation arrangements can provoke hostility in the trade;
(b) in other countries, the law recognises that middlemen invest time and

effort in developing the manufacturer's business and heavy compensation may be payable (27: 5).

10. Channel obsolescence

In any country, there should be a constant watch for channel obsolescence, which will usually occur when a competitor steals a march by opening up entirely new channels. This is perhaps more difficult in foreign markets, but it is just as important.

11. New channels

Similarly, the manufacturer should itself actively seek possible additional or alternative channels as market conditions change. This is particularly important in the smaller developing countries.

Progress test 17

1. Why do distribution channels vary so markedly between one country and another?

2. What market information would you require to assist you in designing a channel of distribution for your products in a foreign country?

3. What factors would you take into account in evaluating the various alternative channels open to you in a foreign country?

4. What methods of middlemen motivation are of particular relevance in markets abroad?

5. Why is it especially difficult abroad to terminate distribution agreements?

6. Indicate some special problems the international marketer might encounter in relation to the establishment of distribution channels in a developing country. How might he or she endeavour to overcome them?

7. You are commissioning market research in Spain covering low unit price packaged consumer goods. You are seriously concerned about the distribution channel possibilities. Specifically what information would you ask the researcher to seek on this aspect?

18

International pricing decisions I: Pricing strategies

1. Introduction

The alternative pricing strategies discussed in most marketing textbooks are, of course, relevant to both domestic and international markets. They are briefly reviewed in this chapter, with special emphasis on their international application.

2. Pricing orientation

Three different approaches are usually distinguished in relation to pricing policy: competitor orientation, cost orientation and demand orientation.

The extreme example of competitor-oriented pricing is found in the commodity markets, where world market prices are known and prevail. These prices are established through the collective interaction of a large number of buyers and sellers. For any one individual producer to quote above the prevailing price would merely invite a catastrophic fall in orders; to quote below it would mean a pointless reduction in profit.

In commodity marketing and similar situations, the company really has no pricing decision to take, except to concentrate on cost reduction. The strategies discussed below are not open to it.

The cost-oriented company will quote as its price its total unit cost plus a percentage of profit, demand considerations having little influence on the final price. The approach is not unusual for those industrial goods where differentiation between products, in terms of value to the customer, is often difficult.

Some of the pricing strategies discussed below (4–8), however, are open to the cost-oriented producer.

Demand-oriented pricing requires an assessment of the intensity of demand: high prices are charged when and where demand is buoyant, and low prices are charged when and where demand is weak, even if unit costs are the same in both cases. Price-setting is flexible, several alternative strategies, including those discussed below (4–8), are open to the company, and pricing becomes an effective weapon in the marketer's armoury. Demand-oriented prices are usual in the case of branded consumer goods and are a practical possibility with many industrial goods.

3. The long-run pricing objective

The long-run objective of commercial organisations may be taken to be profit maximisation, subject to ethical or legal constraints which are often merely implicit.

In pursuing the objective of profit maximisation, however, a company may adopt several different short-run strategies, including a market penetration strategy, a market skimming strategy, early cash recovery, and a strategy aimed at ensuring a satisfactory rate of return on investment. The international marketer is faced with an additional dimension: standardisation or differentiation of prices between countries.

4.   Market penetration

A market penetration strategy implies the establishment of a relatively low price, with the aims of stimulating market growth, capturing a high market share and discouraging competition. Essential preconditions for such a strategy are a price sensitive market and significant manufacturing economies of scale.

Some degree of courage is also required: by definition, results in terms of profits are not quickly achieved. The export marketer, in particular, will think carefully before adopting a market penetration strategy; the market may be lost by, for instance, significant variations in exchange rates or import restrictions before a satisfactory profit position has been achieved.

5.   Market skimming

The aim of market skimming is initially to obtain a premium price from buyers to whom the product has a high present value; prices are subsequently reduced to attract the more price-conscious market segments. Books, for instance, are usually produced first in a limited hard-cover edition; the cheap paperback edition follows later in the light of demand indications.

A market skimming strategy is particularly relevant to the international marketer who has selected a policy of undifferentiated marketing rather than concentration. With limited commitment, and possibly only through limited distribution channels, the marketer can offer the goods profitably in several markets.

Example _____

A UK manufacturer of men's suits decided he was unable to compete on a price basis in export markets. A fundamental problem of high production costs was exacerbated by fashion differences which implied, at least initially, uneconomic short-run production. He therefore promoted a range of standard UK-style suits as the 'British Look' at a premium price in the USA, restricting sales efforts to the better department stores. Results were sufficiently encouraging to justify the extension of this strategy to selected European markets.

_____

6.   Early cash recovery

A cash recovery strategy aims at rapid cash generation. The company may simply be short of funds, or it may regard its future in the market as too uncertain to justify patient market cultivation. The international marketer who rejects a market penetration strategy for fear of import restrictions, for instance, may incline towards a policy of early cash recovery.

7.   Satisfactory rate of return

The aim of this strategy is to achieve a satisfactory rate of return but no more: a level of profit that may be considered normal for a given amount of investment and a given level of risk. It is often the strategy (at least implicit) of the cost-oriented industrial goods company.

At first sight this strategy may seem to be at variance with the long-term objective of profit maximisation, but in the domestic market this is not necessarily so; manufacturing costs of all companies in the domestic industry are likely to be broadly similar, so the approach makes for market stabilisation and avoidance of damaging price wars.

This advantage will often not apply internationally, however, since manufacturing costs can vary significantly between one country and another. It might be thought, therefore, that exporters would avoid a policy of satisfactory rate of return and the resultant near standardisation of price quotations. Nevertheless, there can still be found many companies who are content to quote prices in export markets which provide a uniform rate of return on a given product. Some will even quote the same ex-works price for both domestic and export markets.

8.   Differential pricing opportunities

Many companies, particularly in the consumer goods field, set a different price in each market segment, charging as much as the market will bear. This, the strategy of the demand-oriented company, is the nearest possible approach to the simultaneous achievement of both short-run and long-run profit maximisation. It is only possible, however, when:

(a) the market is clearly segmentable;
(b) the segments show differing elasticities of demand;
(c) there is effective separation between market segments, so that the lower priced segments cannot re-sell the product to the higher priced segments.

These requirements are often easier to meet in international, as opposed to domestic, marketing. The international marketer has a real opportunity to maximise profit by taking advantage of varying price levels in different countries.

9.   Difficulties of differential pricing

Effective separation of markets, however, is becoming increasingly difficult for a number of reasons:

(a) governments exert an influence towards price uniformity by their purchasing practices (many make it a condition of purchase contracts that the prices quoted are at least as favourable as those quoted to any other customer);

(b) many governments have introduced legislation to promote free competition;

(c) regional economic groupings facilitate parallel imports.

10. Parallel imports

Once price differentials between countries become significant, distributors, independent entrepreneurs or individuals may buy the product in low price countries and re-export it to high price countries, usually undercutting the market price in the high price country but still making a profit from the price differential. The process is variously described as parallel importing, parallel exporting, grey market trading or product arbitrage.

Manufacturers, not unnaturally, disapprove of the practice, sometimes referring to it as illicit trading, but there is nothing illegal or unethical in parallel trading provided all import and other regulations are observed. It does, however, have an adverse impact on the manufacturer's sales and profits, and it may damage the product's standing in the market-place, given that price is often perceived as an indicator of quality.

In countries where there is no legislation to prevent it, manufacturers may put pressure on their authorised distributors to dissuade them from engaging in parallel trade; but when other distributors enter the trade it becomes unreasonable to expect the authorised distributors to stand idly by as the business slips away from them. Manufacturers have sometimes gone as far as to withdraw, or at least threaten to withdraw, warranty coverage from products not sold through authorised distributors; but the individual consumer can hardly be expected to understand or sympathise with such a move, and the possible consequences in public relations terms hardly bear contemplating.

In countries where free competition rules are in force, the manufacturer is in an even weaker position: the only real defence against parallel imports is product differentiation which justifies, or appears to justify, the difference in price. When this is not possible, manufacturers have, on occasion, simply withdrawn the cheaper product from its market.

Example
(1) Distillers Co. sold its Johnnie Walker Red Label brand of whisky in West Germany at a price significantly higher than that obtaining in the UK, where competition in whisky is especially keen. One of its authorised distributors in Scotland began to buy large quantities at UK prices and export to West German retail outlets. Distillers threatened to withhold supplies, but the distributor took the matter to the EC court, which held that withholding supply was contrary to EC rules of competition and therefore illegal. After exhausting all legal possibilities, Distillers withdrew Red Label from the UK, maintaining the German price level for the rest of the EC. The brand was reintroduced into the UK several years later, but at a higher price than before.
(2) The UK may be regarded as a distinct and separate market for cars, if only because it is the only EC country that drives on the left. Demand in the UK is

clearly inelastic in relation to price, as compared with other countries; this may not be entirely unconnected with the fact that, in contrast with other EC countries, well over half of new cars in the UK are bought by companies rather than by individuals. UK prices have historically been high in comparison with continental prices.

In the early 1980s UK consumers began to look to distributors in mainland Europe for cheaper cars but found them unwilling to supply: right-hand drive cars were subject to surcharges; it was 'not the maker's policy' to supply right-hand drive cars to continental dealers; delivery might take as long as a year. The EC Commission made its position clear: private individuals had the right to buy a car wherever in the EC they found the best terms. A number of entrepreneurs set themselves up as car importers, relieving individuals of the complicated task of importation, but their popularity declined after one or two of them absconded with customers' deposits.

The EC introduced rules to the effect that basic prices for a particular model should not vary by more than 18 per cent at any given moment and by no more than 12 per cent over a period. But in 1992 some models cost in the UK 32 per cent and 44 per cent more than in the cheapest EC country. How far this is due to a policy of differential pricing is a matter for debate. Car manufacturers point out that what are optional extras in some countries are, in others, standard fittings included in the basic price; in any case, exchange movements obscure price comparisons. The EC Commission, on the other hand, is clearly unhappy with the 1992 level of differentials; suggestions have been made that the UK system of exclusive dealerships for cars might be reviewed. What is undeniable is that, if UK car manufacturers *are* operating a differential pricing policy, then they – together, of course, with importers into the UK – have enjoyed considerable success with it for many years.

Progress test 18

1. 'Exporters should charge what the market will bear.' Is this invariably true? What factors may make such a policy difficult to achieve?

2. 'Underpricing a product can be a serious mistake. The French earn more than we do and are willing to pay for quality. If the British exporter does not make the profit, the French agent or retailer will do so by putting on a higher mark-up' (DTI, *Marketing Consumer Goods in France*). Comment on this statement with reference to both pricing policy and distribution policy.

3. What considerations would you take into account in arriving at a pricing policy for a range of clothing products to be sold in a wide variety of foreign markets? Choose (but specify) any country of origin. *(CIM)*

4. What are parallel imports? What steps can a manufacturer take to limit the problems they cause?

19

International pricing decisions II: Export pricing

The export quotation

1. Build-up of the export price

Whatever the pricing strategy adopted, every price must be set with cost considerations in mind. The true cost of the goods in the market-place is, at the least, a yardstick against which pricing decisions can be made on an informed basis.

In some companies the export price is based on the domestic price, plus appropriate additions for freight, duty, channel mark-ups, etc. The domestic price, however, will usually include cost elements inapplicable to export sales, such as the cost of the home sales force, advertising and publicity in the home market, domestic transport fleet, warehousing and storage charges, cost of financing stocks, etc.

Conversely, exports attract additional costs not incurred in the home market. Some of these costs, such as freight, duty, etc., will be immediately obvious; others are not so obvious and may be overlooked.

2. Profitability of export sales

The level of profitability of export sales has implications not merely for short-term profit, but for pricing policy and overall marketing policy. It is vital that it should be correctly calculated. It may be the case that an export price lower than the home market price is nevertheless more profitable.

Example

An important element in this context (of export profitability) is the way prices for the home and export markets are determined and the way overheads are allocated as between home and export sales. We noted earlier that many companies would reject an order from abroad if it were, say, 5 per cent or 10 per cent lower than that ruling in the home market. Yet the company might have to devote vastly more time and effort to the sale of the same product in the home market. Many elements of cost – if rationally apportioned – would present an entirely different picture of the relative profitability of operations in the home and export markets. In fact, on statistical grounds alone, a solid logical case could be made out for the proposition that, where a company exports only a small proportion (say, 10 per cent or 20 per cent) of its output at the same price as in the home market, exports subsidise the home market sales.

(Source: *Concentration on Key Markets: A Development Plan for Exports*, Betro Trust Report, Royal Society of Arts, 1977)

Table 19.1 is a checklist that will help to avoid the more serious errors and omissions in calculating the profitability of exports.

Marginal cost pricing

3. Relevance of marginal cost pricing to exports

Manufacturing costs may be divided into two categories which can be defined, though with admitted over-simplification, as follows:

(a) *fixed costs*, those costs, such as factory rental, which, at least in the short or medium term, remain unchanged regardless of the level of output;

(b) *variable costs*, those costs, such as raw material purchases, which vary directly according to the level of output.

Once the company has reached an output which gives sufficient revenue to cover *all* the fixed costs, *plus* all the variable costs incurred in achieving the output, it is said to have reached break-even point.

At break-even, total revenue is equal to total cost. Above break-even, since *fixed* costs have already been fully covered, *any* price which is above the *variable* cost per unit will be a profit.

In its established markets, however, the company will continue to sell at the price already fixed. It may wish to offer a price reduction to gain extra sales, but any price reduction would merely depress the general level of prices to all customers, thus increasing the volume of output required to reach break-even. If, however, the company can find an isolated market or market segment in which, without jeopardising price levels in its established market, it can quote prices based on marginal cost (below the established market level but still above the variable cost per unit), the additional sales to these isolated segments will increase the *total* profit of the company, though *percentage* profit per unit would clearly be reduced.

It is difficult to find an isolated market segment within any one country. In the export field, however, communications difficulties, import restrictions, tariffs, etc., tend to divide one country from another, so that marginal-price selling has become common practice. The typical situation is that a manufacturer maintains high prices in the domestic market, sheltering behind high tariff barriers, and from time to time sells any surplus capacity abroad at marginal prices.

4. When to quote marginal prices

The profit-conscious export marketer will realise that marginal-cost pricing is worthwhile only when:

(a) all decisions on marginal business are taken against an agreed profit plan to ensure that it does not form too high a proportion of total business;

(b) it is unlikely that there will be speedy intervention by the government of

Table 19.1 Build-up of the export price (carriage by sea)

Ex-works (EXW)	Direct cost of manufacture, including the cost of any special modifications required by the particular export market.
	Appropriate allocation of company overheads, *excluding any overhead expenditure of relevance solely to domestic sales or to sales in other markets.*
	Allocation of an appropriate portion of total export overheads (e.g. part cost of export department).
	Allocation of overheads specific to the market, such as local advertising costs.
	Allocation of an appropriate proportion of the company's total research and development costs.
	Relevant agency commission.
	Special export packing costs.
	Export credit and political risk insurance.
	Forward exchange cover where appropriate.
	Documentation costs, where these become significant (as with unduly high consular invoice fees).
	Financing costs, bearing in mind that even with a straightforward export contract delays in payment are sometimes unavoidable and often, as with government contracts, routine.
	Appropriate profit margin, *taking into account both competing price levels and strength of demand.*
Free on board (FOB)	Transport and insurance as far as the ship's rail.
	Handling and other FOB charges.
	Cost of all customs formalities necessary for the export of the goods, if significant.
	Export taxes, if any.
Cost and freight (CFR) or	Carriage by sea to a specific port of destination.
cost, insurance and freight (CIF)	If CIF, marine insurance charges.
Delivered ex quay, duty paid (DEQ)	Any landing charges not included in CFR/CIF (e.g. lighterage).
	Customs charges, if significant.
	Import duties.
	Value-added tax.
Delivered duty paid (DDP)	Transport costs to a specified place in the country of destination.
	Insurance in transit if not included under earlier policies.
Retail price	Main distributor mark-up.
	Wholesaler mark-up(s).
	Retail mark-up

the importing country such as the imposition of anti-dumping duties (5);

(c) there is no more profitable use of resources such as an alternative market which might offer a higher price level, or an alternative and more profitable product that could be manufactured on the same plant (the true cost of marginal pricing is the opportunity of more profitable business that is foregone);

(d) as already explained, the markets are clearly segmentable, so that price levels in the principal market(s) are not depressed. In this context not only the domestic but all major export markets not protected by tariffs should be considered.

Example

A UK manufacturer of razor blades enjoyed a lucrative trade in the USA. He also seized an opportunity to sell in bulk to Eastern Europe at marginal prices. These Eastern European blades subsequently appeared in US retail outlets at prices significantly below the established market level.

It should be noted that all the above conditions must be met simultaneously before a decision is made to seek marginal business. Most companies would probably add one further condition: that it should be short-term business aimed at remedying, for example, a purely seasonal fall-off in orders or temporary over-capacity after the construction of new plant.

5. Dumping

The beneficiary of goods exported at marginal prices is, of course, the importing country, which is able to buy on highly favourable terms. Where the importing country has a competing industry, however, the government may try to protect that industry from low price and, arguably, unfair competition by the imposition of an anti-dumping duty.

One rather loose definition of dumping is the export of goods at prices below their full cost of production (i.e. at marginal prices). From a legal viewpoint, however, such a definition is less than adequate: it is difficult to ascertain a foreign company's costs and the reasonableness or otherwise of its allocation of such overheads as marketing expenditure. Article VI of the General Agreement on Tariffs and Trade (GATT), which is incorporated in the anti-dumping legislation of most of the major free-market industrialised nations, therefore concentrates first on the concept of 'normal value':

> ... a product is to be considered as being introduced into the commerce of an importing country at less than its normal value if the price of the product exported from one country to another is less than the comparable price, in the ordinary course of trade, for the like product when destined for consumption in the exporting country; or, in the absence of such domestic price, is less than either: the highest comparable price for the like product for export to any third country in the ordinary course of trade; or, the cost of production of the product in

the country of origin plus a reasonable addition for selling cost and profit.

The investigative procedures needed to establish dumping are lengthy and involved, and the exporter must be allowed to present his side of the case. As a result, anti-dumping legislation poses less of a threat to the exporter than might have been feared, at least for the occasional or short-term dumper.

The GATT rules, however, do permit the imposition, in certain circumstances, of provisional duties. The UK, for instance, is prepared to impose provisional duties, especially in the case of seasonal products or where irreversible damage to the domestic industry may occur before the necessary investigations have been completed.

Devaluation

6. Devaluation and the exporter

When a country changes the value of its currency by devaluation (or revaluation), a company exporting to that country will suddenly find that its competitive position has been radically altered. With floating exchange rates, currency movements are less sudden, but the performance of the pound sterling in 1992 showed that even a floating currency can decline in value with disconcerting speed. The exporter must be alert to take the maximum possible advantage of any change in currency values.

The alternative courses of action open to a UK exporter in the event of a sterling devaluation are, in respect of any given market:

(a) to leave the sterling price unchanged, thus reducing the price to the foreign buyer;
(b) to maintain unchanged the price in foreign currency, increasing the sterling price accordingly;
(c) to set an intermediate price somewhere between these two extremes.

7. Maintaining the sterling price

This course requires no positive action by the UK exporter, but it can only be sustained in the short term since cost increases resulting from devaluation, such as increases in prices of imported raw materials and pressure for cost-of-living wage increases, are likely to force price increases within months. In fact this first alternative makes sense only if:

(a) price elasticity of demand in the market is such that the increase in sales at the new (reduced) price will be of sufficient magnitude to increase total profits even after the inevitable cost increases have been incurred;
(b) there is available manufacturing capacity to support such an increase.

8.   Maintaining the price in foreign currency

This course results in an immediate increase in profit and automatically more than covers the cost increases which can be expected to result eventually from the devaluation. Unfortunately, however, it will often be impracticable since:

(a) distributors and customers will be expecting some price reduction as a result of the devaluation, and some goodwill – and orders – may be lost unless at least a gesture is made;
(b) other UK competitors may reduce their prices in the market, with a resulting loss of business for those UK companies that maintain their prices;
(c) local competitors and exporters in third countries, anticipating UK companies' price reductions, may reduce their own prices, even though this is at some sacrifice to profit.

9.   Setting an intermediate price

The most appropriate course of action, therefore, will usually lie somewhere between the two extremes. Ideally, the exporter will:

(a) estimate the cost increases which will eventually result from the devaluation, consider the timing of such increases, and prepare cost estimates accordingly;
(b) compare the new estimated costs with the elasticity of demand in the market, and establish the price which maximises profit contribution, considering also the possible effect of increased advertising on the demand curve;
(c) take into account the actions or likely actions of competitors, and adjust the price accordingly.

In practice, each of these three requirements presents too many imponderables for the ideal ever to be achievable. Quantitative techniques in marketing, however, can be of assistance, and the exporter's task is to arrive somewhere near the ideal in those markets of real significance.

10.   Quoting in a foreign currency

See 5:**5**.

Progress test 19

1. If the US exchange rate against sterling stood at 1.75 at the beginning of the year but subsequently fell to 1.50 six months later, what price changes, if any, should a UK exporter decide upon when compiling a price list for the next six months? Give reasons for your answer. *(IEx)*

2. Discuss the factors which must be taken into account when determining the selling price for a product to be sold overseas. *(IEx)*

3. At a time when the pound sterling has been falling in value relative to many other currencies, many British exporters would have gained by quoting prices in a foreign currency. Yet they have often been reluctant to do this. Suggest reasons for this reluctance and outline the arguments which indicate that they are not valid in such circumstances. *(CIM)*

4. 'The trouble with our export department is that their minds never rise above marginal cost prices. Now we have to keep them out of the accounts department altogether.' Comment on this attitude, and indicate the circumstances in which marginal cost pricing might be justifiable.

5. What is dumping? Why is it difficult to prove? How far should an exporter bear in mind anti-dumping legislation when setting his price levels?

6. You are an export manager selling knitwear, principally, and with considerable success, into the USA. The pound sterling is devalued by about 15 per cent against the US dollar, and you decide you must reconsider your price levels. What alternative courses of action are open to you?

20

International pricing decisions III: Foreign-market pricing decisions

1. Introduction

This chapter discusses foreign-market pricing decisions, i.e. those pricing decisions that relate to products that are both produced and marketed in the same country, but with some centralised guidance or direction from outside that country, as is the case, for example, with multinational companies.

Government influences on pricing

2. Government influences on pricing and the international marketer

The exporter and, to a much greater extent, the multinational company face a bewildering maze of legislation imposed by government. Pricing decisions cannot safely be made in ignorance of such legislation.

3. Price control

Some years ago continuing price control was associated largely with countries facing constant and serious inflation. In other countries, price control was limited to temporary 'freezes'. With the spread of inflation, however, price control was encountered with increasing frequency and permanency.

Governments have also intervened:

(a) to set minimum prices, as with California's Unfair Practices Act;
(b) to set price ceilings, usually on staple food products;
(c) to lay down specified mark-ups in the distribution channel, as in Norway;
(d) to control manufacturers' profit margins.

4. Restrictive trade practices and monopolies

Restrictive trade practices may be broadly defined as all agreements or concerted practices tending to prevent, restrict or distort competition. They include:

(a) horizontal price fixing, that is, price agreements between competitors;
(b) allocation of markets between competitors;
(c) discriminatory pricing or terms of sale;

(d) refusal to supply.

Monopolies are usually taken to mean not merely a monopoly in the literal sense but mere market dominance, or mergers and acquisitions that might lead to market dominance.

5. Government attitudes to restrictive trade practices and monopolies

The views of governments vary according to the national attitudes to free competition and the economic state of the nation. Most governments, however, have introduced some form of legislation against both restrictive trade practices and monopolies.

In the USA, for example, any restrictive trade practice is illegal. Penalties for contravention are heavy, both for a company and its responsible corporate officials. Landmarks in US legislation include:

(a) the Sherman Antitrust Act 1890, which prohibited 'monopolies or attempts to monopolise' and 'contracts, combinations or conspiracies in restraint of trade';

(b) the Federal Trade Commission Act 1914, which established a commission to investigate unfair methods of competition and issue 'cease and desist' orders;

(c) the Clayton Act 1914, which prohibited price discrimination, exclusive dealing and tying arrangements, and inter-corporate stockholdings where the effect was substantially to lessen competition;

(d) the Robinson Patman Act 1936, which strengthened the Clayton Act and gave the Federal Trade Commission the right to place limits on quantity discounts and other discriminatory allowances against price;

(e) the Anti-Merger Act 1950, which extended the powers under the Clayton Act to permit the prohibition of mergers where these might have a substantial adverse effect on competition;

(f) the Consumer Goods Pricing Act 1975, which forbids price maintenance agreements among manufacturers and distributors in interstate commerce.

These laws apply only within the USA. The Webb Pomerene Act of 1918 specifically permits, between US companies competing in foreign markets, all forms of cooperation including price-fixing and allocation of export business.

For the position within the European Community, *see* 28:**6**.

International transfer pricing

6. Definition of transfer pricing

When a company decentralises, organising itself into separate profit centres, it will usually find it necessary to transfer components or finished products between units. To enable the profit performance of each unit to be evaluated, a transfer price must be established for each inter-unit transaction.

7.   Fixing the transfer price

Transfer prices may be established on a number of bases such as cost, cost plus a standard margin, or arm's length transfer (the price that would be quoted to an independent customer). Central corporate management will usually establish the basis of the transfer price, with the aim of ensuring both a realistic assessment of the contribution of any one unit and the maximisation of the profit of the enterprise as a whole (narrow unit interests may not coincide with this latter aim).

Even within a single country, transfer pricing can give rise to problems in terms of accounting systems, inter-unit cooperation and motivation of executives. When products are transferred across national frontiers, however, entirely new considerations arise, both financial and strategic, which can have a major impact on total corporate profit.

8.   Financial aspects of international transfer pricing

The transfer price between nations can be manipulated to minimise tax or import duty liability, or (in effect) to transfer funds. For example:

(a) products may be transferred into high duty countries at an artificially low transfer price so that, assuming duty is charged *ad valorem*, the duty paid will be low;

(b) products may be transferred into high tax countries at high transfer prices so that profits in the high tax country are virtually eliminated and, in effect, transferred to low tax countries;

(c) products may be transferred at high prices into a country from which dividend repatriation is restricted or subject to government taxes – in effect, invisible income replaces a formal dividend;

(d) similarly, it is possible to avoid an accumulation of funds in a country with high inflation rates, or where an early devaluation is thought to be a probability, or where expropriation is feared.

9.   Strategic aspects of international transfer pricing

International transfer pricing can also be used as a weapon in the overall marketing strategy; profits can be concentrated, by vertically integrated corporations, at the stage of production where there is least competition. Competitors operating at other stages of production can thus be discouraged by the relatively low profits to be earned.

Example

The integrated oil companies keep the prices of crude oil, and, hence, profits of crude production, at high levels. There are many reasons for high crude oil transfer prices, not the least of which is pressure from the governments of crude oil producing countries, and the desire by the companies to take maximum advantage of oil depletion allowances. Another reason for keeping transfer prices and market prices of crude oil at relatively high levels, however, is to discourage entry into refining and distribution by firms without captive sources of crude oil. Since entry into refining and distribution is easier than entry into crude production, the transfer-pricing strategy pursued by integrated producers helps to reduce competition all along the line.

(Source: H.R. Mason, R.R. Miller and D.R. Weigel, *The Economics of International Business*, John Wiley & Sons, 1975)

---

10. Government attitudes to transfer pricing

The manipulation of international transfer prices clearly offers the prospect of very significant financial gain. Such manipulations, however, whether practised for financial reasons or for reasons of marketing strategy, have attracted the attention of governments. For instance:

(a) the government of the *exporting* country has an interest in seeing that the transfer price is not artificially low, and it will endeavour to ensure that appropriate profits are made – and taxes paid – within its jurisdiction;

(b) in the *importing* country, the tax authorities are usually on the look-out for unreasonably high transfer prices which will reduce local profits – and, consequently, liability to income tax – while the customs authorities will, in contrast, be watching for low transfer prices designed to minimise duty liability.

11. Company attitudes to international transfer pricing

It will now be clear that the financial and strategic aims of international transfer pricing will usually be irreconcilable with the initial aim of good corporate management.

In these circumstances, international companies adopt varying attitudes towards transfer pricing. Some regard it solely as a means of encouraging and measuring corporate efficiency; others emphasise the opportunities for financial gain or market manipulation.

Either way, the international marketer must be aware of the alternatives available, both in formulating marketing strategy and in setting market prices.

Progress test 20

1. Discuss the various ways in which governments attempt to influence prices. Give examples from one or two markets other than the UK.

2. In setting prices for intra-company sales across national boundaries it is possible to minimise tax or import duty liability. Explain exactly how this can be achieved.

3. It has been suggested that manipulation of international transfer prices with the aim of reducing tax or import duty liabilities is, though legal, unethical. How far would you agree with this view?

21

International communications I: Media advertising

Introduction

1. Communications

Communications is a general term covering all methods of influencing a target audience. In a marketing sense it will include advertising (**2**), sales promotion (**22:1**), public relations (**22:2**) and personal selling (**23:1**).

2. Advertising

Advertising has been defined as 'any paid form of non-personal presentation and promotion of ideas, goods or services by an identified sponsor'.

3. International advertising

The principles and concepts of advertising are the same the world over. Internationally, advertising is modelled very much on the US pattern and the American influence is strengthened by the proliferation of branches of US advertising agencies throughout the world. Thus the international marketer requires a good knowledge of basic advertising principles.

Paradoxically, in its application and practice, advertising internationally offers greater problems than almost any other aspect of international marketing simply as a result of the environmental differences between nations. Differences of particular relevance to advertising are culture, language, government attitudes towards advertising, and the availability or otherwise of certain advertising media.

The environmental differences present special problems for the international marketer. These may be examined under the following headings:

(a) standardisation;
(b) the advertising message;
(c) the selection of appropriate media;
(d) the selection of advertising agencies.

Standardisation

4. Extent of standardisation

Complete standardisation of all aspects of a campaign over several different countries is rarely practicable – language difficulties alone would often make such an approach impossible. Standardisation usually implies a common advertising strategy, a common creative idea and message and, as far as possible, similar media. In this respect the Esso 'Tiger in your Tank' campaign proved to be a landmark.

Example

Two days of earnest persuasion failed to overcome the European affiliates' reluctance to accept that what had been successful advertising half the world away was an ideal ready-made package for their own market. A similar reception for the Esso 'Tiger in your Tank' campaign was a prospect never far from the minds of the planners in New York five years later; they did their homework accordingly. Returning to square one, what, they asked themselves, was the definition of a coordinated, multinational advertising programme? They came to the conclusion that it was a programme which expressed, in different countries and different languages, a common creative idea – an idea based on a commonly-established strategy. This did not imply that the advertisements appearing in any one country should be exact reproductions of those running elsewhere, but the programme should be such that the advertiser was satisfied that, in all the different countries concerned, he was directing the same message through the same illustrative material, sound effects, and verbal expression – translated as necessary – in all the markets where his product was available.

(Source: B. Ash, *Tiger in your Tank*, Cassell, 1969)

5. Advantages of standardisation

Like any other businessman, the advertiser should select that course of action which is most likely to prove profitable in terms of sales achieved in relation to costs incurred.

At first sight it might seem that sales would invariably be maximised by a campaign tailored to the cultural influences and buying motives of each specific market. Often, however, buying motives are identical in all or many markets. In such cases, genuine creativity in advertising – a scarce commodity the world over – may more than compensate for a standardised theme. Thus, by taking international advantage of creativity wherever it may originate, standardisation may actually improve sales.

Example

The Avis Rent-a-Car Co. used its theme 'We try harder' in the USA and (translated) throughout Europe, with such success that the slogan is still used today.

Standardisation will certainly reduce costs in terms of artwork, copywriting, block production, printing, creative staff and television film production costs. The latter, in particular, offer real economies. Taking £200,000 as a reasonable average production cost for a television commercial, the savings when that commercial can be used in, say, ten countries instead of one can be seen to add up to a sizeable figure.

6. The standardisation decision

There can be no universal solution to the problem of standardisation; each campaign must be separately considered. The following factors should be taken into account:

(a) the general similarity or otherwise of the markets to be covered by the campaign (for instance, where cultural differences are limited and income, education, etc., are similar, buying motives may well be the same);
(b) the nature of the product (industrial goods, for instance, are purchased more on objective criteria and are therefore particularly suitable to a standardised approach, as are 'tourist' products such as films and petrol);
(c) local advertising agency standards, especially in terms of creativity;
(d) government and other restrictions, which may prohibit certain copy themes (**8**) or the use of certain media (**14**);
(e) the non-availability of media such as television in certain countries (**14**);
(f) media spillover possibilities (**12**);
(g) the availability of suitable international media (**12**).

7. The prototype campaign

Where standardised campaigns prove impossible, prototype campaigns may be a useful alternative. Such campaigns are normally prepared by corporate headquarters and are based on common denominators drawn from consumer research in a number of markets regarded as generally representative. The prototypes are then modified by local subsidiaries, licensees or distributors to suit each particular market. In this way the subsidiaries can benefit from the central creative approach, while at least some cost savings can be achieved, even if only in terms of creative staff.

The advertising message

8. Legal restrictions

As in the UK, so in most other countries the law restricts the advertiser's freedom, particularly with regard to the advertising message. Regulations vary from country to country and must be checked in every individual case. It is unsafe to assume a general similarity with English law; some of the regulations, even in Europe, would appear surprising to the UK marketer.

Example
Germany forbids superlatives or comparative claims: 'better' and 'best' are words to be avoided. In the case of product comparisons, the manufacturer with whose products the advertised products are compared may be able to sue for damages.

9. Social constraints

Social and other conventions may affect both the advertising message and the way it is expressed.

Example

What to British eyes would be a quite normal illustration of men and women dining together is quite unacceptable in some Middle East countries.

10. Translation of advertising copy

Where there is no advantage in standardisation, the question of translation of the advertising message will not arise, since copy can be prepared in each individual country.

Often, however, ideas will be generated in the UK and used in many different countries; this is particularly the case, of course, with exporting companies.

Seemingly straightforward translation offers a number of far from obvious pitfalls which can negate the value of the entire campaign. The apparently correctly translated message may become incomprehensible or, worse, may make both the advertiser and his product look ridiculous.

Example

Consider this observation of a Danish executive working for a European trading company in Indonesia: 'I have read many sales pieces written by Americans that were translated into the local language. Often they miss the point entirely. Sales psychology is different in every country and you can get the feel of it only if you know the language.' A countryman of his, based in Thailand, echoed that point. 'Check them out,' he suggested, 'by having a different translator put back into English what you've translated from the English. You'll get the shock of your life. Once, I remember, "Out of sight, out of mind" had become "Invisible things are insane."'

(Source: Ferdinand F. Mauser, *Harvard Business Review*, July / August, 1977)

11. Some rules for copy translation

(a) Understand that the task of the translator is to translate the thought and ideas, not to provide a literal translation from the English. The latter can only rarely be a success as advertising copy.

Example

Once it had been agreed [by Esso] in Washington that all the European affiliates would adopt the original Tiger artwork, the difficulties of rendering exact translations of the slogan 'Put a Tiger in your Tank' became only too apparent. As research had established, it was the crispness and alliteration of the slogan which had contributed significantly to the campaign's success in the United States. It was essential that, where possible, these qualities should be carried over into the European translations, but not if it meant departing from the basic exhortation to the motorist to put a tiger in his tank. In Italy, the word 'tank' could not be literally translated; and 'motor' was chosen as a substitute ... Finally, their slogan emerged as 'Metti un tigre nel motore,' retaining the alliteration of the original and the same pithy delivery.

(Source: B. Ash, *Tiger in Your Tank*, Cassell, 1969)

(b) Design and write the copy from the outset with possible translation in mind.

(c) Avoid unusual idiomatic expressions or slang.

(d) Select a professional translator whose mother tongue is the language into which the translation is to be made. Ideally, this translator will be living in the country where the advertisement will appear, but this may not always be possible.

(e) Bear in mind that languages common to several countries nevertheless show important national differences. For example, Spanish in Colombia differs from Spanish in neighbouring Venezuela.

(f) Always have the translation checked by local nationals with experience in the relevant product area; agents and distributors are the obvious choice. Alternatively, have the advertisement translated back into English by a different translator, as suggested in an earlier example.

(g) Arrange for printing either by a UK printer specialising in the relevant language or by a printer within the market.

(h) Have the printed proofs re-checked by both the translator and agents or distributors.

Advertising media

12. International media

An option open to the international marketer in a position to standardise his appeal is the use of international media: publications aiming, as a matter of policy, at coverage in several different countries. Such media include:

(a) consumer magazines such as *Reader's Digest* or *Business Week*;

(b) a number of trade and technical magazines;

(c) newspapers in several different countries offering a package deal;

(d) satellite television.

In addition, the international marketer may be able to take advantage of media spillover. For instance, television programmes in the north of the USA can also be seen in Canada.

13. National media

Purely national media, however, account for the vast bulk of world advertising. It is not possible here to discuss the diversity of media available.

14. Media selection

The principles of media selection are universal; the desirable media in every country are those that reach the target market most effectively.

The application of those principles, however, will vary from one country to the next. Some of the points the international marketer will need to bear in mind are discussed below.

(a) Very often what would normally be regarded as the most suitable media are available only on a limited basis or do not exist at all.

(b) Local laws may forbid the advertising of certain products.

(c) There is often a lack of reliable basic information on circulation or audience characteristics, particularly outside the industrialised countries.

(d) Low levels of literacy may mean that the normally appropriate medium is unsuitable. Radio, for instance, is particularly suitable in developing countries, and may be preferred to press advertising.

(e) High taxation on certain media result inevitably in distortion of the media plan.

(f) Distinct regional characteristics, especially linguistic, may require the use of regional media. Switzerland, with three major languages, is an obvious example.

(g) The appropriate media may be unsatisfactory from the point of view of quality of reproduction. This applies particularly in the case of colour reproduction.

Advertising agency selection

15. Options available

The international marketer wishing to advertise abroad will normally have the following principal options available:

(a) selection of a domestic advertising agency, which will work either directly with the overseas media or through the UK representatives of those media;

(b) selection of a domestic agency with branch offices, affiliates or association agreements with agencies abroad;

(c) selection of foreign agencies in each national market.

16. Selection criteria

Again, there can be no general rule, but in selecting an agency the international marketer should take into account the following criteria.

Extent of market coverage
Although many of the larger agencies have a remarkably wide international coverage, that coverage may not coincide with all markets of interest to the advertiser.

Quality of service
The standard of advertising agencies varies from market to market, and even

between branches of the same agency. A company with its own advertising department may find a weak local agency acceptable.

Size of appropriation
A certain minimum appropriation is necessary to interest the major international agencies or to interest any one foreign agency. The smaller advertiser of, say, industrial products may have to rely on a domestic agency.

Need for international coordination
A company aiming at a standardised international campaign will require good coordination and control, which is most likely to be achieved through a single international agency.

Company organisation
International companies organised on a decentralised basis may prefer to leave agency selection to the local subsidiary. Similarly, in joint venture arrangements or cooperative advertising in conjunction with a distributor local influence would be significant in the final choice.

Progress test 21

1. Say what you understand by the term 'marketing communications' and describe briefly any two elements of the function of marketing communications. *(IEx)*

2. Your company wishes to develop a 'global brand' of perfume. What implications would this have for the advertising element of the marketing mix? *(CIM)*

3. Outline the circumstances favouring a standardised as opposed to a non-standardised advertising approach when marketing the same products in a number of different countries. *(CIM)*

4. Advertising methods and practices are different in different countries. Why should this be so, even where habits and living conditions have much in common? *(CIM)*

5. 'A good advertisement is impossible to translate.' Discuss. *(CAM Foundation)*

6. You need to have one of your sales leaflets put into German for distribution in Germany. State how you would get this done and what precautions you would take to ensure that the final result was both accurate and acceptable to the people locally. *(IEx)*

22

International communications II: Sales promotion and public relations

Introduction

1. Sales promotion

Sales promotion consists of those marketing activities, other than personal selling, advertising and public relations, that stimulate consumer purchasing and/or dealer effectiveness, such as demonstrations, exhibitions, catalogues, films, trading stamps, premium offers, contests, coupons and free samples.

2. Public relations

Public relations has been defined as the non-personal stimulation of demand for a product, service or business unit by placing commercially significant news about it in a published medium or by obtaining favourable presentation of it on radio, television or stage that is not paid for by the sponsor.

In an international context two aspects of public relations are of special importance: placing press releases with overseas media – particularly difficult for the exporter; and, for the overseas subsidiary of an international company, earning the reputation of being a 'good citizen' in the host country.

Sales promotion

3. Legal restrictions

Perhaps more than any other aspect of marketing, sales promotion is beset with legal pitfalls. Most industrialised countries have introduced laws to protect their citizens. The variety and ingenuity of sales promotion techniques result in complex legislation which even then leaves grey areas where the law is uncertain. A good rule of thumb is to take legal advice before embarking on major promotions in an unfamiliar country.

There has as yet been no attempt, even in the EC, to introduce uniformity of sales promotion legislation. Table 22.1 gives a good indication of the difficulties to be faced in Western Europe.

Developing countries do not concern themselves unduly with sales

Table 22.1 European sales promotion legislation – what is legal and where

Legend: ● Permitted ○ Not permitted ◀ May be permitted

	UK	Irish Republic	Spain	Germany	France	Denmark	Belgium	Netherlands	Portugal	Italy	Greece	Luxembourg	Austria	Finland	Norway	Sweden	Switzerland
On-pack price reductions	●	●	●	●	●	●	●	●	●	●	●	●	●	●	●	●	●
Banded offers	●	●	●	◀	●	◀	◀	●	●	●	●	○	◀	●	◀	◀	○
In-pack premiums	●	●	●	◀	◀	◀	◀	◀	●	●	●	○	◀	◀	◀	◀	○
Multiple-purchase offers	●	●	●	◀	●	◀	◀	●	●	●	●	○	◀	◀	◀	◀	○
Extra product	●	●	●	◀	●	●	◀	◀	●	●	●	●	●	●	●	◀	◀
Free product	●	●	●	●	●	●	◀	●	●	●	●	●	◀	●	●	●	●
Reusable/alternative use pack	●	●	●	●	●	◀	●	●	●	●	●	●	○	●	●	●	●
Free mail-ins	●	●	●	○	●	◀	◀	●	●	●	●	◀	◀	●	●	●	●
With-purchase premiums	●	●	●	◀	●	◀	●	◀	●	●	●	○	◀	◀	◀	○	○
Cross-product offers	●	●	●	○	◀	◀	○	◀	●	●	●	○	◀	●	◀	◀	○
Collector devices	●	●	●	○	◀	◀	◀	◀	●	●	●	●	○	●	○	◀	○
Competitions	●	●	●	○	●	●	◀	◀	●	●	●	◀	●	●	●	●	●
Self-liquidating premiums	●	●	●	◀	●	○	●	◀	●	●	●	○	○	◀	◀	●	○
Free draws	●	●	◀	●	◀	○	○	○	●	◀	◀	○	◀	●	○	○	○
Share-outs	●	●	●	○	●	○	○	○	●	◀	◀	○	○	●	○	○	○
Sweepstake/lottery	◀	◀	◀	○	◀	○	◀	◀	●	◀	◀	◀	●	●	○	○	○
Money-off vouchers	●	●	●	○	●	◀	●	●	●	◀	●	○	◀	●	●	●	●
Money-off next purchase	●	●	●	◀	●	○	●	●	●	●	●	○	●	●	◀	◀	○
Cash backs	●	●	●	◀	●	●	●	●	●	○	●	○	◀	●	◀	◀	○
In-store demos	●	●	●	●	●	●	●	●	●	●	●	●	●	●	●	●	●

(Source: *IMP Europe*, International Marketing and Promotions Ltd, 197 Knightsbridge, London SW7 1RP.)

promotion; legislation is limited in scope. This does not mean, however, that the position is necessarily any clearer or easier. Table 22.2 offers a few hints on how to set about a sales promotion campaign in the Far East.

4. Retailer cooperation

Promotions will often require retailer support in terms of processing coupons, handling on-pack gifts, setting up display material, etc. Securing cooperation is often much more difficult abroad, as a result not so much of dealer attitude but of lack of space and handling facilities.

Exhibitions

5. International importance of exhibitions

Exhibitions are, of course, a regular feature of the business scene in the UK. Internationally, however, they assume much greater significance since:

(a) they play a much more important role in business in many other countries, particularly Germany:
(b) the ever-present problems of time, distance and cost in meeting customers and potential customers are at least partially solved;
(c) product demonstrations automatically surmount all communications barriers;
(d) until recently, in Eastern Europe, trade fairs were one of the few methods by which face-to-face contact with the end-purchaser was possible. The fairs retain much of their importance.

6. Exhibition planning

Occasional participation in trade fairs on an *ad hoc* basis is usually a recipe for failure. Exhibitions must be:

(a) an integral part of the overall marketing plan;
(b) supported by a planned promotional programme designed to ensure that the maximum possible benefit is derived from participation.

7. Categories of exhibition

Essentially the choice will lie between:

(a) a general trade fair or a specialised (industry) exhibition;
(b) a national or international exhibition;
(c) exhibitions open to the trade only and those open to the general public;
(d) special-event exhibitions (the majority) and permanent exhibitions.

It may also be worthwhile to consider the company's own exhibition, perhaps as a mobile exhibition in a train, or as a 'spin-off' exhibition (one held at the same time as, and in the vicinity of, a major exhibition).

Table 22.2 Sales promotion in the Far East

The Far East is still relatively unencumbered with sales promotion legislation, but this does not make it a simple market to operate in.

The first crucial stop in any Far Eastern market is to get local advice. Before talking to any Ministry or interested party, check the protocol with a local agency. You will probably find that any Ministry you consult becomes an integral part of the proceedings; their involvement rarely speeds things up, so check beforehand on whom you should talk to, and when.

Some countries have introduced very limited legislation: in Hong Kong cash cannot be used as an incentive (but gold can!); in Malaysia, Hong Kong and a number of other countries, lotteries must be registered with the state.

The soundest policy, therefore, is to check the scheme with a local agency, and compare the promotion to what is currently on offer.

It is very easy for an exporter to offer too generous an incentive, simply by replicating the value of a UK offer. The local cost of living is vastly cheaper, and incentives should reflect this. In Thailand, recently, a promotion for a soap powder, that promised 'Win a House', had to be cancelled by the government as locals poured boxes of the soap powder into the street in search of the lucky token.

Promoters should also take advice on the theme and creative execution of the promotion. In most Far Eastern countries, the number 8 is lucky, while the number 4 is notoriously unlucky, and a scheme asking for four proofs of purchase might well cause alarm. This is one example of local customs, and the exporter would do well to check mock-ups and artwork at every stage.

(From: *Marketing without Frontiers, the RMI Guide to International Direct Marketing*, Royal Mail International, Basildon, 1991)

(Source: Ian Arthur, European Federation of Sales Promotion, c/o Tim Arnold Associates, 49 York Street, Twickenham TW1 3LP.)

8.   Selecting an exhibition

Usually, within any one category of exhibition, the intending exhibitor will have a wide choice. Final decision criteria are likely to include:

(a) the relationship between the company's target audience and the composition of the exhibition audience in previous years – organisers should provide appropriate research data on attendance;

(b) the length of time the exhibition has been established – as a rule new fairs attract only a small attendance;

(c) the standing of other exhibitors in past years, and intending exhibitors;

(d) the authority of the exhibition sponsors and their organising competence – efficiency matters;

(e) the timing of the exhibition – it may clash with another similar exhibition, but, on the other hand, it may immediately follow, at a reasonably near venue, another relevant exhibition, thus encouraging a spin-off attendance.

9.   Purpose of exhibiting

At the same time the objectives of exhibiting must be fully and clearly defined. They may include:

(a) taking orders on the stand;

(b) obtaining enquiries for subsequent follow-up;

(c) general market publicity, with a view to securing orders in the longer term;

(d) assistance in meeting a selection of prospective agents or distributors;

(e) assistance in the assessment of market potential or of product acceptability.

10. Advance marketing programme

As mentioned, mere participation in an exhibition is not sufficient. The advance marketing programme should include:

(a) target audience identification;

(b) direct-mail publicity to that audience;

(c) advance press publicity.

11. Evaluation and follow-up

After the exhibition:

(a) results should be compared with the original objectives;

(b) actual costs should be compared with budget;

(c) enquiries should be followed up promptly;

(d) market information obtained should be evaluated;

(e) a decision should be reached as to whether to exhibit at the same exhibition in the following year.

12. Government support for exhibitors

The UK government provides financial support to companies participating in overseas exhibitions, provided such companies are sponsored by an approved trade association or chamber of commerce. Support includes:

(a) a 50 per cent grant towards the cost of space;
(b) a fixed amount towards stand construction;
(c) for exhibitions outside Western Europe, a grant towards the travel costs of up to two representatives from the UK.

Support is available for up to three trade fairs in any given market (five in the case of Germany, Japan and the USA).

Store promotions

13. Definition
The term 'store promotion' can refer to a variety of promotional activities within retail stores. In the international marketing sense, however, it is used specifically to describe the more elaborate promotions staged in favour of consumer goods from one or more countries. Promotions are usually organised on the initiative of the store itself. They are major events, with a level of activity not usually seen in the UK. They are of special importance in the sale of consumer goods in Japan.

Details of future store promotions are given in the DTI's Export Intelligence Service and its *Promotions Guide*. The DTI offers advice in its advance publicity on how to offer products or services to the organising store.

14. Value of store promotions
The long-term value of store promotions is difficult to assess and opinions differ on the subject. A few generalisations, however, can be made:

(a) as with exhibitions, they should be considered only as part of a long-term marketing plan;
(b) the aim should normally be the continuing supply of the products in the future, so evaluation should take place, say, a year afterwards;
(c) they are most likely to be successful if the products concerned are already being purchased and sold by the store, and are not simply purchased specially for the event.

Public relations

15. Press releases in overseas media
A UK company is particularly well situated with regard to obtaining space in overseas media. Several hundred correspondents of overseas news-

papers, periodicals, radio and television are based in London.

The COI will prepare a professional news release from any newsworthy item submitted to it and will distribute it to media in all relevant countries. The service does not use paid-for advertising and cannot guarantee publication: the story is published on the strength of its news value at the discretion of the overseas editor. The COI emphasise that a newsworthy product is one with advantages over its competitors, one with a 'leading edge'. Being new to the market is not enough. A small charge is made.

The BBC World Service broadcasts in English and in 35 other languages. A significant part of its programmes is concerned with developments in British industry.

Example

The BBC means business!

BBC World Service broadcasts to 120 million regular listeners in 120 countries, in English and 35 other languages. It is renowned for its integrity and credibility. What better way of bringing British manufacturers and service industries to the attention of potential buyers and users overseas? The BBC offer you an international showcase – absolutely free!

All we ask is that you have a good, new story to tell. The BBC's worldwide reputation has been won through objective broadcasting, bad news alongside good. So when the news is good it is accepted with complete confidence. Innovatory products and services are, accordingly, judged strictly on their merits.

If your story has news value, tell us and we can tell the world in the appropriate programme or language for your product or service and for our listeners. Tell us about interesting new developments, innovative products and services, export orders won, visits to target areas in sales missions or with trade fairs, joint venture participation and training initiatives.

However technical your offering, so long as it is new and interesting we have specialist writers who can put it across to an overseas audience. The many resulting inquiries will of course be passed on to you.

(Source: Export Liaison, BBC World Service, Bush House, Strand, London WC2B 4PH)

16. Public relations for subsidiary companies

An overseas subsidiary should, as indicated earlier (4:8), endeavour to earn and retain a reputation as a 'good corporate citizen' of the host country. The standards required vary from country to country, but as a general rule most subsidiaries would do well to adhere to the guiding principles laid down by the Government of Canada Foreign Investment Review Agency, an abridged version of which is given in Table 22.3

Table 22.3 Government of Canada Foreign Investment Review Agency: Guidelines for Canadian subsidiaries of foreign companies.

1. Pursue a high degree of autonomy in the exercise of decision-making and risk-taking functions.
2. Develop as an integral part of the Canadian operation an autonomous capability for technological innovation, and for production, marketing, purchasing and accounting.
3. Retain in Canada a sufficient share of earnings to give strong financial support to the growth and entrepreneurial potential of the Canadian operation, having in mind a fair return to shareholders on capital invested.
4. Strive for a full international mandate for innovation and market development, when it will enable the Canadian company to improve its efficiency by specialisation of productive operations.
5. Aggressively pursue and develop market opportunities throughout international markets as well as in Canada.
6. Extend the processing in Canada of natural resource products to the maximum extent feasible on an economic basis.
7. Search out and develop economic sources of supply in Canada for domestically produced goods and for professional and other services.
8. Foster a Canadian outlook within management, as well as enlarge career opportunities within Canada, by promoting Canadians to senior and middle management positions, and by including a majority of Canadians on boards of directors of all Canadian companies.
9. Create a financial structure that provides opportunity for substantial equity participation in the Canadian enterprise by the Canadian public.
10. Pursue a pricing policy designed to assure a fair and reasonable return to the company and to Canada for all goods and services sold abroad, including sales to parent companies and other affiliates.
11. Regularly publish information on the operations and financial position of the firm.
12. Give appropriate support to recognised national objectives and established government programmes, while resisting any direct or indirect pressure from foreign governments or associated companies to act in a contrary manner.
13. Participate in Canadian social and cultural life and support those institutions that are concerned with the intellectual, social, and cultural advancement of the Canadian community.

(Source : Businessman's Guide to the Foreign Investment Review Act, FIRA, 1975.)

Progress test 22

1. What factors would constrain the use of standardised sales promotion campaigns for a multinational enterprise in international markets? *(CIM)*

2. Define the following and explain how they might be used together to form a promotional campaign: sales promotion, publicity (public relations) and advertising. *(IEx)*

3. Describe the steps you would take in order to participate in an overseas trade fair. *(IEx)*

4. Assume that your company is considering participation in an overseas trade fair. Describe in detail the steps which you would take to organise such participation and indicate the benefits which you would hope to achieve from exhibiting overseas. *(IEx)*

5. Explain in detail the role of public relations in marketing overseas and state your view of the difference between public relations and advertising. *(IEx)*

6. 'An expatriate subsidiary should be careful to be, and to be seen to be, a good corporate citizen of the host country.' What do you understand by the phrase 'good corporate citizen'?

23

International communications III: Sales management

Introduction

1. Sales management

Sales management includes the recruitment, training, motivation, compensation, organisation, evaluation and control of a sales force.

For obvious reasons, personal selling, more than any other marketing activity, is closely linked to national, or even regional, social or cultural characteristics and to language. Most face-to-face selling is organised within national frontiers. In the EC for instance, despite the progress made towards integration, few sales forces cross political boundaries; international selling is limited mainly to industrial goods or to quantity sales of consumer goods to wholesalers and major retail groups.

Purely national selling is not further considered.

2. International sales management

The international sales management function may involve:

(a) the management of a team of travelling export sales people based at company headquarters;
(b) the management of a sales force based abroad, within its market area – such a sales force may, of course, consist of either expatriates or nationals of the market country;
(c) ultimate responsibility for the nationally organised and managed sales forces of an overseas subsidiary or branch;
(d) responsibility for sales through agents.

The first three subjects are considered in this chapter. Agencies are discussed in Chapter 24.

The travelling sales force

3. The export sales force

In sales management a prime requisite for success is the selection of the right sales team: a difficult task for any sales manager, but doubly difficult in the export field. Export sales people must possess all the qualities of their domestic counterparts, plus the characteristics discussed below.

Managerial competence
The export salesperson must be able to make prompt decisions, often with limited information and with less consultative support, on risks and opportunities of much greater magnitude than are usual in the home market. Overseas buyers are unlikely to react favourably to someone who is constantly referring back to headquarters for instructions. The export salesperson is also likely to be responsible for guiding agency operations and for training agency staff.

Research competence
Export salespeople must know where to look for advice and information and how to interpret data obtained. They will have many of the characteristics of the market researcher.

Cultural adaptability
The ability to adapt to and, better still, identify with very different cultures is essential in an export salesperson. Much more is required than mere tolerance or acceptance.

Dependability
Far more than a domestic counterpart the export salesperson will be required to work without supervision; business abroad is often frustrating, and temptations to take time off are greater. The export salesperson must be relied upon to persist with the sales task.

Health
Travel in itself is physically demanding. Extremes of climate, strange foods, indifferent hotels and customer entertainment all combine to increase the strain on the constitution.

Linguistic ability
On the one hand, linguistic skills may be overvalued: competence in appropriate languages, without the qualities discussed above, is not enough. Conversely, some companies even today seem not to realise the weakness of a sales approach that relies on a bilingual customer.

4. Size of the export sales force
The size of a sales force is a function of:

(a) market potential;
(b) the extent to which personal selling is the most effective method, in terms of eventual profit, of exploiting that potential;
(c) the work load involved, in terms of sales calls and other related activities, in exploiting the potential.

The basic principles hold good whether sales are national or international. It is necessary to mention them in an international context only because so many companies ignore them in relation to their export markets. The Betro report commented on this fact and on the resultant damaging effect on the sales and profits of UK exporters. Whilst the position must surely have improved immeasurably since the Betro investigation, the report's comments are still worth pondering.

Examples

(1) Even allowing for the use of overseas agents British companies employ a relatively small number of people on the export side of their activities (small in relation to the number employed on the selling side for the home market, and small in relation to the number of countries they have to service).

(2) There are many companies where almost the entire export effort revolves around one man (including a number exporting from 50 per cent to 80 per cent of their production). It is his task to keep in touch with all the markets (often over 100), customers and problems overseas; attend to the problems of administration and finance; appoint and supervise agents and so on.

(Source: *Concentration on Key Markets: A Development Plan for Exports*, Betro Trust Committee, Royal Society of Arts, 1977)

5.   Deployment of the export sales force

Sales forces are normally organised into territories, again on the basis of market potential and work load. In exporting, the same principles hold good, except that the sales contribution of the agent must also be taken into account. Assessing the agency's contribution on a realistic basis is not always easy – it is usually spread over a range of products and may, as a result, be sporadic. Nevertheless, such an assessment must be attempted and the sales force must be deployed accordingly. The Betro report also commented on the deployment of UK export sales staff.

Example

Yet another reason for the small export sales force is that companies organise their selling operations for exports in an entirely different manner from that in the home market. In the latter they split up the country into small sales territories, effectively manageable by one man. In the export markets, as a rule, they hand over their products to an agent who covers an entire country. Thus one export sales specialist can 'look after' ten or more countries. Even allowing for the different situation, this approach would be regarded as monstrously inefficient in the home market.

(Source: *Concentration on Key Markets: A Development Plan for Exports*, Betro Trust Committee, Royal Society of Arts, 1977)

Export sales staff abroad

6. Expatriate sales people

In the case of expatriate sales people the problems of sales management are similar to those of a travelling export sales force. Two additional problems arise: employee conditions of service and the high cost of expatriate staff.

7. Conditions of service

With any sales force, one of the most important problems is the maintenance of morale. This is doubly important when, say, a sales manager is posted overseas with only limited contact with headquarters. Inadequately thought-out conditions of service are a frequent source of dissatisfaction, and it is important to consider salary, expenses and career development before any employee is posted abroad. Table 23.1 gives a checklist of points to be considered.

Actual salary levels, or the allowance for the local cost of living, must, of course, be established separately for each relevant country. The larger company, regularly sending employees overseas, may find it worthwhile to subscribe to the services of Employment Conditions Abroad Ltd, which monitors economic conditions, salaries and tax structures in some 160 countries.

8. Cost of expatriate staff

The advantages of posting an executive abroad are perhaps greater than appear on the surface. Export sales people spend, as a rule, a very limited amount of time actually in the market; they may be out of the UK for perhaps six months of the year, but absences much longer than six months would be unusual. Expatriate sales executives are based in the market and may be regarded as the equivalent of two UK-based staff, while they achieve a significant saving in air fares and hotel bills.

The cost of maintaining an expatriate abroad, however, can be surprisingly high. For the not-too-distant markets the travelling salesperson may be the more cost-effective alternative.

Example

Let us imagine that you are thinking of basing a senior sales executive for the first time in Hong Kong. Let's say the company concerned prides itself on good, as distinct from best, employment practice and is to transfer a 35-year-old sales manager earning £37,200 p.a. from Manchester to Hong Kong. Let's also say he is married, with two children aged 7 and 12, both of whom will attend schools in Hong Kong. Air fares will include the flight to Hong Kong plus one UK leave for the whole family in business class. A Toyota Corolla 1.6 will be provided and insurance, tax and one service will be paid for. Settling-in costs will include on month at a hotel for the family and one month's salary as disturbance allowance. The manager's UK salary will be increased by a 15% expatriate allowance. He will not sell his

Table 23.1 Conditions of service for an expatriate sales manager: some points to consider

---

1. Salary and allowances
How does the proposed salary compare with the local cost of living *for expatriates*?
Is a clothing allowance to be paid? For *all* family members?
Is a car provided? With driver?
How is the salary, if expressed in sterling, to be protected against devaluation?
Is the salary to be linked to the local cost of living? If so, how often will adjustments be made?
If there are exchange controls on remittance of capital to the UK, should part of the salary be paid into a UK bank? Or to a bank in some other country with a convertible currency?

2. Travel
Are all family passages to be paid? Class?
What quantity or value of household goods may be shipped over at company expense? And who pays duty on these items?
If children attend UK boarding schools, how frequently can they fly to join parents at company expense?
Who pays fares home in the event of compassionate leave?
For what regular home leaves will travel be paid for by the company?

3. Local housing
Does the company provide accommodation? If so, of what standard? Furnished? If furnished, exactly what will be provided?
If accommodation is not provided, what allowance will be made towards its cost? And what hotel expenses will be paid to enable an employee to look around for accommodation? For how long?
Who pays for electricity, water and other utilities? And local property taxes? And maintenance charges?

4. UK housing
If the expatriate is to sell the UK house, will the company pay legal fees, estate agent's charges, etc.?
If the house is retained but let, will the company contribute to any shortfall between outgoings and rental income?
Who pays for any furniture storage?

5. Education
Will the company pay local school fees? Or UK boarding school fees?
What exactly will such fees include? For example, what optional subjects are allowed?

6. Medical
Are appropriate medical and hospital facilities available locally? And who pays?
Will all dental treatment be paid for? Or merely emergency treatment?

7. Social
Who pays club entrance fees and annual membership fees?
Is an entertainment allowance desirable?
Will the company pay for language courses?

8. Career prospects
How long are the employees expected to serve abroad?
Where are they likely to fit in at headquarters after their tour of duty abroad?

---

house; whether he rents it or not is a matter for him. In these circumstances the total cost for the first year might be as given below.

Pre-posting: medical, expatriate briefing	600
Relocation: excess baggage and insurance	550
Installation: hotel and settling-in	7,300
Remuneration: pay, pension, etc.	48,900
Accommodation: furnished 3-bedroom flat	32,700
Education: local schools	5,100
Leave: original flights + 1 return	11,450
Car: purchase + road tax and 1 service	11,400
Other: family subscription to clubs (excluding corporate debenture), medical insurance, etc.	1,900
	£119,900

This calculation takes no account of expenses such as office services, business travel in the Far East, or entertaining.

(Source: Employment Conditions Abroad Ltd, 15 Britten Street, London SW3 3TY (December 1992))

9. The national sales force

Partly on the grounds of cost, but also on the grounds of language and cultural compatibility, exporters are turning increasingly to the local national sales force, already based in the market. Again, a superficial estimate of costs can be deceptive: apart from the higher salary probably needed, the increased cost of supervision of a newly established sales force, based a long way from headquarters, can be significant.

Many of the comments made throughout this chapter are relevant to such an appointment.

The national sales force

10. Organisation

A full sales force abroad will usually be managed through a branch office or subsidiary company. For obvious reasons it will normally consist of local nationals.

11. Recruitment

Simply because personal selling varies so much with the social and business environment, recruitment is best undertaken within the foreign market by local managers. If a sales force is being recruited from scratch, and, therefore, without the benefit of local sales management advice, it will usually prove advisable to rely on local personnel recruitment agencies.

Regional differences within the country should, of course, be taken into account at the recruitment stage. For example, a French Canadian would be recruited in Quebec.

12. Managing the sales force

No hard and fast rules can be laid down; face-to-face selling varies so much not merely between nations and between regions, but also between industries and individual companies. Generally, however, international sales managers are likely to find that:

(a) training, motivation, methods of remuneration, organisation and control of the sales force are best left in the hands of local managers;
(b) in all these areas they have a significant role to play as an adviser on sales management techniques and in facilitating the international exchange of experience.

Progress test 23

1. What criteria would you use in the selection of sales representatives for a UK manufacturer? The sales representatives will be permanently based in Germany. *(CIM)*

2. Explain why a UK-based sales representative operating overseas has heavier responsibilities than a counterpart operating in the home trade. *(IEx)*

3. Write notes on three types of sales organisation which could be used for overseas marketing. *(IEx)*

4. As a manufacturer of optical instruments such as microscopes you decide to have a company representative to work with your distributors in:
    (a) the Caribbean markets, based in Jamaica;
    (b) the Far East markets, based in Hong Kong.
What kind of persons would you appoint? What special qualities should they possess? *(IEx)*

International communications IV: Agency sales

Agency search

1. Consideration of alternative channels

Before seeking any agent the exporter should have undertaken sufficient research, or have sufficient experience of the market, to be sure that, among all the alternatives available, an agent is the channel most appropriate to profit and other objectives.

2. Agency profile

Exporters should be clear in their own minds as to exactly what type of agency is being sought; similarly, they must give as detailed a brief as possible to those organisations who are likely to assist in the search. Preparation of a formal and detailed profile of the ideal agency is a useful step, even if in practice the ideal is unlikely to be achieved.

Such a profile will vary from one company to the next, but is likely to include, as a minimum:

(a) the precise geographical area the agent should already cover;
(b) the types of customers or distribution channels to which the agent should *already* be selling;
(c) the completeness and frequency of the agent's sales coverage;
(d) the types of products ideal as complementary lines;
(e) requirements in terms of servicing, repair and stockholding facilities.

The first three items are particularly important, and are often the basic reason for selecting an agent rather than recruiting local sales staff, yet intending principals often fail to enquire about the extent of sales coverage, let alone its quality. If agents have to introduce themselves to a new range of customers, they incur a significant outlay, while the principal, at best, has an expensive delay before sales result.

3. Principal profile

Any competent agent who is seriously interested will require the fullest possible information on the prospective principal. Such information is best drawn up initially in the form of a profile of the principal. The profile should be a selling document, designed to interest as many prospective agencies as possible. It should cover not merely the usual and obvious subjects such as product range, factories, number of employees etc., but as far as possible:

(a) the company's recent performance in the home and other export markets;
(b) the special advantages and selling points of the product range offered;
(c) the recommended marketing approach;
(d) the assistance the company normally provides in the marketing of the products, such as cooperative advertising, the provision of sales literature, and training of agency's technical and sales staff.

Commission rates payable are often best left for more detailed discussion with agents at the face-to-face negotiation stage.

4. Finding the agency
The more usual sources of information on likely candidates for the agency are the Overseas Trade Services of the DTI, chambers of commerce, banks and trade associations. Advertisements in appropriate trade magazines may prove helpful.

5. DTI Overseas Trade Services
The DTI now offers a comprehensive agency or distributor search service.

Example
_____

Start your search with us. We can play a key role in helping you identify the best person to represent your business. Staff in the Diplomatic Service Posts have extensive knowledge of individual markets and can provide high quality information and advice.

In our computers we hold details – regularly updated by Posts overseas – of potential business contacts. We can rapidly produce for you a short list of names who handle your product. You could approach them direct to see whether they would be interested in doing business with you.

Or if you prefer we can undertake for you, with our Export Representative Service, a detailed investigation through Diplomatic Service Posts, who are uniquely well placed to help, drawing on their local contacts and expertise. Armed with information about your product, including trade literature and prices, they can determine which representatives would be interested in handling it. And they can advise you on their suitability, reporting on their trading interests, capabilities, scope of activities, other agencies held, territory they can cover effectively, warehousing and distribution facilities, sales force, technical know-how, and after-sales support.

(Source: DTI Overseas Trade Services, *Guide to Export Services*, 1992)
_____

A small charge is made for the service.

6. Chambers of commerce
The functions and importance of chambers of commerce vary significantly according to country, some being very much official bodies with legal standing, others being fairly informal trade bodies. Similarly, the value of the

assistance they can give to companies in search of agencies will vary.

Many chambers of commerce, however, will make efforts to provide introductions, or will pass on enquiries to other chambers abroad. The London Chamber of Commerce and Industry offers an 'Openings for Trade' service to which members can subscribe for a small additional fee. The service issues a regular publication which includes the names of overseas agencies interested in representing UK principals.

Chambers of commerce abroad may also be contacted direct. These include specialist two-country chambers, such as the Anglo-Venezuelan Chamber of Commerce in Caracas.

7. Banks

Most of the major banks have an overseas business development service, whose task it is to help customers *or prospective customers* of the bank to enter or to expand in foreign markets. It is not as a rule necessary to have an account at the bank to take advantage of such a service.

Bank information is not limited to financial status reports. Many banks are specially organised to provide introductions between principals and agents.

8. Trade associations

Trade associations can assist in the agency search by contacting their equivalents abroad and by publishing agency opportunities in their newsletters.

The service may cover not only equivalent associations (those covering the same product) but also associations covering the complementary side of the industry. For example, an electrical manufacturers' association might contact an association of electrical wholesalers abroad.

9. Advertising

Appropriate trade and technical magazines can be identified from the international or national press guides used by advertising agencies, such as *Tarif Media* in France.

Agency selection

10. Market visit

A visit to the market is absolutely essential. A company which lacks either the financial resources or the management time necessary for such a visit should seriously ask itself whether it should be contemplating entering, or remaining in, the market at all. Further, the visit should be made by a senior executive, who will be either immediately or ultimately responsible for the subsequent results from the territory.

11. Selection procedure

Essentially the selection decision should be based on:

(a) the fullest possible discussion with agency executives, sales and other relevant staff such as service engineers;

(b) whenever possible, discussions with customers and potential customers, the companies to which the agents will sell your products and to which they are already selling, or should be selling, other lines.

12. Agency selection checklist

Some companies have also found it helpful to establish a formal comparison procedure or checklist. Such checklists will vary from company to company, but are likely to include the points listed below.

(a) Ownership of agency.

(b) Career histories of executives.

(c) Other agencies held, and extent of success with those agencies.

(d) Geographical area genuinely and regularly covered.

(e) Types of outlet covered.

(f) Frequency of visits per outlet.

(g) Number of sales staff and their length of service.

(h) Agency's knowledge of the market.

(i) Agency's apparent marketing competence, particularly in relation to how it is intended to market the new product line.

(j) If required, servicing and spares facilities.

(k) If relevant, number and qualifications of service staff.

(l) Bank and other trade references.

(m) Agency's interest in and enthusiasm for the new product.

The agency agreement

13. Nature of the agreement

The agency agreement is a commercial contract and is quite properly the subject of detailed negotiation between the parties. Agreements are likely, therefore, to vary significantly between one company and another, or between markets. Nevertheless, there are a number of common features that should be taken into account in drawing up almost any agency agreement. These features are summarised in Table 24.1.

The checklist given in Table 24.1 is necessarily an over-simplification. Many of the points listed require the most careful and detailed consideration; some brief indication of problems that may arise is given below.

Further, the laws of many countries make special provisions for agency contracts, usually with a view to protecting the position of local agents or defining the position of the principal in relation to any possible liability to local taxation. Some reference is made below to the more important and more

Table 24.1 Checklist of points to include in an agency agreement

1. Parties
Identification of parties to the agreement and their capacity to contract.

2. Purpose
One party appoints the other as agent and the other agrees to act.

3. Products (**14**)
Definition of products subject to the agreement.
Position regarding other products sold by the principal, now and in the future.

4. Territory (**15**)
Definition of territory in which agent is entitled to act.

5. Exclusivity (**16**)
Agent's sole and exclusive right to represent principal.
Extent to which principal may operate in the territory without the agent's assistance.
Agent's right, if any, to commission on orders placed direct with principal.

6. Duties of principal (**17**)
Sales and marketing assistance, training of agent's staff, provision of information, etc.

7. Duties of agent (**18**)
Right, if any, to enter into binding agreements on behalf of principal, and, if so, to what extent.
Extent to which agent is bound to comply with principal's instructions on prices and other conditions of sale.
Stipulation of minimum turnover required, if any.

8. Consignment stocks (**19**)
Provision for sale of, and payment for, such stocks, and their storage, maintenance and insurance.

9. Servicing
Provision of after-sales and spares service by agent, if required, and agency's remuneration.

10. Commission (**20**)
Percentage rate of commission.
Variations in rate for different origins of orders (e.g. for orders through a London export house).
Basis of calculation of commission (e.g. FOB price, CIF, etc.).
Indication of when commission is earned: on receipt of order, on delivery of goods, on payment by customer, etc.
Position in event of subsequent order cancellation, buyer bankruptcy, etc.
Dates for payment of commission by principal.

11. Duration (**21**)
Date agreement comes into force and *expiry date*.

12. Termination (**21**)
Provisions for termination before expiry date in case of breach of agreement, bankruptcy, etc.

13. Arbitration
Provision for arbitration in event of disagreement.

14. Assignment
Stipulation that agent cannot assign the benefit of the contract.

15. Authentic text
Indication of which text is authentic, if agreement in two languages.

16. Law of agreement
Indication of the national law that governs the agreement.

usual of such provisions, but it is emphasised that no international agency contract should be entered into without the benefit of professional legal and fiscal advice from lawyers in the country concerned.

For details of EC agency legislation, *see* 28:15.

14. Products

In many markets the exporter is unlikely to find one single agent suitable for the entire product range. Two or more agents may need to be appointed if adequate market coverage is to be secured.

There should be no implication whatever in the agreement that new products to be introduced by the principal in the future will automatically be included in the agreement. Such products may bear no relation to existing products in terms of sales outlets or marketing programmes.

15. Territory

The territory should normally relate to the agent's existing sales areas, as has already been emphasised. This area will not necessarily coincide with national boundaries, and may require careful definition in geographical terms.

It may also be desirable to define the territory in terms of sales outlets. For instance, two agents could quite validly be appointed to cover the same products and the same area, one covering retail outlets and the other covering industrial outlets.

16. Exclusivity

It is not normally in the principal's interest to grant exclusivity – this leaves the entire rights to the market in the hands of an independent party who may fail to exploit its potential. On the other hand, agents cannot really be expected to invest time and money in the sale of the principal's product unless they are granted exclusivity for a reasonable period of time. Normally the principal's aim should be to grant exclusivity but to limit the duration of the agreement to the shortest reasonable period.

17. Duties of principal

The agreement should consider in detail all likely future marketing activities and indicate who is expected to foot the bill. Constantly recurring areas of friction include:

(a) servicing and repairs;
(b) guarantee arrangements;
(c) local advertising;
(d) the provision of promotional material;
(e) translation costs;
(f) training of agent's staff; and
(g) stockholding, especially consignment stocks.

18. Duties of agent

The agency agreement should specifically state whether the agent has any power to enter into binding agreements on behalf of the principal and, if so, to what extent. It should be borne in mind that in some countries if an agent has, and exercises, a general authority to negotiate and conclude contracts on behalf of the principal, the principal becomes liable to tax *in the agent's country*.

A frequent clause in agency agreements is that the agent must maintain the prices and conditions of sale quoted by the principal, but in some countries such a clause is not legally valid.

Another favourite clause stipulates a minimum acceptable turnover from the territory, below which either the agreement is terminated or the agent loses exclusivity. Such clauses often take up much valuable negotiating time and then are finally fixed at so low a level of turnover that they are virtually useless as a form of motivation. A competent principal will offer a better approach to agency motivation.

19. Consignment stocks

Consignment stocks remain the property of the principal but are physically within the agent's territory, under agency control. The possible causes of friction under such an arrangement are legion, and any agreement covering consignment stocks must make the most careful and detailed provision for storage, maintenance, insurance, terms of sale, stock checks, etc.

A further danger is that in some countries the establishment of a consignment stock may render the principal liable to taxation in the country in which the stock is held.

20. Commission rate

These days few sales managers would pay a fixed percentage of turnover to their domestic sales force; most would vary the commission so as to achieve maximum incentive effect. Nevertheless, such a fixed percentage of turnover is still very much the normal and expected form of remuneration for overseas agents.

It is often worthwhile to devise a scheme which acts as a genuine incentive to the agent to direct selling effort into the channels desired by the principal, at the same time increasing profits for both parties. For instance, higher percentage rates can be paid on orders from new clients, or for particularly profitable items in the range.

21. Termination

The termination clause is of vital importance. Termination of agency agreements offers special difficulties in many countries and heavy compensation may be payable. It requires the most careful consideration in the light of local laws before the contract is even signed. *See* 27:5.

Agency motivation

22. The need for motivation

For principals, the fundamental problem of agency distribution is that of ensuring that their products, among all the different lines the agent handles, receive at least their fair share of attention, and preferably much more. The agency agreement is important for the avoidance of disputes that might damage the agent's goodwill, but it is only the starting point, the base from which a positive programme of motivation can be launched.

23. Market visits

The first essential is frequent visits to the territory by the principal. Interest and support simply must be demonstrated in this way if success is to be achieved, a point which might seem obvious if it were not for the fact that so many UK exporters still seem to ignore it.

Example
_____

The relatively few export salesmen are away from their home bases for 5 to 7 months of the year. But because they have so many countries to look after, even the best markets are visited once or at most twice a year only – seldom more. The others, once every two or three years – or never.

(Source: *Concentration on Key Markets: A Development Plan for Exports*, Betro Trust Committee, Royal Society of Arts, 1977)
_____

Again, the position has doubtless improved since the Betro Report, but there are indications that there is still room for improvement in regard to this very basic requirement.

24. Profit

The fundamental motive of the agent is, of course, profit. The principal must work closely with the agents and help them to make money.

This is especially important with a newly appointed agency. Many agents tend to be salespeople at heart; in any case, they are, not unnaturally, unwilling to invest time in market enquiries. The principal, with the advantage of the market research that should have been undertaken, may be able to suggest one or two hitherto neglected possibilities and assist in initial sales.

25. Marketing plans

The principal can provide valuable assistance in preparing annual plans covering all aspects of the marketing of the product.

26. Communications

Quite apart from market visits, regular two-way communication is essential. The uninformed agent soon becomes uninvolved and uninterested;

the uninformed principal directs attention to other markets where opportunities seem more obvious.

The communications system should cover:

(a) formalised and regular reporting of results, not merely by the agent, but also by the principal to the agent (e.g. of overall company results);
(b) essential information such as changes in agency executives or new product developments by the principal;
(c) informal personal matters, preferably in an informal manner.

27. Interpretation of agreement

However carefully the agreement is drafted, some difficulties of interpretation, or some unforeseen special circumstances, will occasionally arise. Whenever possible the agreement should be interpreted in favour of the agency; its goodwill is worth much more than the commission paid in borderline cases.

Progress test 24

1. In search of an agent, it is quite usual to draw up a profile of the ideal agency. What points should such a profile cover?

2. What organisations are likely to be of help in the search for agents abroad?

3. When appointing an overseas sales agent, what are the specific points which must be included in the agreement? Give your views on the relationship between principal and agent. *(IEx)*

4. A company marketing a range of electric welding equipment uses agents to sell its products in various countries in Asia, Africa and South America. Results have been disappointing and the new international marketing manager believes it is because the agents all sell other products. How could he confirm whether this view is correct and, if it proves to be so, how might he be able to motivate the agents to be more effective? *(CIM)*

25

International marketing planning

1. Marketing planning

McDonald has defined marketing planning as 'a structured way of identifying a range of options for the company, of making them explicit in writing, of formulating marketing objectives which are consistent with the company's overall objectives and of scheduling and costing out the specific activities most likely to bring about the achievement of the objectives.'

The essential characteristic of a plan is that it sets out the *means* by which the objectives will be achieved. This is the significant difference between a plan on the one hand and a budget, sales target or forecast on the other.

The real value of marketing planning is that it enables *alternative* marketing strategies to be identified and evaluated. A marketing plan which is merely an update of last year's figures, based on an unthinking acceptance of last year's strategies, is unlikely to be of real value. Effective marketing planning demands an active, even creative, search for alternative strategies that will have a major impact on profit or other objectives. Evaluation of these strategies may require market research.

This in turn means that a marketing plan cannot be the result of a once-a-year meeting. The plan in terms of calendar time will require much of the year to complete and contributing to its preparation should be regarded as a normal and continuing part of the duties of any marketing executive.

Marketing objectives should not consist merely of sales or profit targets. In particular, some evaluation of competitive position, such as market share, should be among the key objectives; it is fatally easy to achieve short-term profit targets by running down long-term competitiveness. Other objectives might include percentage brand awareness, a target number of new distribution outlets or a new-product introduction with a specific sales or distribution level.

2. Marketing planning procedure

Figure 25.1 gives a broad outline of the marketing planning process. This is useful for the purpose of definition, but it does not offer much practical guidance towards the detailed and structured planning procedure that each company must develop for itself if it is to produce a worthwhile plan. Such a procedure would indicate, for instance, who will participate in the preparation of the plan, what contribution they make to which planning decisions, what stage of the plan should be reached by which date, who commissions any research required, what coordination meetings should be held and when,

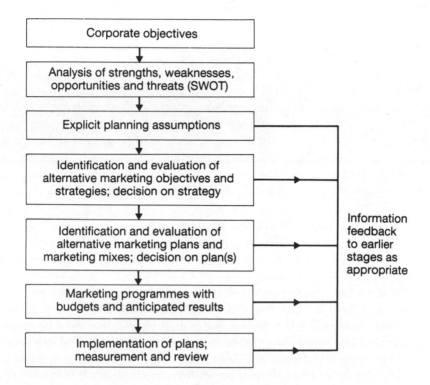

Figure 25.1 *An outline of the marketing planning process.*
NOTE: The marketing audit, which convention demands as an early stage in the marketing planning process, has been ignored. The student may find it advisable to remedy this omission. The marketer, on the other hand, may feel that the marketing audit, so often accompanied by a profusion of checklists, is a distraction from the creative process that is at the heart of marketing planning: the search for broad alternative strategies and new marketing approaches that are likely to have a major impact on profit. The marketing function is in any case considered in the SWOT analysis. The marketing audit has its place as an aid to marketing efficiency, but is perhaps best undertaken on an occasional basis, say every few years, preferably by an outside consultant.

how to spark off those creative ideas leading to changes in strategies, and how best to organise interaction between disparate groups.

Sometimes one particular individual is appointed as marketing planning officer: a useful role. If, however, that role is to produce the marketing plan itself and present it to colleagues more or less as a *fait accompli*, then it may be doubted whether the plan will ever be satisfactorily implemented. Preparation of an effective marketing plan demands the enthusiastic involvement of all marketing executives responsible for its eventual implementation, to say nothing of the support and involvement of the chief executive.

3. International marketing planning

The planning procedure outlined above presents organisational problems in any context. In an international context, and especially in relation to multinational companies, the problems are multiplied: distance and travel costs may mean that coordination meetings become extremely expensive; the diversity of management backgrounds may lead to greater differences of opinion than usual; the necessarily decentralised structure of many multinational companies encourages independence of thought to an extent sometimes detrimental to the overall success of the company.

4. 'Top-down' and 'bottom-up' planning

Three approaches to marketing planning can be distinguished.

The first, 'top-down' planning, implies that the plan is decided by top management and then communicated to subordinates and subsidiary companies. The disadvantages of an international marketing plan prepared without an input from the agents, distributors and overseas subsidiaries who will eventually be required to implement it will be clear. It seems likely that any such 'plan' will consist of no more than a profit target handed down to the subsidiaries of a decentralised organisation.

Under a 'bottom-up' planning system middle management or subsidiary companies prepare their plans and submit them to top management for approval or amendment. This might be regarded as an improvement on top-down planning and might *perhaps* appeal in the case of the traditional Japanese company, where major decisions are often expected to originate at the level of middle management and work their way upwards.

The international marketer may prefer the 'top-down, bottom-up' approach. In an international context this implies that, after agreement on objectives, headquarters and subsidiaries would each prepare marketing plans from their own respective viewpoints, the various plans being then coordinated and amended to produce a final version. The advantages here are obvious. Major Japanese firms are reported as having adopted this approach.

5. International marketing planning procedure

As mentioned (*see* 2), each organisation must develop its own *structured* planning procedure. This applies with even more force in an international context. However, Fig. 25.2 suggests in outline a planning procedure for a multinational company which may perhaps be helpful as a starting point.

6. Content of a marketing plan

Again, the content of the plan will vary according to the preferences of the planning company. Table 25.1 gives as an example the basic format of the marketing plan of a Scandinavian ethical pharmaceutical manufacturer.

7. International marketing strategies

As mentioned (*see* 1), effective marketing planning demands an active and creative search for alternative strategies that will have a major impact on profit or other objectives.

There are, however, a number of strategies which the international marketer will have in mind during the preparation of any marketing plan. Some are of relevance only to major multinationals, others only to the exporter. They are briefly reviewed in the remainder of this chapter.

8. Globalisation

Porter has defined a global industry as 'one in which the strategic positions of competitors in major geographic or national markets are fundamentally affected by their overall global positions.' IBM, for instance, held for many years a dominant position in the world computer market by virtue of its technological lead, its marketing skills, and its manufacturing operations coordinated on a world-wide basis. 'Global industries require a firm to compete on a world-wide coordinated basis or face strategic disadvantages.'

A global industry will be characterised, for example, by manufacturing economies of scale extending beyond the size of major national markets, by very high R&D costs which must be spread over many markets, or the facility to extend marketing techniques learned and successfully applied in one market to other markets elsewhere.

A global strategy does *not* imply a single marketing strategy in all national markets – usually quite the reverse. In one market, for instance, a company may set high return-on-investment targets, in another it may rely on those profits to challenge strong local competition, in yet another it may be content merely to establish a market presence in anticipation of the day when the market becomes more attractive.

9. 'Multi-domestic' or 'multi-local' strategy

Not all industries have the essential characteristics of a global industry. For many industries in which multinational companies operate, globalisation is *not* a feasible strategy.

Such industries are often characterised by, for example, significant differences in product requirements between one market and the next, differing national technical standards, high transport and storage costs that more than

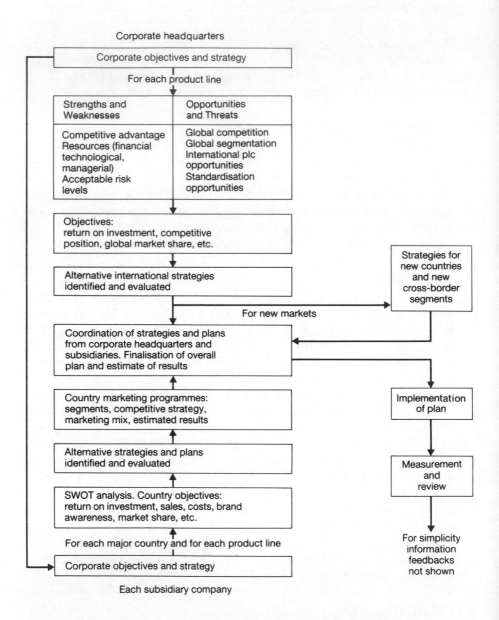

Corporate headquarters

Corporate objectives and strategy

For each product line

Strengths and Weaknesses	Opportunities and Threats
Competitive advantage Resources (financial technological, managerial) Acceptable risk levels	Global competition Global segmentation International plc opportunities Standardisation opportunities

Objectives:
return on investment, competitive
position, global market share, etc.

Alternative international strategies
identified and evaluated

Strategies for
new countries
and new
cross-border
segments

For new markets

Coordination of strategies and plans
from corporate headquarters and
subsidiaries. Finalisation of overall
plan and estimate of results

Country marketing programmes:
segments, competitive strategy,
marketing mix, estimated results

Implementation
of plan

Alternative strategies and plans
identified and evaluated

Measurement
and
review

SWOT analysis. Country objectives:
return on investment, sales, costs, brand
awareness, market share, etc.

For each major country and for each product line

For simplicity
information
feedbacks
not shown

Corporate objectives and strategy

Each subsidiary company

Figure 25.2 *Starting point for the development of a marketing planning procedure for a multinational company.*
NOTE: The top-down bottom-up procedure is not a continuous sequence. A global overview, with its expectations for each country, is agreed with each subsidiary as input to the early stages of the planning procedure
See also 26:**18**

Table 25.1 Contents headings for the marketing plan of a Scandinavian manufacturer of ethical pharmaceuticals

1. Executive summary
2. Summary of supporting information and research findings
   - Planning assumptions
   - Results of SWOT analysis
   - Market descriptions, history and anticipated developments
   - Summary of market research findings
   - Competitor analysis
   - Contingency plans
3. Market segmentation methods and segments selected
4. Competitive strategy
5. Product policy
   - Products/market segments
   - Product sales history
   - Product positioning
   - Forms/sizes
   - Patent position
   - Trade marks/brand names
   - Registration status/launch
   - Budget:
     - sales volume
     - price per unit
     - sales value
     - product costs
     - pre-tax income
   - Anticipated market shares
6. Distribution policy
7. Pricing
   - Review of market pricing opportunities
   - Cost considerations
   - Competitor considerations
   - Government regulations
   - Pricing objectives
   - Pricing policies
   - Allocation of R&D costs
8. Promotion
   - Objectives
   - Promotional messages
   - Promotional methods:
     - sales force
     - seminars
     - brochures
     - public relations
     - packaging
     - clinical trials
9. Production capacity/sourcing
10. Guidance to and liaison with R&D
11. Implementation
    - Responsibilities of named individuals
    - Monitoring system (performance against plan)
12. Strategic alternatives considered in preparation of the plan (for possible reconsideration next year)

offset the economies of scale of centralised production, difficulty in gaining access to established distribution channels, and high tariff barriers. Many fast-moving consumer goods industries are in this category.

In such industries multinational companies can quite safely and successfully leave each national subsidiary, except to some extent in product development, as an autonomous unit. Such an arrangement has been called, for want of a better term, a 'multi-domestic' or 'multi-local' strategy.

10. Regional expansion strategy

A company may decide to concentrate on a particular region, often a particular free trade area such as the EC. The reasons for such a policy are clear, but the international marketer should at least check that there are not better opportunities outside the region. For an EC member it may be, for example, that Canada offers more potential than Greece.

11. Protected niche markets

This strategy quite deliberately looks for relatively small markets which offer local producers a high degree of government protection behind, for instance, high tariff barriers. It requires close attention to the host government's requirements to ensure that tariff and other protection is not removed.

12. Concentration on key markets

The Betro Report (19:**2** and 23:**4, 5**) seemed to suggest that many British exporters attempted to cover too many markets, and that they were as a result engaged in haphazard export selling rather than a planned and profit-maximising marketing operation.

A subsequent report prepared by Industrial Market Research Ltd compared British exporters in this respect with French and German exporters. Its results tended to support the suggestion made in the original Betro report.

Since then there has been some debate as to the advisability of concentrating on key markets. In favour of concentration it has been suggested that:

(a) higher market shares are often associated with a competitive advantage and higher profitability;
(b) a more intimate knowledge of the market permits competition on non-price factors such as product differentiation and customer service;
(c) there are often significant savings to be made in management time and administration costs.

Conversely, strong arguments can be put forward in favour of looking for a small share of a large number of export markets:

(a) the risk of over-dependence on a few markets is avoided;
(b) it may be possible in each market to select those segments that respond best to the existing product, so that expensive product modification can be avoided;

(c) a small market share is less likely to attract retaliation from competitors;
(d) marketing costs are lower.

In practice, the nature of the product and its market are likely to lead to fairly clear-cut decisions. Consumer goods requiring distribution facilities, local stockholding and extensive advertising support would indicate concentration on a few markets; conversely, heavy capital goods sold direct to customers would suggest a large number of markets. What can be said is that exporters between these two extremes should not let this decision go by default.

13. The 'triad' markets

Ohmae has argued that it is hardly worthwhile for multinational companies to develop markets in the third world. The major markets, accounting for a very high proportion of total world demand, are the triad markets: Japan, Europe and the USA. These three areas offer the fastest-growing market for most products and an increasingly homogeneous one. Multinationals would therefore do well to invest more resources in ensuring the rapid introduction of new products into all triad markets simultaneously, entering into long-term cooperation agreements (licensing, joint ventures, etc.) with other companies that operate in the triad markets. In this way they can steal a march on the competition, establish triad market leadership, and aim right from the start at high initial plant investment and lower unit costs.

The triad markets, however, are mature markets where growth opportunities are not always easy to find and where competition is well entrenched. Further, high investment in production facilities for a new product is a high-risk strategy, given that so many new products fail.

14. Domestic strategy

Not all companies are well advised to involve themselves in international marketing: very small companies might find even the costs of exporting too high, some service companies are by definition local in nature, and a newly established company might at first find life easier in the familiar home environment.

Outside categories such as these, however, a company should be reasonably sure, before it decides on a purely domestic strategy, that there are not better profit opportunities outside its home market and that those home market opportunities are not themselves under threat from imports. Again, this is not a decision that should be allowed to go by default.

Progress test 25

1. Examine the view that marketing planning and control is essentially the same for multinational business as it is for domestic business. *(CIM)*

2. You are the export marketing manager of a major manufacturer of yachts, cabin cruisers and small sail boats and your marketing director has asked you to prepare an export marketing plan for the next year. Outline the areas that you would cover in your plan and explain how you would monitor its progress. *(IEx)*

3. Explain why market concentration is a favoured approach to market spreading in international marketing. *(CIM)*

4. Why is export marketing likely to be a superior approach to export selling? *(CIM)*

5. UK Culture Tours Ltd is a company that has concentrated on marketing package holidays in the UK to the USA market and in 1987 its turnover had increased to 18,000 visitors with a package tour value of £25 million. It is now proposing to expand its business into Northern Europe. Draw up a marketing plan to meet this objective, to include market research, promotion and distribution, with a monitoring system to give regular feedback on performance. *(IEx)*

6. Your company produces a range of cosmetics and skin care products which, to date, has only been marketed in the UK. What factors should the company take into account before launching into an overseas market? *(CAM Foundation)*

7. It is frequently said that the marketing strategy depends largely on the product and the market-place involved. Choose two examples from different product fields and demonstrate why the differences occur. *(CAM Foundation)*

26

Organising for international marketing

1. Company organisation

Company organisation includes:

(a) the analysis of the work that needs to be accomplished in order to meet company profit and other objectives;

(b) the division of that work into manageable tasks;

(c) grouping those tasks together on a logical basis and defining the relationships between them;

(d) the appointment of staff to control the tasks and ensure that the work is carried out as planned.

The aim of any organisation structure is to achieve maximum operating efficiency and, hence, maximum profit.

2. Marketing organisation structure

A company's marketing activities will usually be organised on the basis of marketing functions, geographical regions or product groups.

Each of these alternative approaches is illustrated in simplified form in Fig. 26.1. In practice, in a company of any significant size, the organisation structure will usually combine two or more of the basic alternatives.

Key to Figure 26.1 (*overleaf*)

(a) *Functional organisation*. Activities are organised by function (sales, advertising, etc.). All geographical areas and products are covered by each function. The approach offers good coordination and cooperation between managers, but its value declines as the company expands geographically or extends its product range.

(b) *Regional organisation*. Activities are organised by geographical region, each region covering all functions, including marketing. The approach is appropriate where significant differences exist between regions.

(c) *Product organisation*. Activities are organised by product group, each product group controlling all functions, including marketing. The approach is appropriate where the products are quite separate, requiring entirely separate marketing programmes, or where product groups coincide with customer groupings or distinct marketing channels.

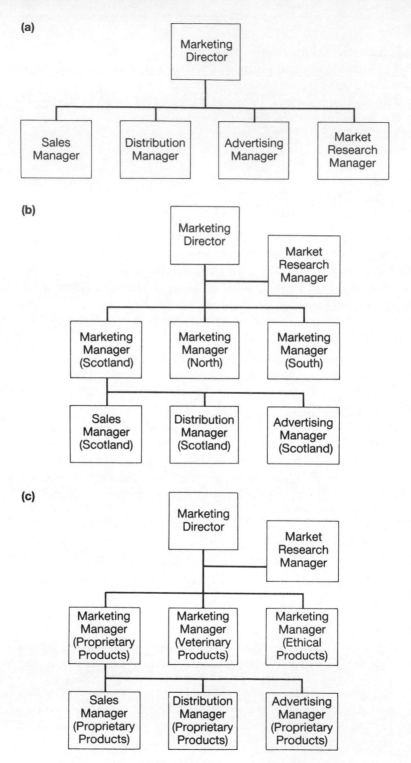

Figure 26.1 *Marketing organisation structures: simplified illustrations of the three principal alternatives.*

3. International marketing organisation

It is possible to distinguish, in international marketing, three principal stages as regards organisation structure: the export department, the international division and the multinational organisation.

It is these three organisational stages that are considered in this chapter, against a background of the general principles of marketing organisation illustrated in Fig.26.1.

The export department

4. The occasional exporter

Many companies begin their international marketing activities by responding to one or two initial orders received from abroad, with little or no marketing effort. At this stage, the order will be processed by the existing (home) sales administration.

5. The exporting company

If international sales increase, the company, recognising the special nature of exporting, will usually organise a small export department consisting of an export sales manager and the necessary administrative assistance, perhaps a secretary and a sales clerk. The danger at this point is that, as sales continue to expand, the company may fail to realise the need for corresponding changes in the organisation of the department: the export manager is allowed to struggle unaided with an ever-increasing volume of business. Just as the field sales organisation should develop with increasing business, so must the export department develop back at headquarters. What might be a typical export department for a company with a significant export turnover is illustrated in Fig. 26.2. Such a department has its own functional specialists for export market intelligence, publicity, etc., and can seek export business more independently and more aggressively than it could if it depended on the part-time services of home marketing staff that are, perhaps, already over-extended. The example given is, of course, only one of many possible alternatives, but, *however the export department is organised, it must be a marketing, not merely a sales, organisation*.

6. Licensing operations

In Fig. 26.2 the export manager is shown as not being responsible for licensing operations. Licensing agreements go beyond marketing, involving manufacturing at least to the extent of quality control and probably well beyond that. When a company becomes seriously involved in licensing, a separate manager for licensing will probably be appointed.

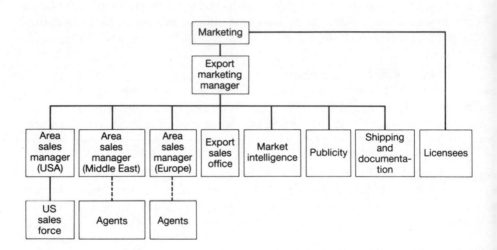

Figure 26.2 *An exporting company: development of the exporting function as export sales increase.*

The international division

7. Need for an international division

When a company moves beyond exports into manufacturing abroad, on either an independent or joint venture basis, an export department no longer serves its purpose, and an international division should probably take its place. Essentially, the aim of establishing such a division will be to minimise the problems arising from the great distances separating the various units within the organisation and the diversity of operating conditions and personnel.

8. Organisation of an international division

The international division may be organised in a variety of ways. Usually, however, it will have a central headquarters staff consisting of functional specialists in marketing, manufacturing, finance, personnel, etc. This staff will plan for, and provide services to, the various operating units located around the world.

Decentralisation may be organised on any of the three bases discussed in Fig. 26.1, i.e. function, region or product. Regional organisations are the most common, however, while a functionally organised division is perhaps most appropriate as a first development from an export department organisation. Regional and functional divisional organisations are illustrated with explanatory comment in Fig.26.3. The examples shown are again highly simplified; in practice, of course, it is again possible to combine two or more of the basic organisational principles.

Key to Figure 26.3 (*overleaf*)

(a) *Functional organisation.* For supervisory purposes, foreign units are grouped by the nature of their activities. Executives can develop their skills in exporting, licensing, etc. The approach is usually best adopted where the operations in any one country are all of one type; problems are likely to arise if a company has a plant in a country and also exports to that country. It is for this reason that the functionally organised division is most suitable as a first step from exporting. As international operations grow, problems of coordination arise.

(b) *Regional organisation.* The regional managers are the key executives at headquarters: they have full and sole responsibility for all activities in their area. Marketing and other functional executives support the regional operations with information, analysis and advice, applying the know-how of the parent for the benefit of the foreign units. The supply manager is responsible for the deliveries from home plants to foreign units. Unlike the functional organisation, the international division organised on regional lines is capable of indefinite expansion.

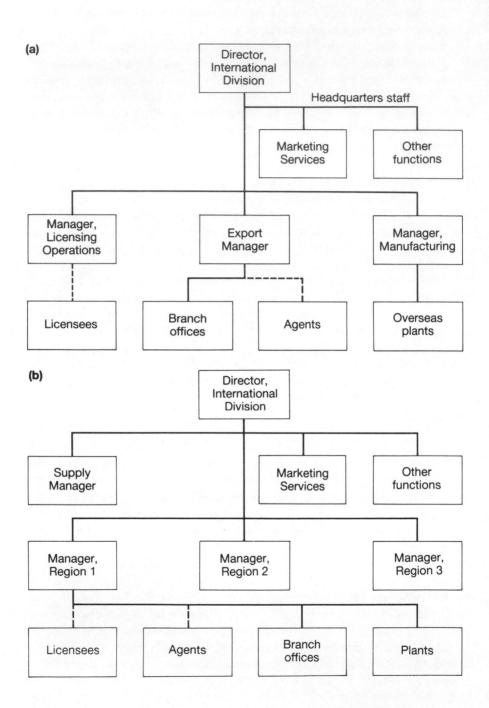

Figure 26.3 *The international division: simplified illustrations of functional and regional organisation structures.*

9. Limitations of the international division

The major disadvantage of the international division approach is that higher management may regard the international division merely as one among many, on a par with the various domestic divisions. Ignorant of world market opportunities, they may fail to give the international division the management attention and the resources it merits. The largest international companies tend to think of organising along multinational lines (1:7).

Multinational organisation

10. The nature of multinational organisation structure

In a multinational company, corporate management and staff are *fully* involved in the world-wide planning of manufacturing facilities, marketing policies and financial flows. All the operating units around the world report directly to the chief executive of the group, not to an international division.

Multinational organisation structure is a major management subject which is still developing as the multinational companies seek improved organisation approaches. Here it can only be touched upon, with the emphasis largely on the marketing function.

11. The aim of the multinational organisation structure

The basic aim of the organisation structure of a multinational company is to capitalise on the advantages of internationalism while at the same time minimising its inherent disadvantages. More specifically, the objectives are:

(a) to maximise the operating performance of the individual units by making available the resources of company headquarters in terms of management expertise, technical know-how, financial assets, market intelligence, etc.;
(b) to minimise the problems that arise from the distances between operating units and from the diversity of operating conditions and personnel, such as, for example, the exercise of too much or too little initiative, or actions taken with inadequate knowledge of the local market;
(c) to coordinate the activities of individual companies where these are interdependent.

12. Interdependence of individual companies

Interdependence of companies is most obvious, perhaps, in the case of manufacturing operations; for instance, one plant may supply components to another. It is important to consider also the extent of *marketing* interdependence.

Marketing activities may be competitive, now or in the future. The organisational implications should be considered in advance, and not when both companies find themselves in competition in the same export market.

Marketing activities may be complementary, when, for instance, common marketing channels can be utilised for different products from different manufacturing units or when standardisation of advertising and promotion is possible (21:4).

13. Centralisation

For an organisation structure to achieve its objectives some degree of centralisation is clearly essential. At the very least central management will wish to retain control over what are regarded as the three key areas of:

(a) basic policy decisions, such as product elimination or introduction, or expansion of manufacturing facilities;
(b) major capital expenditure;
(c) appointment of key executives.

Usually this limited degree of centralisation will be quite inadequate to capitalise on the advantages of internationalism. On the other hand, centralisation of decision-making offers serious drawbacks. In fact, the problem of centralisation versus decentralisation is fundamental to any consideration of a multinational organisation structure.

14. Disadvantages of centralisation

The principal disadvantages of centralisation of decision-making may be summed up under two headings: motivation and communication.

Centralisation of the important decisions is likely to have an adverse effect on the motivation of senior managers in the individual operating units. Most managers are motivated by the need to achieve results in profit terms, and they expect to be judged on those results. When the decisions most vitally affecting profits are taken out of their hands, they not unnaturally tend to lose interest.

Centralisation requires international communication, which in turn leads to expense (though not usually significant), possible misunderstandings and certain delays. Delay, of course, is particularly important in a marketing context: opportunities may be missed that could have been seized by a decentralised or independent organisation.

15. The usual approaches to multinational organisation

Most multinationals adopt one or more of the three basic approaches to decentralisation already mentioned: the functional, regional or product approach.

The functional organisation is more likely to be favoured when the company offers a limited or homogeneous product line, with few modifications required for international markets, or when variations between countries are not significant in marketing terms. These conditions are rarely met in the case of multinational companies and the functional organisation is uncommon.

The regional organisation is more likely to be favoured when the company is exploiting regional market groupings such as the European Community, the market countries are grouped in close proximity but at some distance from headquarters, or the product line is limited or homogeneous.

It will now be evident that the product organisation is most likely to be favoured when the company offers several quite unrelated products, or when modification of products to meet various national requirements is of fundamental importance. The real danger of a product organisation is that international market opportunities are likely to be missed, especially if the domestic market has been historically important and the product division staff lack international marketing experience and expertise.

Any organisation structure, of course, must allow for functional, regional and product inputs, and reliance on only one of the above organisational approaches would, in a multinational context, be highly improbable. The organisation structures of most multinational companies are likely to show either initial reliance on product decentralisation with subsequent regional groupings; or initial reliance on regional decentralisation with subsequent product groupings.

In both cases, a functional input will be required from corporate headquarters staff. The principle of product decentralisation followed by regional groupings is illustrated in Fig. 26.4.

16. Matrix structure

All the approaches so far mentioned provide for the coordination of activities in only one dimension: for instance, a regional organisation permits coordination of all activities within a region. Interdependence, however, may not be confined within one region; in marketing, in particular, a decision taken within a region may have world-wide implications for the company as a whole. The traditional organisation structures are not always adequate when coping with multidimensional interdependence. For this reason some multinational companies have adopted structures that permit simultaneous coordination in terms of product, area and function, while still, it is hoped, achieving the benefits of decentralisation. These structures, known as matrix structures, involve the overseas executive in reporting not merely to his regional superior but also to a functional superior. The matrix approach helps cut through organisational complexities, encouraging team work and cooperation between managers.

However, many companies have found that the matrix structure gives rise to problems. The dual reporting channel inevitably causes conflict, and even minor issues may be resolved only by committee decision, with resultant delays. Multinationals are still searching for the ideal organisation structure.

17. The global corporation

All the organisation structures so far discussed have one thing in common: they all envisage a central headquarters, usually situated in the organisation's country of origin, that is the ultimate authority. Ohmae pro-

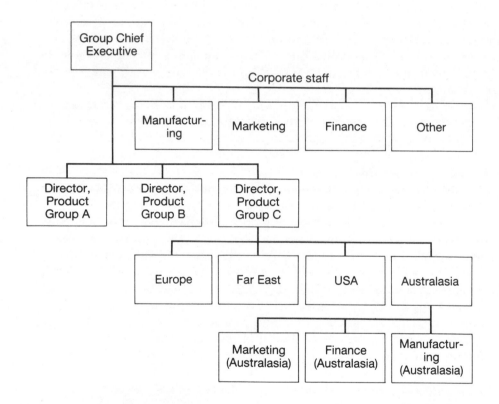

Figure 26.4 *Multinational company organisation (simplified): product basis, with subsequent regional and functional decentralisation.*

poses a stage beyond this, where companies that want to move into a genuinely global mode of operation transcend their country of origin, replacing the corporate centre by several regional headquarters. The link between those regional headquarters is not a line of command but a system of values shared by company executives around the globe.

As an example, Ohmae cites his own company, McKinsey, a firm of international management consultants, that has long experimented with this form of global organisation. A corporate centre does exist in the USA, but it performs only a few corporate functions. Consulting work is carried out through a network of offices connected by criss-crossing lines of communication rather than lines of authority. Similarly, a number of Japanese multinationals, such as Nissan, Honda, Sony and Matsushita, have decentralised responsibility for strategy and operations.

Such an approach is not appropriate for all multinationals. Coca-Cola, for example, is a multinational company still dominated by decisions made in Atlanta.

18. The network organisation

A similar approach to global organisation is the network corporation. The emphasis changes from concern with organisation structure to the need to take into account the differing perspectives of the various corporate entities around the world. What may still legally be subsidiary companies become fully involved in the development and execution of world-wide strategies. International teams of managers from appropriate subsidiaries meet regularly to develop these strategies, so that local input to decisions is automatic. The lead role in ensuring implementation will not necessarily lie with head office; it could be delegated to, say, a regional headquarters, even for a policy involving the whole corporation world-wide.

Progress test 26

1. Within an exporting company, who should be concerned with and involved in the marketing process? *(IEx)*

2. Show how a multinational enterprise (MNE) might modify its organisational structure to accommodate various marketing influences. *(CIM)*

3. 'However the export department is organised, it must be a marketing, not merely a sales, organisation.' What do you understand by this statement? What characteristics, in terms of organisation structure, would distinguish the marketing organisation from the sales organisation?

4. 'The functionally organised international division is probably the best organisational approach for a company that has just moved into limited manufacturing overseas.' Discuss.

5. 'Organisation is only a means to an end, it does not constitute an end in itself.' What do you consider are the ends that should be furthered in the organisation of a multinational company?

6. The organisation structure of many industrial goods companies shows international decentralisation primarily on a product basis, while consumer goods companies tend to decentralise primarily on a regional basis. Why should this be so?

Part four

Marketing in selected countries and the European Community

The principles of international marketing as set out in Part three are of world-wide application. From a marketing viewpoint, however, every country has its own special national characteristics, deriving usually from social and cultural differences, a political philosophy, varying distribution channels, or legal restrictions (often designed to protect a country's economic independence or the interests of its nationals). Part four examines these special characteristics in relation to Brazil, Japan, Nigeria, Russia, the USA and the EC.

Each of the countries selected offers, together with the EC, real opportunities to the international marketer: that has been the first criterion for their selection. Thereafter, however, the aim has been to illustrate the divergences between countries and to indicate how such divergences might affect marketing decision-making.

No attempt has been made – or, in a few short chapters, could be made – to provide a complete treatise on marketing in any of the countries selected. The intention has been more to highlight in each country aspects of special interest or difficulty.

In some instances it has been necessary to quote specific figures, such as percentage rates of import duty. Such figures can, of course, change at short notice.

Accounts of national or EC law are of necessity severely compressed. They are intended to do no more than draw initial attention to the nature and scope of legislation that may be of relevance to marketing.

27

Marketing in Brazil

1. Size and regional nature

Brazil is the largest country in Latin America, being about the size of the whole of Europe including Russia. The population is around 155 million; about half are under the age of 18. Population is increasing at an annual rate of over 2 per cent.

Inevitably in a country of this size, there are marked differences between one region and another. Economic activity and growth are heavily concentrated in the states of Rio de Janeiro, São Paulo and Minas Gerais; the north-east has been referred to, in contrast, as an 'underdeveloped country within a country', while the centre-west and northern regions, vast as they are, account for only 10 per cent of the total population.

2. Inflation

Like so many South American nations, Brazil has for many years suffered from an extremely high level of inflation. Throughout the 1980s price and wage controls were imposed periodically in an attempt to reduce the inflation rate, but 1990 still saw runaway inflation at 85 per cent per month and the world's largest external debt. In March 1990 the new democratic government brought in stringent anti-inflation measures, including the freezing of 80 per cent of money in bank accounts for a period of 18 months. At the same time the government demonstrated its determination not to allow the huge wage increases which had been regularly awarded in the past as a necessary compensation for inflation.

3. Competition

For decades Brazil was a highly protected economy. A long list of prohibited imports was accompanied by tariffs so high that exporting to Brazil, for many companies, was not a practical proposition.

In 1990 the situation changed. Some 1,200 products have now been removed from the prohibited list, and a new tariff policy has been announced with the aim of improving the efficiency of Brazilian industry by exposing it to foreign competition. The modal tariff will fall from the 1990 rate of 40 per cent to 20 per cent by 1994. For example, the 1990 rates for toys (105 per cent), cars (85 per cent) and numerically controlled machine tools (65 per cent) were set to fall to 20 per cent, 35 per cent and 20 per cent respectively by 1994. By 1992 this programme of tariff reductions was more or less on course.

The new tariffs, plus shipping costs and local taxes, which are levied on the duty-paid value, will still give Brazilian industry a degree of protection. Nevertheless, for the first time in decades, Brazil is becoming a market in which many British exporters could find their goods competitive in terms of both quality and price.

A national privatisation programme has been introduced with a view to privatising state-owned industries. A list of the first companies to be privatised has been published.

4.   Free trade areas

Brazil is a member of the Latin American Integration Association (*see* Table 2.2). Brazil, Argentina, Paraguay and Uruguay have agreed to form the Southern Cone Common Market (Mercosul) by the end of 1994.

A free-trade zone has long been established at the river port of Manaus. Land is provided in industrial areas at nominal rates for factory and warehousing use.

5.   Agents

Few agents can hope to cover the whole country, but concentration on Rio de Janeiro, São Paulo and Minas Gerais is clearly an acceptable approach for many UK companies.

Brazilian law protects the agent from unilateral termination of his or her contract by a foreign principal without just cause. Compensation for such termination may, under certain circumstances, amount to a significant percentage of *total* sales effected during the life of the contract.

Brazil is one of the countries in which an agency agreement granting to the agent a general authority to conclude contracts may render the exporter liable to local income tax on the grounds that the exporter has a 'presence' in the country (24:**18**). If payable, the tax is levied on 20 per cent of the invoiced value of the products. It is therefore advisable to state expressly in the agency agreement that the agent has no power to bind the principal in sales contracts.

6.   Licensing, patents and trade marks

Agreements with foreign companies for the protection of industrial property must be registered with the Brazilian Central Bank and with the National Institute for Industrial Property (INPI), the equivalent of the UK Patent Office. INPI assesses the value of the technology and sets a limit on the percentage rate of remittance, each contract being separately considered. A licence agreement may not forbid export of the product from Brazil.

Patent licences have a maximum term of registration of 15 years, and a permitted royalty level between 1 and 5 per cent of total sales. Patents registered with INPI must be worked on an industrial scale within the first three years from registration. If this does not occur, or if exploitation of the patent is suspended for more than a year, interested parties may apply for a compulsory licence.

Contracts for the sale of industrial know-how not covered by patents or for technical industrial cooperation are for a maximum term of five years, with royalties of between 1 and 5 per cent of sales.

The maximum term for trade mark licences is ten years, though the licence may be renewed indefinitely for further ten-year terms. Only 1 per cent of sales may be remitted to the foreign trade mark owner. The first applicant for a trade mark is entitled to registration, but that registration may be cancelled on the grounds of non-use for a period of two years or more.

INPI's general approach and the tenor of legislation is that the Brazilian licensee has paid for technology and that it is free to use it, and even transfer it to third parties, once the patent or agreement has expired. Similarly, a trade mark licensee must be given the option of using his or her own trade mark together with that of the licensor on the products covered by the licence; the licensee may also use the trade mark separately on goods other than those of the licensor. In effect, licensors of technology or trade marks may find that they have created their own competitor.

7. Manufacture in Brazil

A manufacturing company may be the equivalent of a UK private company (a *limitada*) or a public company (SA). The form normally preferred for a foreign company is the SA. Branch offices of foreign companies are permitted but are difficult to form.

Restrictions are placed on foreign investment in certain strategic sectors of the economy such as banks, telecommunications, informatics, oil refining, hydroelectric or nuclear power generation and development of rural land. Otherwise the Brazilian government's attitude towards foreign investment has always been one of encouragement, especially for joint ventures involving the transfer of technology or offering export potential. Foreign capital is treated in the same way as local capital.

Debt-equity swaps are these days the favoured means of importing new capital into Brazil (*see* 30:**10**).

8. Exchange control: remittance of profits

To qualify for the remittance of profits abroad, foreign capital must be registered with the Central Bank of Brazil.

Profit remittances are subject to a 25 per cent withholding tax, provided they do not exceed in each year (calculated on a three-year average) 12 per cent of the registered foreign investment. Remittances above the 12 per cent figure attract withholding tax deductions on a steeply rising scale.

Repatriation of *capital* (original investment plus reinvestment of profits) may be made at any time. Repatriation of the original investment is always tax-free; repatriation of reinvestment of profits is normally tax-free if made more than five years after the reinvestment has taken place.

9. Investment incentives

The federal government offers tax concessions to both local and foreign investors in the North-East and Amazon regions, subject to approval by the development agencies SUDENE and SUDAM. The concessions take the form of exemption from charges on imported equipment for new industries, a tax holiday of 10–15 years for industrial investments that are the first of their kind, and where the investment is not eligible for the tax holiday a 50 per cent reduction in tax. The tax savings in the two latter categories are conditional on the reinvestment of the tax saved. Low-cost loans are also available to companies in these same two regions.

Incentives are also available at state and municipal level. Concessions are not mutually exclusive and may be secured from several sources for the same investment. A very careful enquiry into available incentives from all sources should be made before any investment takes place.

10. Export incentives
Incentives available to exporters include exemption from federal excise tax and states' sales taxes, low-cost export finance, and land for industrial development at reduced prices provided a commitment is made to maintain agreed levels of employment within the municipality that offered the land.

11. Price control
Throughout the 1980s, severe price and wage controls were imposed periodically in an endeavour to limit inflation. The new democratic government lifted almost all controls in 1990, but was forced to reintroduce them in 1991.

12. Monopolies and anti-trust legislation
CADE, the equivalent of the UK Monopolies Commission, is responsible for the suppression of any abuse of economic power. New and wide-ranging measures were introduced in 1990 in defence of competition. Cartels and monopolies are being increasingly challenged under the new regulations.

13. Conclusion
Probably most foreign companies will find licensing under present regulations an unattractive proposition. Brazil is now becoming, however, a market to be considered seriously by exporters.

Until 1990, foreign investors might well have regarded Brazil, despite its size, as a niche market, where infant industries were protected behind very high tariffs and could sometimes be cushioned by cartels. In the 1990s, the economic climate is likely to prove more bracing, with success going to those companies which, by their efficiency, earn it.

Progress test 27

1. Burgess, Meredith plc manufacture and market surgical instruments and hospital operating theatre equipment to UK and other EC markets.

The sales within the EC have shown a steady growth rate over the past five years of 6 per cent p.a. Research into other market territories has indicated potential sales to Brazil of £10 million p.a. but, if this indication were realised, limited production capacity would restrict the continued growth in EC markets, where sales are currently running at £75 million p.a. Your company IMC Ltd has been retained as market development consultants. Prepare a report to your clients with your recommendations on how to proceed. *(IEx)*

2. Discuss the advantages and disadvantages of selecting an agent versus using a licensing agreement for your textile machinery in less developed countries such as those of Latin America. *(CIM)*

3. 'Most foreign companies will find licensing in Brazil under present regulations an unattractive proposition.' Why?

28

Marketing in the European Community

1. Introduction

This chapter after a brief account of the development and workings of the EC, selects and summarises only those aspects of the Community that are of special relevance to marketing.

2. Development of the EC

The first step towards the formation of the EC was taken in 1951 when the European Coal and Steel Community (ECSC) was established with the aim of placing the coal and steel production of six countries, Belgium, France, West Germany, Italy, Luxembourg and the Netherlands, under a single authority. In 1958 these six countries signed the Treaty of Rome to establish what was then known as the European Economic Community with the objective of increasing trade among member states. Customs duties between member states were progressively abolished over the next few years and a common external tariff was established.

Denmark, Ireland and the UK joined the EC in 1973, Greece in 1981, and Spain and Portugal in 1986. With the reunification of Germany in 1990, the total population of the member states reached 340 million.

In 1985, member states agreed to remove all remaining barriers to trade within the EC by the end of 1992, with the aim of creating a single European market permitting the free movement of goods, services, capital and people.

Austria, Finland and Sweden joined the EC in 1995.

3. The European Economic Area

Political agreement on the establishment of the European Economic Area (EEA) was reached in 1991. The aim was to extend most of the single-market principles to most of the countries of the European Free Trade Area (EFTA): Austria, Finland, Iceland, Liechtenstein, Norway and Sweden. EEA countries adopted much of the EC single-market legislation and will be expected to adopt relevant new legislation as it is introduced. They will be consulted on such new legislation but will have no voting or veto rights. They will also 'cooperate' on environmental policies, R & D and social policy, as these develop within the EC. In effect the EEA arrangements combined most of EFTA and the EC into a single market. The enlargement of the EC in 1995 (*see* **2**) leaves only Iceland, Liechtenstein and Norway as EEA members.

4. EC institutions

There are four main EC institutions: the Commission, the Council of Ministers, the European Parliament and the Court of Justice.

The Commission proposes policy and legislation, puts into effect decisions taken by the Council, and ensures that member states comply with the rules. It has 17 members nominated by the governments of each member state.

The Council of Ministers is the EC's decision-making body; it adopts legislation proposed by the Commission. It consists of appropriate ministers from each member state.

The European Parliament is a directly elected body of 518 members. Its opinion is required on many proposals before the Council can adopt them. It does not yet have the power to introduce or veto legislation.

The Court of Justice rules on the interpretation and application of EC laws. Its judgements are binding on each member state and take precedence over national law.

5. EC legislation

The Council and Commission make regulations, issue directives, take decisions, make recommendations or deliver opinions.

Regulations do not have to be confirmed by national parliaments in order to have binding legal effect. Where there is a conflict between a regulation and existing national law, the regulation prevails.

Directives are binding on member states as to the result to be achieved within a stated period but leave the method of implementation to national governments. A directive does not in itself have legal force in member states but particular provisions may take direct effect if the directive is not implemented by a national government.

Decisions are binding on those to whom they are addressed, whether member states, companies or individuals.

Recommendations and *opinions* have no binding force; they merely state the view of the institution that issues them.

6. Competition policy and the Treaty of Rome

A fundamental principle of the Treaty of Rome is the maintenance of fair competition.

Article 85(1) of the Treaty prohibits agreements between firms which prevent, restrict or distort competition within the EC. In particular price-fixing, market sharing and territorial restrictions which divide up the market are prohibited. Agreements in breach of Article 85(1) are void and unenforceable; the parties to such agreements may be liable to heavy fines.

Article 86 of the Treaty forbids the *abuse* of a dominant position within the EC. Such abuse might include predatory pricing, limiting production or technical development, a refusal to supply , or discrimination against others to their competitive disadvantage.

Article 30 of the Treaty lays down that governments, national or local, and government bodies may not impose quantitative limits or similar restrictive measures on products from other member states. The European Court of Justice has decided that this requirement debars not only import licensing but also any discrimination between domestic and foreign goods.

7.   Public purchasing

Public purchasing is a large and lucrative market where it has proved especially difficult to introduce a measure of cross-border competition. Government and local authorities tended to restrict the issue of tenders to their own nationals, failed to advertise contracts properly, or laid down specifications that discriminated in favour of national suppliers.

Directives were issued requiring either open tendering (under which any supplier may bid) or restricted tendering (under which only approved suppliers may bid but any supplier may apply for approved status). Single or negotiated tenders were limited to special cases such as extreme urgency. Summary advertisements regarding tenders had to be placed in the EC's *Official Journal*, and discrimination by means of technical specification was banned.

These measures proved to be considerably less effective than had been hoped. The Supplies Directive 1989 tightened up public procurement, limiting even further the use of single tendering and requiring justification of the use of restricted or negotiated tenders. The Works Directive 1990, covering public works contracts, required purchasers to give reasons for the rejection of a contractor's tender. The Utilities Directive 1993 extended tender rules to water, energy, transport, telecommunications and other utilities. The Compliance Directive 1991 allows for action against purchasing bodies in breach of the regulations.

8.   Technical standards

The differing technical standards of member states can be a serious barrier to cross-border trade, especially when governments will not accept other states' testing procedures. Products have to be modified, and product testing can prove expensive. The problem is more difficult to solve than the 'buy national' prejudices of government bodies: national standards are a guarantee of quality for customers and have usually stood the test of time. German retailers, for example, are unwilling to sell goods that do not conform to German (DIN) standards.

The EC objective is that ultimately all products sold in any one member state shall be freely marketable in all others, unhindered by differing technical standards or testing requirements. To this end, new European standards will be introduced, and testing and inspection procedures will be approved throughout the EC. Progress has been made, but inevitably it is a long, slow haul.

9. Patent protection and licensing agreements

Member states have their own national patent registration systems, but these differ significantly in terms of procedural requirements and in definitions of what is or is not patentable. An inventor applying for patent protection in each country is likely to find the procedures cumbersome and expensive.

The alternative route is through the European Patent Convention, which is subscribed to by all member states and certain other West European countries. Under the convention, a single application to the European Patent Office in Munich will, once granted, permit registration in all participating countries. The resultant patents, however, are national patents, and must be defended, if necessary, in the courts of each individual country.

The EC has also devised a Community Patent Convention, under which Community patents would be granted; these patents would be defended in special Community Patent Courts whose judgements would be valid throughout the EC. Arrangements for the Community patent have been signed but ratification has been delayed.

The EC does not concern itself with the terms of licensing agreements provided they are not used to prevent the free movement of goods or to support a policy of differential pricing within the Community.

10. Trade marks

The EC has ten different systems of trade mark registration: with the exception of the Benelux countries, which have a unified system, each member state has its own arrangements.

Member states are now required to harmonise their national laws in terms of the rights conferred by a trade mark and the tests of what may be registered.

Proposals have been made for Community trade mark protection, along lines broadly similar to the European Patent Convention.

11. Fiscal barriers to trade

Member states have now agreed that, where VAT is charged, the minimum rate shall be 15 per cent. Zero rating, however, is still permitted.

12. Merger control

The EC is now in a position to rule on the acceptability or otherwise of proposed mergers between companies meeting certain size criteria. Mergers which will lead to the establishment or reinforcement of a dominant position, and which will significantly impede competition within the EC, will be prohibited.

13. Company law

The EC aims at minimising any difficulties which may arise for businesses operating in two or more member states as a result of the differing systems of company law in each country. A number of directives have been issued and more are under discussion.

A proposal has been put forward to enable businesses active in two or more member states to form a Societas Europaea (SE or European Company) subject to a new European level of company law. Progress so far has been limited. Mandatory worker participation in management is a particular difficulty.

14. Investment incentives

Any form of aid granted by individual member states is subject to EC scrutiny and approval. Such approval will not be granted if the aid is likely to distort competition within the Community. The Community has been applying the rules with increasing stringency in recent years, restricting the level of aid and in some cases demanding repayment of grants already made.

The Commission, however, controls its own Structural Funds, which are intended to support investment in infrastructure, industry and agriculture in the less developed regions of the Community. There is increasing emphasis here on Corsica, Greece, the Republic of Ireland, Northern Ireland, Southern Italy, Portugal and certain areas of Spain. The regulations on public procurement (*see* 7) should enable UK firms to tender for contracts arising from aid granted from the Structural Funds to any member state or region.

15. Commercial agents

A Commercial Agents Directive sets out to regulate the relationship between commercial agents and their principals. It applies essentially to commission agents; distributors buying and selling on their own account are specifically excluded.

The directive covers most aspects of agency agreements, including those especially likely to give rise to conflict. For instance, the directive specifies:

(a) that commission is payable on repeat orders from customers acquired by the agents, even if those orders were not placed through the agent;
(b) that, where an agent has an exclusive territory, the agent is entitled to commission on orders from that territory even if he did not negotiate the orders and the customers were not originally acquired by him;
(c) that an agent is entitled to commission even after the agency contract has come to an end if the transaction was mainly the result of the agent's efforts during the period of the agency contract;
(d) that on termination of the contract the agent is entitled in certain specified circumstances either to a lump-sum indemnity or compensation for damages;
(e) that agreements in restraint of trade (which restrict the agent's business activities after termination of the contract) are acceptable only in certain circumstances and in any case for no longer than two years from termination.

The UK has previously had little or no statute law relating to agents. To allow time for discussion, therefore, it was allowed until 1994 to implement the legislation.

16. Block exemption

Sole agency and exclusive distribution agreements necessarily include restrictions on the territories in which the parties may operate. Such restrictions may bring the agreements within the scope of Article 85(1) of the Treaty of Rome (*see* 6).

However, special 'block exemption' regulations permit a supplier to agree not to supply products direct to users in the contract territory and not to appoint other distributors for the territory. The supplier also has the right to prevent distributors from engaging in *active* selling of the products outside their own territories.

Distributors must, however, retain the right to respond on a *passive* basis to unsolicited requests by customers in other territories for the supply of the products, and no attempt must be made to prevent goods sold by a distributor in one territory from being transhipped by the customer to another territory. Users must also be free to obtain the products from a source of supply other than the exclusive distributor, either from the manufacturer or a dealer in another territory.

17. Consumer protection

The EC has issued a number of directives aimed at establishing common levels of consumer protection throughout the Community. Those of special interest to marketers include the directives on misleading advertising, doorstep selling, consumer credit and price marking.

For product liability legislation *see* 11:24.

18. The Exchange Rate Mechanism

Perhaps the most serious remaining hindrance to free trade is the instability and uncertainty caused by variations in the exchange rates of member states. The Exchange Rate Mechanism (ERM) was established with the aim of keeping such variations within reasonable limits.

Each ERM currency had a central rate of exchange against the other ERM currencies. Member states had to keep their currencies within an agreed percentage of this rate, either within a narrow band (fluctuation permitted up to 2.25 per cent either side of the central rate) or within a wide band (fluctuation up to 6 per cent). In the short term, currencies were to be kept within their designated bands by coordinated intervention in the foreign exchange market by the central banks; in the longer term, member states would need to adopt economic policies consistent with maintaining the currency within its designated band. Changes in the central rate – known as realignments – were permitted, but only as a last resort and only with the agreement of all ERM members.

By 1990 all EC member states other than Greece had joined the ERM. By mid-1993, however, several states, including the UK, had been forced to leave, while France had been permitted a new wide band permitting fluctuations up to 15 per cent, one so wide as to be meaningless.

The ERM is now of little effect. Optimistic sounds regarding its future still emanate from Brussels and elsewhere, but the UK government has made it clear that it will not contemplate a return to the ERM for a matter of years ahead.

19. Extent of progress towards the single market

Most of the single market legislation envisaged in the '1992' single market programme is now in place in terms of EC regulations or directives. There are some exceptions, such as the SE legislation already mentioned (*see* 13).

Directives, as mentioned, must be confirmed by legislation in member states. The UK has been diligent here, with, reportedly, 80 per cent of directives passed into national law by the end of 1991; only Denmark and France have a better record. In contrast, up to the same date Italy had included only 40 per cent of directives in national legislation.

Further, to be effective, legislation must be not only in place but also enforced. The UK prides itself, with some justification, on its record of enforcement. It has been suggested that other member states are perhaps not always so conscientious. The EC itself has no direct means of enforcing compliance.

Examples

(1) Many Brussels regulations have a devastating effect on British interests, and are designed to do so, because Brussels knows that the British authorities, believing in the rule of law, apply them, whereas the countries behind the Brussels system, chiefly France, do not. As one French farmer put it, not unkindly, 'les règles sont pour les Anglais, pas pour les Français.'

(Source: Paul Johnson, *The Spectator*, 7.11.92)

(2) Press reports suggest that in Italy small firms are able to evade value-added tax. The Spanish authorities are said to be lax in enforcing EC rules on mesh sizes in fishing nets. The UK Civil Aviation Authority has claimed that air fares are far too high because EC rules are 'totally ineffective'.

The EC competition commissioner has expressed very serious concern about disparities between UK car prices and those elsewhere in the EC: according to present EC rules, the basic prices for any particular model of car are permitted to vary across the Community by no more than 18% at any given moment and by no more than 12% over a period; yet some models cost 32% and 44% more in the UK than in the cheapest EC country. Cars made in the UK by Japanese companies, defined under EC rules as wholly British, are said to face secret restrictions designed to prevent them from making further inroads into other EC countries.

The EC Commission has announced proposals to allow Germany to charge a new annual road-use tax of £3600 on all heavy goods vehicles travelling through the country; the revenue gained would be used to reduce German vehicle excise duty by up to 80%, thus giving German haulage companies a cost advantage against foreign hauliers.

20. The future

In 1992, with the Maastricht Treaty on European Union, EC member states formally turned their attention to matters of even greater import than the single market. The treaty was finally ratified in 1993, after a stormy passage in certain member states, notably Denmark and the UK. Widely divergent prophecies have been made as to when and how fully its provisions will be implemented, or whether they will be implemented at all. An examination of the main points of the treaty, however, gives at least some indication of intended future policy.

Under the treaty, a single European currency is to be created. The currency will be issued and controlled by a central Euro-bank. All member states able and willing to do so will be expected to join this new monetary system. The UK has arranged to be specifically excluded, although it has the right to join if it so wishes.

The UK will join, however, the proposed European Monetary Institute, the precursor of the Euro-bank. The institute will have the responsibility of overseeing exchange rates.

The UK has also opted out of the Social Chapter, so that new EC laws on workers' pay, hours and conditions will not take effect in the UK. It has been suggested that this opt-out will give the UK an unfair cost advantage. It is, however, possible that some of the requirements of the Social Chapter could be introduced under the guise of health and safety requirements; in such circumstances they would be binding on the UK.

21. The European Union

One effect of the Maastricht Treaty was the creation of the European Union (EU). The treaty outlined activities which member states could undertake not, as hitherto, on the basis of supranational integration but on the fundamentally different basis of intergovernmental cooperation. These activities have come to include a common foreign and security policy and cooperation in the fields of justice and home affairs. According to the treaty 'the European Union' is the term both for this intergovernmental cooperation and for a declaration that a new stage has been reached in creating 'an ever-closer union among the peoples of Europe'.

When, therefore, member states act on trade policy or take steps towards economic and monetary union, they are using powers that derive from the Treaty of Rome (*see* 2) and should be described as the EC; when they collaborate on foreign and security policy or on justice and home affairs, they are the EU.

It is UK government policy to maintain this careful distinction. This chapter follows that policy: since it is concerned entirely with the trade and economic matters it refers throughout to the EC.

It does seem, however, that the term EU is coming increasingly, if loosely, to be used to describe the EC, perhaps with some encouragement from governments and individuals who are strong supporters of closer political integration between member states.

Progress test 28

1. 'The EC is now our home market.' Is it really?

2. What marketing problems do you envisage for British Industry that may arise from foreign competition within the European Community? *(CIM)*

3. 'The EC is still very far from its declared ideal of a single market. In any case, whatever Brussels may say or do, the EC will never be a single market in the way the USA is.' Discuss.

4. Evaluate the value of membership of the European Community Exchange Rate Mechanism (ERM) to a UK reporter. *(CIM)*

5. You have been asked to give a talk on '1992: Threat or Opportunity?' to members of your branch of the Charted Institute of Marketing. Suggest, with justification, the main areas you would cover. *(CIM)*

6. A senior politician told the House of Lords that, with hindsight EFTA had judged it right by staying out of the EC while the UK had 'muffed it'. The EFTA countries were now, through the EEA, 'enjoying all the benefits of free trade but not paying all the costs of the Common Agricultural Policy'. Put forward, from the point of view of a marketer, an opposing view.

7. In what ways might the completion of the EC single market be of benefit to businesses outside the Community – for instance, in the USA?

29

Marketing in Japan

1. Size and population

Japan comprises four main islands, Hokkaido, Honshu, Shikoku and Kyushu, together with over 3,000 smaller islands. It covers some 142,000 square miles (almost half as large again as the UK) but well over 70 per cent of this area is mountainous.

The estimated population figure for 1990 was over 121 million. The birth rate is declining; senior citizens account for 11 per cent of total population. This figure is expected to reach 20 per cent in twenty years' time. About half the population live in what are known as the 'three metropolitan regions' centred on Tokyo, Osaka and Nagoya.

Per capita income has overtaken that of the USA. The Japanese economy is second only to the USA in size.

2. The Japanese cultural and business environment

The Japanese cultural and business environment presents, for the European, unusual difficulties (*see* Table 29.1).

3. Japanese government import promotion

Japan has now embarked upon a policy, unique in the world, of active encouragement of imports. Under a scheme introduced by the Ministry of International Trade and Industry (MITI):

(a) tariffs have been eliminated on more than 1,000 manufactured imports since 1990, bringing the total of zero-tariff items to over 2,300, about half of all manufactured imports;
(b) tax incentives have been offered to importers of manufactured goods;
(c) low-interest finance is being made available to Japanese importers, distributors, wholesalers and retailers of imported products to support new inspection and display facilities;
(d) a budget of US $100 million has been allocated to import promotion.

Overseas, much of the import promotion effort rests with the government-supported Japan External Trade Organisation (JETRO) and its network of offices in industrial countries. JETRO's trade specialists respond daily to a flow of enquiries from local exporters. In particular, JETRO offers two database services: the potential exporters' database, by which the details of foreign exporters become immediately available to Japanese importers via an on-line system connecting forty-nine 'local internationalisation centres' throughout Japan; and the trade opportunity service, which matches the

Table 29.1 Doing business in Japan

Many people come back from a trip in Japan wondering exactly what they have achieved, because there are two sorts of communication between people in Japan: public and private. Private communication is restricted to Japanese people only and no foreigner is very likely to be included in conversations of that sort. In public, confrontation is absolutely unacceptable and everything must be polite and agreeable. The great disaster of George Bush's visit to Japan, from a commercial point of view, was not that he was sick in a public place, but that he confronted his hosts publicly in arguments over trade matters.

Japan is very much a consensus society in which the group is far more important than the individual, and the good of the group is the supreme objective. Negotiations may progress very slowly because it is important for Japanese negotiators to be certain that they have a workable agreement with all those who will be involved in the decision. An unfortunate result of this from the point of view of Western negotiators is that their Japanese counterparts can and will expect almost immediate action once the final agreement is signed. To a Japanese businessman, the signature on the bottom of the contract is irrelevant unless he is certain that you can immediately fulfil all the terms. Therefore a lot of time is spent finding out whether you are able to commit your organisation to any agreement which is negotiated and if there is any doubt about this, then there will be a lot of polite talk but no substantive negotiation.

Japanese negotiators tend to operate in teams and to spend a lot of time discussing points in front of visitors, feeling safe in their assumption that the visitors will not understand what is being said and that their interpreter will feel part of the Japanese group. Answers to your questions may be short and uninformative when finally translated, after what will clearly seem to have been a more extensive discussion; this can be frustrating to the non-Japanese-speaking business person.

Status is very important in Japan and age and seniority are respected. When operating as a group the senior person will be deferred to, even though he may not be the authority on the particular subject being discussed. Good manners are a sign of good breeding and of status and are, therefore, very important as indicators to the Japanese of the seniority and importance of particular individuals among the visiting group. Senior people sit and stand straight, never make hurried or excessive movement, never raise their voices, and expect others to bow lower to them than they do in return. Any attempt to make a senior Japanese businessman feel at ease by relaxing in a chair, or any attempt to stress a point by excessive or animated hand movements, will tend to show that you are of low status and, therefore, not able to complete negotiations satisfactorily on your own authority.

The family comes very much in second place for a Japanese businessman during the working week. He will work long hours, and often late into the evening, socialising with fellow businessmen. Groups of company men are very common; they see these evening sessions as part of the bonding process, to the organisation or to the objective for which the group is aiming. But family is important, and the traditional wife is very much in charge of the home and also manages the family's income, which the husband earns. Japanese wives are very submissive publicly but rather dominant within the family, in private. Unless a couple is rather Westernized, the wife is not likely to be involved in business entertaining.

Some knowledge of the Japanese language can be very useful if you are to have any chance of understanding what is going on. Even a rather basic knowledge of Japanese will give some idea about the way in which a discussion is going, but it would be unwise to attempt to speak Japanese in negotiations unless you are really fluent. The Japanese are not particularly grateful that you have made an effort to learn their language; perfection is admired, but an attempt is not particularly impressive. Japanese culture is very different in many ways from European culture; this is particularly evident by the continual appearance of agreeable assent, which may hide anything from total disagreement and hostility to complete understanding and agreement. A thorough briefing can open the eyes of a businessman before he has any dealings with Japanese managers and will greatly increase the chances of a successful conclusion to any negotiations.

(Source: Richard Hobbs, Director of the Centre for International Briefing, Farnham Castle, Surrey GU9 0AG.)

needs of registered overseas exporters with suitable partners in Japan.

JETRO also offers general information on the Japanese market, on specific market sectors and products and on trade fairs. It offers assistance to selling missions to Japan, organises seminars on selling to the Japanese market, and runs a complaints service for exporters who believe they have come up against non-tariff barriers. JETRO has also posted abroad a number of specialists to conduct research into local businesses in order to identify products suited to the Japanese market. These specialists will also offer one-to-one consultancy to appropriate companies.

JETRO's services are mostly free of charge.

4. Promotion of UK exports in Japan

The DTI has established a special Exports to Japan Unit to assist UK exporters. The Unit commissions market studies on product areas believed to offer potential.

5. The traditional wholesale-retail distribution system

The Japanese distribution system has long been notorious for its length and complexity. Its outstanding characteristics are still an excessive number of small retail outlets and two or even three intermediate wholesale levels.

Relationships between manufacturers, wholesalers and retailers are close for a number of reasons:

(a) the Japanese have traditionally placed much importance on strong and continuing personal relationships in business;

(b) manufacturers supply goods to wholesalers on several months' credit, reducing very significantly wholesalers' need for working capital;

(c) wholesalers will often be prepared to take back unsold goods from retailers;

(d) wholesalers offer special rebates to retailers according to the total value of the retailer's business over a given period;

(e) some suppliers are prepared to maintain stocks at or near the wholesaler's warehouse so as to offer immediate delivery.

As a result, it is immensely difficult for a newcomer, whether Japanese or foreign, to break into the system.

The system arises from tradition, good service and value for money rather from any desire to exclude outsiders. Yet it is through this traditional wholesale-retail set-up that the Japanese retain their dominance over their domestic market. The would-be exporter to Japan can be forgiven for regarding it as a non-tariff barrier of the most serious kind.

Rationalisation is gradually taking place as both the Japanese businessman and the consumer become more price-conscious. Voluntary chains have been organised and the development of self-service outlets is something of a breakthrough. Nevertheless, the bulk of Japanese consumer goods still passes through the traditional lengthy channels.

Exporters content to have their products regarded as low-volume speciality or prestige items need not concern themselves; they can achieve a satisfactory turnover through the department stores (*see* 6) and, possibly, supermarkets (*see* 7).

Other exporters can secure, through JETRO, the all-important introductions to wholesalers, but these can only be the starting point of a very long haul.

In theory, it is open to any exporter to by-pass the system completely and set up his or her own distribution network. In practice, only the largest companies, and then only those confident of eventual high-volume sales, could contemplate the heavy investment in time and money that would be required. A few companies have succeeded.

A specific example of the distribution system for food products is given in Fig. 29.1.

6. Department stores

There are a dozen or more department store groups in Japan. Such stores are leisure, cultural and entertainment centres as well as important outlets for quality goods of all kinds. They have been described as part of the Japanese way of life. With supermarkets, they account for a very high proportion of the sales of all *imported* consumer goods.

Purchases are often made direct from European suppliers. Most of the larger stores maintain a buying office in London or have appointed a London buying house as their purchasing agent. An up-to-date list can be obtained from the Exports to Japan Unit.

7. Supermarkets

Supermarkets represent a most significant change in Japanese purchasing habits. Their total sales now well exceed those of the department stores. Food and drink predominate, but most supermarkets sell a wide range of household goods and hardware as well, and some offer clothing and furniture.

As might be expected, the supermarkets are fiercely price-competitive. British goods have not so far achieved any significant volume successes.

8. Japanese trading companies

The trading companies are another unique and prominent feature of the Japanese scene. *See* 14:4.

9. UK export-import houses in Japan

A number of British export-import trading houses have offices in Japan. Most have been established in Japan for many years. They are involved in various commercial and industrial activities and can offer agency representation services. They include Dodwell and Co. Ltd, and Jardine, Matheson and Co. (Japan) Ltd.

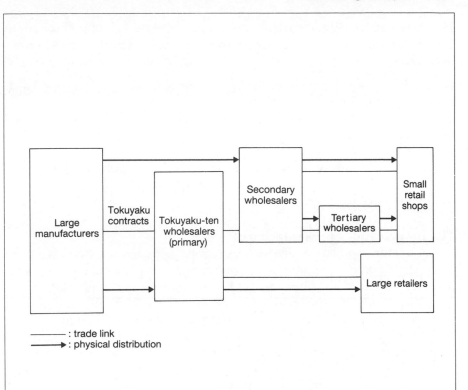

Many large food manufacturers employ the Tokuyaku-ten system. In this system, a manufacturer makes supply contracts with only selected wholesalers and transactions are limited to these wholesalers. This contract is called Tokuyaku (literally 'special contract'). The selected wholesalers are called Tokuyaku-ten. Large wholesalers, such as Kokubu, Meidi-ya and Ryoshoku, have many Tokuyaku contracts with manufacturers and distribute their products to smaller local wholesalers. (Wholesalers who trade directly with manufacturers are called primary wholesalers in contrast to smaller secondary and still smaller tertiary wholesalers.) Sales activities are divided between the primary and secondary wholesalers. Primary wholesalers trade with large retailers and secondary wholesalers with small independent stores.

Figure 29.1 *The wholesale–retail distribution of food products in Japan: the Tokuyaku-ten system.*
(Source: *Retail Distribution in Japan*, 4th edition, Dodwell Marketing Consultants, Tokyo. Copies available in UK from Proplan, Amersham, Bucks.)

10. Agents and distributors

In Japan, the choice of an agent or distributor will usually lie between:

(a) one of the large Japanese trading companies (most appropriate, perhaps, in high volume or high value items);
(b) a specialist Japanese trading company (especially appropriate for sophisticated industrial products);
(c) a UK export-import house;
(d) a Japanese producer of complementary products (Japanese manufacturers are showing an increasing interest in taking advantage of their established distribution networks in this way).

11. Branch and representative office

A foreign company which intends to engage in commercial transactions within Japan on a continuous basis must appoint a representative and establish a *branch* office. Branches are taxed on income from sources in Japan.

A *representative* office may be established as an alternative to a branch, provided the representative does not engage directly in trading activities. The registration procedure is similar, but corporation tax is not payable. Activities acceptable for a representative office include providing information on market conditions, maintaining business contacts, carrying on a purchasing operation or seeking a suitable joint venture partner.

12. Licensing

Patents are granted for a period of 15 years from the date of publication of the application. Compulsory licensing may be required if a patent has not been industrially exploited for three years.

Licensing agreements with foreign organisations are subject to government approval under the Foreign Exchange and Foreign Trade Control Law, but in practice most agreements are automatically approved. No restrictions are placed on the amount of the down payment or the royalty payable, which has ranged from 2 per cent to 8 per cent and more. Royalties may be freely remitted abroad after payment of a withholding income tax.

The Japanese licensee, however, must file a report with the Fair Trade Commission (FTC). The FTC will scrutinise the licensing agreement to see that it conforms with its guidelines on fair business practices. In particular, a licensing agreement should not:

(a) restrict the territory to which a licensee can export patented products, except in the case of territories already being directly or indirectly exploited by the licensor;
(b) restrict the licensee's export price or export quantity, or the re-sale price in Japan;
(c) restrict the handling of competitive products or the utilisation of competitive technology;

(d) impose upon licensees an obligation to purchase materials or components from the licensor;

(e) impose upon licensees an obligation to sell products through the licensor;

(f) require the licensee to vest in the licensor the rights in improvements in the licensed technology developed by the licensee, unless the licensor accepts in return similar obligations towards the licensee.

13. Trade marks

The first applicant is entitled to register a trade mark, irrespective of prior use in Japan. Trade mark piracy (11:22) is not uncommon.

Registration is valid for ten years in the first instance and is renewable indefinitely, but if the mark has not been used in Japan for three consecutive years it may be cancelled on application from a third party.

14. Foreign investment

Up to 100 per cent foreign ownership of new or existing corporations is permitted, except in certain sectors of strategic importance such as petroleum and agriculture. The government may also prohibit foreign investment on such grounds as national security but has rarely done so.

Joint ventures in any country offer lower cost of entry and lower risk. In Japan, they also offer a means of entry to distribution channels that would otherwise prove inaccessible (*see* 5). In addition, they make it easier to secure the services of good local staff. Japanese employment practices are very different from those in the UK. Great importance is attached to job security, promotion according to length of service, and a strong sense of corporate belonging. Many Japanese spend their entire lives with a single company and social relationships with their colleagues are important to them. This situation is gradually changing, especially among the younger generation, but recruitment of good staff by a new foreign company is still likely to present serious difficulties.

The wholly-owned subsidiary, offering none of these advantages, has nevertheless become more popular in recent years. It is likely to be the preferred choice of companies that regard Japan as a crucial element in their global strategy and are prepared to take a long-term view.

There are no government restrictions on use or remittance of profits for either a joint venture or a wholly-owned subsidiary.

Investment incentives available to foreign companies include tax concessions, grants, interest-free loans and industrial land and premises sold at low prices. They are offered at national, regional and local government level. In practice most are available only to subsidiary companies and not to branches.

15. Conclusion

For years exports to Japan consisted mainly of niche-market high-quality goods, often bought by department stores and supermarkets, while investment was limited largely to joint ventures.

It would be too much to say that the market is now wide open. But the vast bulk of restrictions have been removed. Foreign investment and imports are actively encouraged by the Japanese government. For the efficient, competent and confident, Japan offers potential as never before.

Progress test 29

1. Select two contrasting countries and then explain differences in their retailing systems. *(CIM)*

2. Your chairman is making his first sales visit to Japan. Write a brief to advise him on the cultural adjustments he might consider making to improve the chances of sales success. *(CIM)*

3. Your company advises on the design of recreational areas such as golf courses, sports complexes, leisure parks, etc. It has established that there are opportunities in the Far East. How would you try to develop these opportunities? *(IEx)*

4. A Japanese soap manufacturer spent ten years building up a company-controlled network of regional distributors to replace the traditional wholesale outlets in the toiletry industry. Why do you think it took so long? What chance do you think a non-Japanese company might have of successfully setting up a company-controlled distribution network in Japan in a consumer goods industry?

5. 'A Japanese joint venture? If I'm going to have a nervous breakdown, I might as well have it at home.' What might have brought about this attitude?

6. 'Unless we can contain the Japanese by taking a share of their market, we can't expect to beat them abroad.' Discuss.

7. Exporters now have more help than ever before in tackling the Japanese market. Outline that help. What problems remain?

8. 'Although a variety of importing methods exist side by side in Japan, overshadowing all others is still the pervasive influence of the ubiquitous Japanese trading company.'
  (a) Outline the activities of these trading companies.
  (b) Describe briefly the alternative 'importing methods' available.

9. The Japanese retail distribution system has been described as 'complex, somewhat archaic in foreigners' eyes, but showing signs of adapting to modern trends'. Give a brief account of this system and say how far you would agree with the description quoted.

30

Marketing in Nigeria

1. Introduction

Nigeria's population is variously estimated as being between 90 and 120 million; it is believed that about half the population is below 20 years of age.

There are some 400 different tribes and very many different languages and dialects. The four main languages are Yoruba, Hausa, Ibo and Fulani. English is the official common language.

The country was divided into 12 states in 1967 in place of the original four regions. The number of states has been increased on several occasions since; there are now 30 states in all.

2. The Nigerian economy

Nigeria is one of the world's major oil exporting countries and a member of OPEC. Oil accounts for the vast bulk of export earnings. The USA buys most of Nigeria's oil and is Nigeria's most important customer by far. The UK is Nigeria's tenth most important customer, but its most important supplier.

Nigeria's boom years coincided, naturally, with the oil price rises of the 1970s. As oil prices declined, however, economic difficulties became acute. To tackle the crisis, Nigeria introduced in the mid-1980s a Structural Adjustment Programme (SAP), which is still continuing. Most import and export restrictions were lifted and price controls were abolished. Efforts have been made to expand non-oil exports. A privatisation scheme has been put forward covering almost 100 government enterprises in sectors such as hotels, insurance and agriculture. Other major government enterprises are to be placed on a more commercial footing.

3. Foreign exchange and terms of payment

Nigerian exchange control regulations are complex and subject to repeated change. Business should take place only on the basis of irrevocable letters of credit confirmed by a British bank in the UK.

4. Pre-shipment inspection

Nigeria is one of about 30 countries that operate a system of pre-shipment inspection, known in Nigeria as the Comprehensive Import Supervision Scheme (CISS). It applies to all goods in excess of US $1,000 in value, and to all containerised goods regardless of value.

The CISS includes: a physical check on product quantity and quality; a price comparison to ensure that the price charged is in line with the prevailing price for similar goods; a legal check to ensure that the transaction complies with Nigerian law; and a check on the tariff code and rate of duty. The checks are undertaken by an officially appointed inspection agency.

The essential purpose of the CISS is to prevent an uncontrolled outflow of Nigeria's much needed foreign exchange. Exchange reserves can be depleted by excessively high prices (which may conceal illegal money transfer), short-shipment of goods, or by shipment of substandard goods. The inspection also facilitates import duty collection in Nigeria.

A Clean Report of Findings (CRF) is issued by the inspection agency when all aspects of the transaction are found to be satisfactory. The CRF is among the documents required before any payment can be made from a confirmed and irrevocable letter of credit (CILC).

Inevitably, the inspection and the issue of the CRF take time and the exporter should ensure that this is allowed for when fixing the expiry date of the CILC. Any problems that arise over the issue of a CRF will give rise to further delay and possible payment problems.

5. Government purchases

Federal government departments are required by law to purchase goods manufactured in Nigeria, provided that the local product is competitive on quality, price and delivery.

Each state government places its own orders. Purchasing offices are located in the state capitals.

6. Merchants and agency houses

Most merchant and agency houses have been established for many years, often originally as international trading companies. They have their own retail outlets in major towns and offer facilities for after-sales service and the supply of spares. They are especially suitable as outlets for high-quality consumer durables.

7. Commission agents

Few Nigerian agencies are in a position to offer effective coverage of the whole country and it is probably best to appoint a number of regional agents.

Nigerian law makes no specific provision for agency agreements or their termination. Nigerian company law, however, gives legal validity to written or *verbal* contracts. It is advisable, therefore, to ensure that any agency agreement is in writing.

8. Patents and trade marks

The life of a patent is 20 years. Compulsory licences may be granted if the patent has not been sufficiently worked within four years of filing or three years from the grant of the patent.

The first user of a trade mark is entitled to registration, which lasts initially for seven years. Registration may be renewed for further periods of 14 years.

9. Branch offices

Branch operations of foreign companies are not normally permitted.

10. Local manufacture

The Nigerian Enterprise Promotion Act of 1977 initiated a programme of indigenisation. Industries were placed in one of three categories, requiring respectively 100 per cent, 60 per cent and 40 per cent Nigerian ownership.

A 1989 amendment to the Act listed only 40 industries reserved exclusively for Nigerians. Foreigners may now own up to 100 per cent of *new* enterprises in industries not listed in the amendment, and not in the banking, insurance, mining or oil exploration business. Enterprises in existence before the 1989 amendment remain subject to the 1977 Act.

In a further endeavour to encourage foreign investment, restrictions on the amount of profit that can be declared as dividend, and on the repatriation of capital and earnings, have been removed. Tax and export incentives are available.

In 1988, the government initiated a debt-for-equity swap scheme. Nigerian foreign debt can be purchased for local investment purposes at regular auctions. Investment capital thus becomes available at a discount, often as high as 50 per cent.

11. ECOWAS

Nigeria is a member of the Economic Community of West African States (ECOWAS), which aims for the reduction and eventual elimination of import duties between member states.

12. Fraud

Recent years have seen an alarming increase in trade-related fraud, much of it centred on Nigeria.

Example

What has become known as 'Nigerian crime' has become so serious that the Lagos government has taken out advertisements to warn the business community and the Nigerian High Commission in London has issued its own warnings.

One continuing fraud attempt involves fake letters of credit allegedly issued by Standard Chartered Bank and advised by NatWest. Current examples of the documents list the Standard Chartered Bank as at Bradford St., Leeds, and advised by NatWest of Caxton Rd., London. All addresses are fictitious.

Another scam is designed to gain access to details of a company's bank account and to get copies of a company's letterhead. Unsolicited letters from Nigerian individuals arrive offering deals on the movement of money allegedly blocked in Nigeria and said to relate to excess claims on foreign contracts awarded between 1979 and 1983. Recipients of these letters are offered up to 40% of the sums involved, which can range as high as US $50 million, in return for supplying blank proforma invoices, company letterheads and details of company bank accounts.

A further type of fraud concerns Nigerian oil cargoes. Companies are offered Nigerian crude, but the cargoes are either fictitious or do not belong to the people offering them for sale. The victims are usually middlemen or small companies, often with little or no experience in oil trading. They are induced to pay a large sum up-front to secure rights to an oil cargo on which they expect to make a profit by on-selling.

(Source: *The International Trade Bulletin*, NatWest Bank, July/August 1992).

In many cases the UK victim is asked to connive at a breach of Nigerian law. The supposed oil cargoes, for instance, are offered at a significant discount from world prices on the grounds that they are 'grey' oil outside Nigeria's OPEC quota. Whilst the Nigerian government is anxious to stamp out the frauds, it cannot in such cases be expected to extend sympathy to the victims; a Presidential statement speaks forthrightly of 'crooks losing money to crooks'. The banks, of course, cannot be held responsible for losses incurred through fraud of this nature.

13. Conclusion

Over the last few years, Nigeria has become an increasingly difficult market, both for exports and for local manufacture. Some British companies have sold off their Nigerian assets.

However, recent reforms of foreign exchange arrangements, relaxation of import restrictions, reductions in some import duties and the more positive encouragement of foreign investment, together with the availability of debt-for-equity swaps, offer promise for the future. Assuming that present policies will continue, trading opportunities with Nigeria appear increasingly attractive.

Progress test 30

1. In what ways would the marketing plans developed for mature products for less developed countries (LDCs) differ from plans relating to markets in more industrially advanced countries? Use examples to illustrate your answer. (*CIM*)

2. You supply agricultural equipment through a distributor to Nigeria. This distributor wishes to set up a joint venture between your company, his company and another local Nigerian company in order to expand sales there. Nigerian sales have in your case been expanding steadily for the past few years. What would you recommend your company to do? (*IEx*)

3. You have agreed to appoint I. Yoruba as your sole distributor in Nigeria. What essential points would you include in the agency agreement you draw up for him to sign? (*IEx*)

4. 'Assuming that present policies will continue, trading opportunities with Nigeria appear increasingly attractive.' Why is this so? And what serious difficulties remain?

5. Nigeria does not permit the establishment of branch offices of foreign firms. Many other countries legislate specifically for them. Can you suggest reasons for this difference in attitude?

31

Marketing in Russia

1. Background

Russia is now, for the first and only time in its long history, at least a fledgling democratic state, a situation unimaginable only a few years ago. But the country has already seen attempts at a coup. Will any political forecaster be brave enough to predict that over the next ten years it will not see another? Perhaps, next time around, one that is more successful?

The workforce is skilled, the market is large, the demand unsatisfied. But, as of 1992, the Russian economy is shrinking, inflation is at levels astonishing even by Latin American standards, and there is a desperate shortage of foreign exchange.

It is against this background that the rest of this chapter should be read.

2. Foreign Trade Organisations

Under the centrally planned economy of the former Soviet Union virtually all foreign trade was conducted through about 100 Foreign Trade Organisations (FTOs). Marketing consisted mainly of establishing a reputation with the appropriate FTO. FTO officials were usually professionals who had served abroad and understood international trade. For those who had the skill and patience to deal with their hard-nosed negotiating tactics the rewards could be high. Payment was invariably made on the nail in hard currency.

In November 1991 all legal entities in Russia were granted the right to conduct foreign trade on their own behalf; the 70-year FTO monopoly was at last broken. The FTOs continue to exist; many are being transformed into companies with the aim of developing into umbrella bodies for their industries. Their long-term future must, however, be in doubt.

3. Market research

The problem for many companies interested in doing business in Russia will be to locate appropriate organisations as customers or joint venture partners among the many thousands who are now empowered to do business on their own behalf.

Conventional research methods, Western-style, are not really applicable. Former Soviet organisations are still not helpful, beyond officially published statistics. The East European Trade Council, certain UK chambers of commerce and trade associations may be of help. A number of merchant houses specialise in trade with Russia; Rainbow Commercial Centre, with offices in Windsor and St Petersburg, seem especially active.

Exhibitions remain popular. They are useful not only for promotion but for making contact with potential customers. British trade missions to Russia are jointly sponsored by the DTI and chambers of commerce. The BSCC (formerly the British-Soviet Chamber of Commerce) organises missions independently of the DTI. Seminars and inward missions are also continuing.

4. Agents
Apart from the specialist merchant houses already mentioned, Russian enterprises may now act as agents for foreign companies.

Individual Russian citizens can be employed as local representatives. There are no longer any legal problems in opening a representative office.

5. Licensing
Inventions are protected by patents or certificates. Patents give the inventor exclusive rights to the invention for 15 years, subject to renewal fees. Certificates recognise the 'authorship' of the invention but give the right to use it to the state. State use entitles the inventor to remuneration.

6. Trade marks
The first applicant is entitled to registration and exclusive use. Registration is compulsory.

Registration is for ten years, subject to use within the first five years. Renewals may be made for further periods of ten years.

7. Joint ventures
Joint ventures are now encouraged as a means of attracting foreign capital, technology, and management and marketing expertise. By 1992, 1,200 were in operation, 126 of them British.

8. Subsidiary companies
One hundred per cent foreign ownership of companies in Russia is now permitted.

Foreign ownership of land and property is still not permitted, but long-term leases are available.

9. Payment terms
Chronic shortages of foreign exchange have resulted in lengthy delays in payment. Cash in advance or confirmed and irrevocable letter of credit terms have been recommended.

In the light of these payment delays ECGD withdrew export credit and investment insurance. Reinstatement of limited export credit facilities was announced at the end of 1992.

Understandably, countertrade (6:6) retains its popularity with Russian enterprises.

10. Foreign exchange

The rouble remains essentially a non-convertible currency, though *limited* amounts of roubles can be changed into hard currency at bank auctions. Because of the demand, auction rates are high.

The essential aim of the Russian government is to achieve full convertibility of the rouble. In 1992, however, there were no fewer than nine different rates of exchange for different types of transactions. The two most important were the market (floating) rate, which is the rate at which roubles can be purchased for cash for personal use, and the commercial rate, the rate adopted for business transactions.

11. Hard currency levies and export taxes

Russian enterprises engaged in the export of certain listed products must sell 40 per cent of their hard currency profits to the state. An additional 10 per cent levy is charged on the export earnings of all goods and services.

Subsidiaries of foreign companies and joint ventures with foreign companies may be exempted from these arrangements.

12. Conclusion

Present prospects of finding customers for direct exports, paid for in hard currency, are very limited. Exporters willing to engage in the complexities of countertrade may have greater success.

Siren voices are urging investment in joint ventures, stressing the need 'to get in on the ground floor'. Such investments must be regarded as long term. Profits from investment in Russia are best ploughed back into the business; it makes little sense at present to repatriate profit earned in roubles.

Taking also into account the political uncertainties, Russia would seem to be a market for the major multinational both willing to cast its bread upon the waters and able to withstand the loss of its investment.

Progress test 31

1. How would you undertake market research in Russia at the present time?

2. You are the export manager of a medium-size company that successfully exports its high-technology electronic equipment to five continents. You have received from your managing director a memo, a touch peremptory in tone, enquiring why you have made no attempt to sell to Russia. Draft out your reply.

32

Marketing in the USA

1. Size and regional nature

The USA is the world's largest single-country market. Its population is around 250 million.

The UK is the USA's seventh largest supplier and fourth largest customer.

From a marketing viewpoint the most striking feature of the USA is its sheer size. Although for some industrial products the market may be regarded as a homogeneous whole, for most consumer products – such as clothing – there will be a distinct regional pattern. Most companies will wish to make a start in one particular region rather than on the country as a whole. Very often a regional success can add up to a higher total profit than that available from any one European country.

2. The US legal system

The USA has a system of federal laws, applicable throughout the entire country. Each of the 50 states, plus the District of Columbia and the Commonwealth of Puerto Rico, also has its own state law. Most areas of commercial law fall within the competence of the states rather than of the federal government. Inevitably, the system is complicated.

Further, Americans must surely be among the most litigious of nations; they certainly have more lawyers per capita than any other country. Their business people are thrusting and aggressive in the pursuit of profit and a resort to law, or the threat of it, comes naturally to them.

In the UK, the legal costs of both parties to an action are usually borne by the loser. In the USA, in contrast, each party will normally bear its own costs, regardless of the result of the case. In actions for damages, lawyers are often willing to take a case on a contingency basis (no win, no fee) in return for a significant proportion of the damages that may eventually be awarded. Those damages will usually be much higher than might be expected from a court in the UK. For instance, damages in excess of a million pounds in the UK will give rise to press comment; in one US case, in compensation for injuries sustained in a car accident, a plaintiff was awarded $105 million. Naturally, not all damages awards are on that scale, but US citizens in a position to sue for damages have an almost risk-free chance of securing a substantial award. It is not surprising that they are so often willing to take advantage of it.

The message must be that in the USA legal advice should be sought before any problem arises and certainly before any commercial agreement is drafted, let alone signed.

Two areas of US law offering especially dangerous pitfalls for the international marketer are the anti-trust laws and product liability legislation. Both are discussed later in this chapter (6 and 12).

3. Import regulations

There are no foreign exchange restrictions on payments for imports. There is no general licensing of imports, though there are import restrictions on a small number of products and a prohibition on all products originating from Cuba, North Korea, Kampuchea and Vietnam.

Special technical regulations concerning quality and safety apply to goods such as motor vehicles and electrical equipment. The US food and drug legislation is widely regarded as a formidable and expensive non-tariff barrier.

The USA has now adopted the Harmonised Tariff System. This brings classification of goods for duty purposes into line with the EC and other members of the Customs Cooperation Council.

4. Direct selling

Department and chain stores play a significant role in US retailing; they account for a large proportion of the sales of British consumer goods. Many such stores maintain buying offices in London; others buy direct from representatives of foreign manufacturers who call on them.

Mail order houses offer similar direct sales opportunities, but they normally purchase in large quantities and at very keen prices.

5. Federal and other government purchases

The US Federal Government is a major purchaser of goods of all kinds, though the emphasis is on military procurement. Non-military purchases are subject to the Buy American Act, under which federal agencies may buy foreign goods only if US goods are not available, if it would not be in the public interest to buy US goods, or if the cost of US goods is unreasonable. 'Unreasonable' US prices have been defined as those 6 per cent above the foreign price, or 12 per cent if the US tenderer is located in a designated area of high unemployment or is classed officially as a small business.

Each state, county or municipality has its own independent purchasing organisation, all of which provide a huge and readily identifiable market for a wide range of goods, especially capital goods. The Buy American Act applies only to Federal Government purchases, but many states have adopted similar regulations. These apply to state, county and municipal bodies.

6. Agents and distributors

The size of the market means that very few US agents or distributors can offer genuine national coverage. Nevertheless, this will not always deter them from seeking nationwide representation. The granting of an agency on a national basis to a purely regional distributor is the most elementary error that a UK exporter can commit.

Except in Puerto Rico, there is no special Federal or state legislation relating to agency or distributor agreements, but exporters must ensure that the terms of the agreement do not come into conflict with US Federal or state anti-trust laws. These laws (*see* 20:5) have as their objective the encouragement of competition and the avoidance of price fixing or monopoly. In this they are similar to Articles 85 and 86 of the Treaty of Rome (28:6), but they may have more serious consequences for the exporter in that they may make certain contractual conditions imposed on the US agent or distributor illegal or potentially illegal. Clauses to be particularly avoided, for example, are those which purport:

(a) to fix a distributor's resale prices;
(b) to impose territorial restrictions on a distributor;
(c) to forbid a distributor to handle competing products.

If any clause in the contract should violate the anti-trust laws, the agent, distributor or other injured party may, even if they signed the contract, sue for treble damages (i.e. damages three times those actually sustained).

Again, except in Puerto Rico, there is no specific provision in US Federal or state law regarding the termination of agency or distributorship agreements. The Uniform Commercial Code (UCC), however, applicable in most states, requires parties to any contract to act in good faith and to allow contracts to remain in force for a reasonable length of time. An agent or distributor may well claim improper termination on the basis of the UCC, on the grounds of violation of anti-trust legislation, or on other, common law, grounds.

Chapter 24:13 suggests that all agency or distributorship agreements should be prepared with the benefit of advice from lawyers in the country concerned. Nowhere is this advice more important than in the USA.

7.   Licensing agreements

Government approval is not required for licensing agreements. Normally, there are no legal limitations on the percentage royalties which a licensor may charge.

As with agency or distributorship agreements, however, licensing agreements may violate anti-trust legislation. Again, the services of a US lawyer are essential.

The life of a patent on an invention is 17 years.

8.   Franchising agreements

In contrast to licensing agreements, franchising agreements are subject to close regulation under the rules of the Federal Trade Commission (FTC) and under state legislation in most states. Often, laws require the issue of a franchise prospectus similar to that which a company might issue when offering its shares to the public. The laws usually also cover unfair termination of the franchise contract.

FTC regulations and most state franchise laws include definitions of a franchise. Some definitions are wide in scope – so wide that they may encompass licensing and distributorship agreements even when that is not the intention of either party to the contract. Again, legal advice should be sought, since the requirements for the establishment of a franchise are onerous and expensive.

Registration of a trade mark is not strictly necessary to establish the exclusive right to its use; for a number of reasons, however, it is highly advisable. Registration may be challenged after two years of non-use.

9. Branches and sales subsidiaries

Increasingly, UK companies have tended to set up branches or sales subsidiaries to undertake local marketing and to maintain stocks in the market-place, thus providing a delivery service competitive with that of local manufacturers. A subsidiary company may be preferable to a branch for tax reasons.

It may prove advantageous to stock goods in one or more of the 150 foreign trade zones (FTZs). These zones, the equivalent of international free-trade areas, operate in almost all states. Importers and exporters may use FTZs to stock, exhibit, package, assemble or manufacture goods. Duty is payable only on goods imported into the US domestic market; the value for duty purposes excludes the cost of work undertaken within the zone.

10. Manufacturing subsidiaries

The declared policy of the US government is to support free enterprise and free trade and 'to admit and treat foreign capital on a basis of equality with domestic capital'. In accordance with this policy there are no price or exchange controls and no foreign investment approval process at the Federal level. There are very few restrictions on foreign ownership of US corporations (100 per cent foreign ownership is permitted) and both capital and earnings may be freely remitted abroad after payment of appropriate US taxes.

However, a company wishing to establish itself in the USA will need to look carefully at:

(a) the consumer protection and product safety laws relevant to its product, and the general question of product liability (12);
(b) the stringent pollution control laws and their enforcement both by the Federal Environmental Protection agency and by individual states;
(c) the immigration laws, which in practice amount to a restriction on the number of foreign managers who can be employed.

Business corporations are formed under state, not Federal, laws. Company law and taxation regulations vary from one state to another; tax and other advantages may be gained by careful choice of the state of incorporation, which need not be the state where the company carries on its main activities. Delaware is often favoured as a state for registration of foreign corporations.

11. Investment incentives

The Federal government offers grants, loans or loan guarantees to encourage location or expansion of businesses in economically distressed areas. These are available to both foreign and US corporations.

Almost all states are interested in promoting foreign manufacturing investment within their borders; they may offer financial assistance, tax allowances and the provision of land, buildings and equipment at favourable rates.

12. Product liability

Product liability legislation is a matter with which the international marketer should concern himself in every country in which his product is sold. It is discussed in general terms in 11:**24**.

In the USA, however, product liability offers special problems. Some of these stem from the nature of the US legal system (*see* **2**). In addition, in some states, the principle of 'joint and several liability' applies; under this principle, damages are payable by those defendants in a position to do so, regardless of the extent to which their products were responsible for the injury.

Again, a UK exporter might expect to be sued in a British court, where damages would certainly be significantly lower, but certain states permit an extension of their jurisdiction to include foreign suppliers whose only connection with the state is the sale of their goods within it. In any case, distributors as well as manufacturers can be sued, and most distributors these days will insist that suppliers accept liability for damages.

In the USA, insurance cover for certain inherently dangerous products such as motor cycles is now either difficult to obtain or simply not available. For other products, insurance premiums are four or five times as high as those for comparable risks in other countries. Companies with relatively low sales in the USA may decide it is not worthwhile to continue operations. Other companies may decide to dispense with insurance cover altogether, but they may then find themselves among the growing number of companies driven into bankruptcy by product liability actions.

*Example*_____

In 1968 the Keene Corporation acquired, for $8 million, Baldwin Ehret Hill, manufacturers of a thermal insulation containing about ten per cent asbestos. In 1972 BEH eliminated asbestos from its product and in 1975 Keene Corporation closed the company down. Since then, Keene has paid out $400 million to resolve asbestos claims brought against it, even though not one of the 8500 plaintiffs in a consolidated trial was ever employed by Keene or BEH – most merely installed the product. Furthermore, most of the plaintiffs are not sick, they are merely worried about what might happen in the future. So far, 16 of Keene's co-defendants have been bankrupted; the remaining defendant companies must now shoulder their burden as well. Under the 'joint-and-several' responsibility rule, the last asbestos supplier standing will be liable for all judgments against all asbestos defendants. Glenn Bailey, chairman of Keene, expects that the remaining suppliers will soon be eliminated, too – they face 2000 new lawsuits every month. The lawyers in the case are paid on the contingency system (no win, no fee) and, of the $400 million paid by Keene, $265 million has gone to lawyers. 'No other country', says Mr Bailey, 'countenances a justice system anything like the United States' ad hoc asbestos law, with its punitive damages, consolidation of entirely diverse cases, junk-science testimony and huge contingency fees.' He is calling for an end to this 'legalised extortion'.

13. Conclusion

The USA must be regarded as one of the world's most open markets. It offers almost none of the restrictions found in so many other markets overseas, and the potential is enormous.

Yet it is not an easy market, and certainly not one for the dilettante or amateur. Americans are demanding customers, taking first-rate quality and service for granted, while competition, both US and foreign, is intense. Legal pitfalls abound, especially in the area of product liability.

Progress test 32

1. 'Too often selling into the US market is centred on one person, without even an office in the market-place. US customers don't like that … they like to see some sort of operation.' What sort of distribution operations might be practicable in the USA?

2. What special local considerations would you take into account in establishing an assembly or manufacturing operation in the USA?

3. 'The USA must be regarded as one of the world's most open markets. It offers almost none of the restrictions found in so many other markets overseas.' Justify this statement, comparing the USA with one other more restrictive market with which you are acquainted. Can you think of any exceptions to the statement?

4. 'If you want to sell in the USA, start by calling on your lawyer.' What might have prompted this statement?

Part five

Case studies

Case study I

The Latinian State Railways tender

'Jim, we need the business. You don't need me to tell you that. We're relying on you.'

Jim hesitated. Tenders were due to be opened that same day. Wasn't it a bit late to open negotiations? Shouldn't he have been in touch with the buyer when tenders were first issued? Or even earlier?

No, it wouldn't do to show his concern. Not so soon after his appointment as export manager. Not on the eve of his first-ever visit to Latin America.

The managing director read his thoughts. 'Don't worry, Jim. Any problems, just do as Pablo says. He knows his way around. That's what agents are for.'

Three days later, in the agency office, Pablo was all smiles. 'Jim, good to meet you at last. Meet Tex. He's acting as our sub-agent, just for this deal.

'Tenders were opened on Friday, as you know. On that desk in the corner you'll find photocopies of all the competing tenders. That's the pile in the middle. At this end of the desk are the two original tenders you submitted, which I have withdrawn, and at the far end are two blank copies of the tender form, stamped and signed by the chief buyer and back-dated to the tender issue date.

'I've only had time to glance through the competing tenders, but it's pretty clear that one or other of our competitors has quoted lower prices than ours on every item. Not by much, but it's enough to lose us the business.

'What I'd like you to do is look through the photocopies and decide on some new prices just a few cents per item below the lowest competing price. Then, if you'll give the new prices to Maria, she'll type them in on the two blank tender forms. Then you just sign the new tenders and we'll do the rest.'

Jim looked doubtfully at the pile of photocopies. 'Is this the usual way you do business here?' he enquired.

Tex grinned. 'Yeah, I guess you could say that.'

'You mean everybody gets copies of competing tenders?'

Tex's grin widened. 'Now I didn't quite say that, did I? Wouldn't be much point if they all got copies, now would there?'

'Then how is it that we ... ?'

'Let's just say this chief buyer's a good friend of mine. So good, I just bought him a new car for Christmas. That might have helped some.'

'A new car! But that's ...' Jim hesitated. 'That's bribery.'

Tex's grin disappeared abruptly. 'You think? Look, I gave him a new car, no strings attached. *Before* tenders were issued. I did him a favour and now he's doing me one That's not bribery, not in my book. Don't you give Christmas presents to buyers in England?'

'Well, yes. But not to that value. Not to anything like that value.'

'No? And when did a buyer last tell you how much his Christmas presents were worth?'

Jim made no reply. Tex turned to Pablo. 'We're wasting time. If the control office copy is found missing, Conchita's in trouble. That tender has got to be back in her files today. With the new prices or the old prices, I don't care which. But make your mind up.'

Jim looked at Pablo. 'Control office?'

'It's a separate office that keeps the second copy of all tenders submitted. It's too complicated to explain now, but the railway buyers have no access to its files. So Tex has an arrangement with a control office secretary.'

Pablo paused. He saw he was merely making matters worse. 'Look, Jim, there's not much time. If you fill in the new prices and sign the tender forms, we'll get the new tenders back in the files today. Then you can take it from me that the order's as good as in the bag.

'You need this order. It'll keep a lot of people in jobs. Back home, they'll see they were right in promoting you, young as you are, to export manager; they'll know you can do the job. Isn't it worth it?

'Tex and I are splitting my commission. It won't cost your company a cent extra. And above all, you do see, don't you, that the railways will be paying less than they otherwise would. Everybody wins, nobody loses. So why don't you sit down at that desk and get started?'

Questions

1. 'Everybody wins, nobody loses.' Is that really so?

2. In Jim's position, would you have signed the new tender forms? Justify your decision.

Case study II

Kwikpak Ltd and La Scatola SpA

NOTE: Company names and certain market data have been changed for reasons of confidentiality.

Kwikpak is a UK manufacturer of packaging machinery whose principal product is a range of flow-wrap machines.

Flow-wrapping is a high-speed and highly cost-effective, if slightly down-market, method of packaging small products in plastic film. It is extensively used for food products, especially biscuits and confectionery – a typical flow-wrapped product is the Mars bar. The system is also used for a very wide range of non-food products such as bandages, surgical swabs, disposable razors, small hardware items, etc.

A typical flow-wrap machine may cost anything from £20,000 upwards; fully electronically controlled versions might cost £50,000 or more. The machines can be expected to have a life of at least ten years, and machines up to 20 years old can still be found in service. Most orders are for one or two machines, although the occasional batch order can offer very significant savings in production costs. Machines are made to order. Manufacture for stock is not really practicable, since each industry, and often each type of product, offers its own special packaging problems which may necessitate adjustments to the basic design of machine. Because of this there is often, though not invariably, some degree of loyalty to the supplier of the machine(s) currently installed in the factory; such a supplier knows the industry, the products and their special problems. Standardisation on one supplier also reduces the stocks of spares that have to be carried, cuts down on operator training costs, and permits greater flexibility in transferring operators between machines. Increasingly, however, purchasers are taking the shorter-term view, and a reasonably significant price difference tends to overcome any preference in favour of standardisation on one supplier.

Kwikpak, with around 250 employees, sells its products world-wide, but about half its turnover derives from the UK. In recent years competition within the UK from both British and foreign manufacturers has intensified.

Only two UK competitors are of any significance: Sanke, Forwood and Greenpak. Sanke, Forwood also manufactures bread slicing-and-wrapping machinery and is a subsidiary of a major industrial group which offers flow-production bread-making plant and other food-processing machinery.

Greenpak is a small but very active company offering one basic design of a no-frills machine at a very competitive price.

A dozen or more foreign manufacturers are to some extent active in the UK, including US and Japanese suppliers. Only three, however, give Kwikpak any cause for concern: Swisswrap, Sleevofilm of Holland and La Scatola. Swisswrap has concentrated almost entirely on a very small number of large biscuit-manufacturing groups, offering them machines claimed to be at the leading edge of technology, at prices as much as three times as high as Kwikpak's. Sleevofilm has similarly concentrated on biscuits, though with a wider range of customers and at much more competitive prices. La Scatola were believed to be interested mainly in the bakery industry, in which Kwikpak had taken little interest except for a dozen or so specialist cake manufacturers. These three competitors had clearly been making inroads into the UK market.

To assess the extent of these inroads, and also to provide a factual basis for market segmentation and the better deployment of the sales force, Kwikpak decided to undertake a survey of the major user industries in the UK market. Annex II.1 lists these user industries and gives an indication of the *minimum* number of establishments classified by the number of employees. In order to limit research costs, Kwikpak decided to confine the enquiry to establishments employing fifty or more people. It was, however, recognised that smaller companies also bought flow-wrap machines, since the savings in labour costs were very significant. Kwikpak staff had fond memories of a muffin manufacturer employing only eight people who bought two machines, one simply as back-up in the event of breakdown (once installed the machine becomes an integral part of the production process, and breakdowns may stop production altogether).

The bakery industry presented special problems, both in terms of the research programme and in terms of sales exploitation. So far, as mentioned, Kwikpak had limited its activities to the dozen or so specialist cake manufacturers. These companies distributed their products nationwide, necessarily all wrapped in some way and usually flow-wrapped. They were, therefore, significant purchasers of flow-wrap machines, often having as many as ten or twelve installed per establishment.

Also significant users were the so-called 'plant' bakers, whose principal activity was the flow-line production of bread, but who also produced cakes and 'morning goods' (bread rolls, croissants, Danish pastries, etc.) for more local distribution. There were about 50–60 such plants, the vast majority owned by only two companies, Allied Bakeries and British Bakeries. Each of these plants required, mainly for morning goods, two, three and sometimes four flow-wrap machines.

The rest of the UK bakery industry is made up of a vast number of smaller (but often significant in size) independent bakeries offering freshly baked bread, cakes and morning goods for very local delivery. Annex II.1 identifies more than 900 establishments in total in the bakery industry, but this almost certainly understates the position.

Many of these independent bakeries delivered their products un-wrapped, on open trays, to local retail stores. Others had found it more convenient to flow-wrap their morning goods, perhaps at the insistence of their retail store customers (retail stores in general, but especially supermarkets, were increasingly demanding wrapped morning goods). Some independent bakeries, however, owned bakers' shops and delivered to them exclusively; there was little chance of persuading such bakeries to start wrapping their products.

The capacity of even the oldest flow-wrap machine was such that for most independent bakeries one, or at the most two, machines per establishment was a more than adequate number.

The Kwikpak survey took due account of these three very different segments in the bakery industry and results were analysed accordingly. An extract from the survey results is given in Annexes II.2 and II.3. (The enquiry was based on a census of establishments employing 50+ staff, so there is no question of sampling error; non-response was low.)

La Scatola's figures aroused particular interest. A Kwikpak executive commented that it was not difficult to infer what had been La Scatola's segmentation policy in relation to the bakery industry. It looked to him as though La Scatola had stolen a march on all its competitors. If the structure of the bakery industry in other countries was even vaguely similar to that in the UK, La Scatola would by now have gained an unassailable competitive advantage in the bakery industry and have created a jumping-off point for the eventual penetration of other market segments.

Questions

1. What specific factor(s) might have led La Scatola to concentrate, as they obviously have, on the bakery industry, and then only on two segments of it?

2. In as much detail as possible, what would you infer was La Scatola's segmentation policy within the bakery industry? In particular, how far is it possible to quantify segments (in terms of numbers of establishments in each segment and subsegment)?

3. Why might this policy be expected to give La Scatola an 'unassailable competitive advantage' in the bakery industry?

4. What are the implications of La Scatola's segmentation policy in relation to:
    (a) the organisation of the sales effort;
    (b) the sales message to customers;
    (c) call frequency on customers?

5. On the basis of the limited information available, how would you categorise the approach to segmentation adopted by:
   (a) Sanke, Forwood;
   (b) Kwikpak?

6. What other segmentation criteria might usefully be considered in relation to the market for flow-wrap machines?

Annex II.1 Industries using flow-wrapping: number of establishments according to number of employees (GB market)

Industries using flow-wrapping		No. of establishments		
SIC no.	Brief description	Total	50+ employees	20+ employees
2570	Pharmaceutical	254	112	162
4122.2	Frozen meat	40	14	24
4196	Bakery	920	230	434
4197	Biscuits	67	34	54
4214.1 and 4214.2	Chocolate and sweets	169	68	80

Notes:
1. These are minimum figures. Not *all* establishments were identified, especially in the bakery industry.
2. Although the industries listed are significant users of flow-wrapping, not *all* establishments will be users. For instance, under the pharmaceutical classification there are few users outside bandage and surgical swab manufacturers.
3. SIC: Standard Industrial Classification 1980.

Annex II.2 Number of flow-wrap machines at present installed in Great Britain

Industries		Establishments having at least one flow-wrap machine installed	Total no. of machines installed	Machine suppliers								
SIC no.	Description			KW	SF	GP	SW	SL	SC	Japan	USA	Others
2570	Pharmaceutical	22	80	42	20	2		9		1	1	5
4122.2	Frozen meat	12	36	14	10	2		6	1	2		1
4196	Bakery: specialist cake	11	110	45	15		1	11	2	19	1	16
4196	Large bakery groups	40	129	2	33	1			88	3	1	1
4196	Independent bakeries	106	190	2	25	1	2	8	148	2		2
4197	Biscuits	33	373	99	43	12	120	44	1	23	10	21
4214.1 and 4214.2	Chocolates and sweets	65	327	148	75	35	21	18		6	2	22
	Total	289	1,245	352	221	53	144	96	240	56	15	68

Notes:
1. These figures include only establishments having 50 or more employees.
2. The Japan column includes two separate Japanese companies; the USA column represents one company only.
3. Abbreviations: KW = Kwikpak; SF = Sanke, Forwood; GP = Greenpak; SW = Swisspak; SL = Sleevofilm; SC = La Scatola.

Annex II.3 Installations of flow-wrap machines effected 'during last 12 months' in Great Britain

SIC no.	Description	Establishments having at least one flow-wrap machine installed	Total no. of installations of new machines effected in last 12 months'	No. of establishments effecting the installations in previous column	Machine suppliers								
					KW	SF	GP	SW	SL	SC	Japan	USA	Others
2570	Pharmaceutical	22	5	3	3		1				1		
4122.2	Frozen meat	12	4	2	1	2	1						
4196	Bakery: specialist cake	11	10	2	3	3		1	1				1
4196	Large bakery groups	40	14	10		5	1			6		1	1
4196	Independent bakeries	106	37	25		4	1		2	28	2		
4197	Biscuits	33	29	5	8	3	1	7	2	1	3	3	1
4214.1 and 4214.2	Chocolates and sweets	65	28	8	9	5	5	3	2		3		1
	Total	289	127	55	24	22	10	11	7	36	9	4	4

Case study III

Letraset distribution in the USA

'Shambles' was the word John Chudley, Letraset's managing director, chose to describe the situation. In the USA, potentially the world's largest and most profitable market for Letraset products, sales had slumped disastrously and the US subsidiary had incurred a swingeing loss. The future appeared hopeless and, despite the importance of the market, the board was seriously considering complete withdrawal. It was the greatest set-back in Letraset's thirteen years of existence.

Those thirteen years, in fact, had shown a history of virtually unbroken success: a success based on an ingenious dry-transfer lettering system brought to technical perfection, on some highly competent financial management and on some innovative marketing.

The early years

The original product idea on which the fortunes of the company were founded was an easily applied transfer of letters and drawings as a substitute for the tedious and expensive hand-drawing that had hitherto been required.

These original transfers were still based on the use of water when manufacture was begun in 1956. The ultimate aim, however, was the development of the infinitely more convenient *dry* transfer, a technical breakthrough that was eventually achieved in 1960 after much research and experiment. The simplicity of the dry-transfer product is clearly demonstrated in the concise but entirely complete instructions given in Annex III.1.

The company realised at the outset that so revolutionary a product offering so many cost and other advantages had a world-wide market, and at an early stage made a positive decision to promote its product throughout the world, selecting initially a few markets of major potential for thorough exploitation. The board recognised, in particular, the importance of the USA.

Major customers were advertising agencies, art studios, architects, television stations, newspaper offices, printers and publishers, and large engineering companies with their own design and drawing offices. Almost any commercial or industrial organisation, however, might find an occasional use for the product, as might the individual consumer.

The US agent

As early as 1961 a 25-year agency contract was signed with a US agent who distributed art requisites to dealers (art requisite retailers) by means of a nationally syndicated catalogue (dealers bought the catalogue and bound it in their own cover before issue to prospective customers). As might be expected when so novel a product achieved such immediate and extensive distribution, the agency was a real success in that it brought significant and much-needed income to the fledgling Letraset Ltd.

Letraset became, however, one of hundreds of different products in a catalogue. Even at that early stage there was some doubt whether such an arrangement was in the best long-term interest of the company, and the agency agreement, which had been signed by a director without the formal approval of the board, led to a boardroom upset.

Licensee

The situation in the USA was unique in that the company faced serious competition from local manufacturers. One US company, Prestype, had developed independently a product similar to Letraset, though on a paper, rather than a plastic, base. Another company, Chartpak, with an already established distribution network in the art requisites field, began to manufacture a plastic-base product, which involved Letraset Ltd in patent litigation. Other competitors were springing up.

In 1963, Letraset decided to go public. It was clearly undesirable to have to report, in the prospectus, pending legal actions relating to patents which were vital to the whole future success of the company. The company was forced to consider licensing Chartpak in the USA. Licensing negotiations were initiated, but were so protracted that, in order to reach an early settlement of the patent actions (which Letraset were assured they would eventually have won), the company licensed competition in its major market for an amount which even then appeared a trivial sum, and which today appears derisory.

Appointment of distributors

Distribution through the syndicated catalogue system continued, and, though sales increased, it was clear that the company was rapidly losing market share, largely as a result of the haphazard and patchy distribution inseparable from any catalogue sale operation. It was decided to appoint a number of authorised distributors as wholesalers, in an endeavour to gain greater control over distribution. This resulted in some improvement in sales, but performance still fell a long way short of that achieved in other less important markets. There was no attempt to extend the official Letraset franchise to dealers, most of whom already handled two or more competing brands of dry transfer.

Letraset USA Inc.

In 1967 Letraset USA Inc. was formed as a sales and distribution subsidiary with headquarters in California. It was decided to mount a major distribution campaign, loading the Letraset wholesalers so as to provide the 'urge of stock on the shelf'. Such a policy, of course, could only be successful provided sales *in* to wholesalers were followed by equivalent sales *out* to dealers and thence on to end users. 'Selling out', however, was given scant attention. The agency organisation was not in any way structured to assist with the selling-out function and necessarily relied on the uniqueness of the product to ensure its passage through the distribution chain. Eventually, the agency agreement had to be bought out – at a cost approaching one million dollars.

Dealer loading

With the cancellation of the agency agreement, Letraset were in a position to exercise much closer control over their market. Nevertheless, there was still no mechanism by which they might assist in the selling-out operation. It was therefore decided to take advantage of the introduction of new and improved format and designs of the instant-lettering product in order to load the distributors with yet more stock.

These new designs were introduced under the Letraset USA name at an increased price per sheet, but all distributors, and consequently all their dealers, were offered a complete exchange of stock on a sheet-for-sheet basis – provided they bought, in addition, an equivalent number of sheets at the new price. As the product changes were not readily apparent, the new range was allocated sheet numbers which differed from the hitherto standard international numbering system. A new US catalogue was to include *only* these special numbers. This, rather ingeniously, put pressure on distributors, and their dealers, to accept the exchange offer, since sheets not exchanged would become very largely unsaleable.

Not surprisingly in these circumstances, most distributors and dealers accepted the exchange offer. US sales soared and it was these sales that largely accounted for the record company profits in 1967–8. Sales *out* to end-users, however, fell far short of sales *in* to distributors and their dealers. Further, the length and diffuse nature of the distribution chain meant that this factor was not suspected for many months, and the full extent of distributor and dealer over-stocking was only realised early in 1969.

Production problems

The new numbering system that had been so effective in persuading distributors to accept the exchange offer brought immediate production problems in its wake. In effect a special product, requiring separate and much shorter production runs, had been created. This in turn gave rise to delivery problems at the UK factory (newly built, and still experiencing teething troubles), reduced stock turn, and increased stock control problems. All this occurred at a time when the standard product could have been offered without difficulty – the sheets withdrawn from the USA were perfectly serviceable.

Technical problems

Worse, in the atmosphere of urgency generated by the sudden upsurge in the US demand a change in product formulation went unnoticed. The supplier of an ingredient of the adhesive used to retain the lettering on the backing sheet altered its composition. The effect of the change was to reduce the satisfactory shelf life of the product, which had up to that point been virtually indefinite – and the high level of stocks forced on distributors had resulted inevitably in a longer storage period.

Clearly, the first priority was the withdrawal of all defective stock from distributors and their dealers by a further one-for-one exchange (there proved eventually to be a million defective sheets in all). Unfortunately, what seemed at first to be a simple and straightforward operation proved to be a lengthy and difficult task. Although, of course, *distributors* were readily identifiable, and although most of them were only too happy to cooperate, by no means all of them were in a position even to identify those of their dealers who stocked Letraset products. Selling a range of perhaps hundreds, even thousands of items, they were quite unable to analyse their sales on a product basis.

Future action

It was at this critical stage, with the US company incurring heavy losses, that the board considered total withdrawal from the market. On reflection, however, it was felt that the problems in the USA all had their origin in the unplanned approach to distribution. In Canada, in contrast, a planned and managed distribution system, established by John Soper, a cousin of John Chudley, seemed to be yielding good results. It was decided to give Soper responsibility for the USA as well as Canada, with a brief to restore the US market to profitability and growth.

Soper reviewed the situation. Clearly there were a number of serious problems to be faced. In the first place, *immediate* availability of the product was vital to many of Letraset's most important customers such as newspapers, television stations and advertising agencies. This implied the maintenance of stocks in every city of any size. There could be absolutely no question of Letraset's financing such stocks, so some form of local intermediary was essential. On the other hand, the present lengthy and diffuse chain of distribution had led to a complete loss of control over the distribution operation, with disastrous results at the time of product failure. That situation would certainly have to be remedied.

Stockholding itself presented serious problems, given the immense variety of type faces, size and colours necessarily offered by Letraset – to say nothing of whole ranges specially devised for certain categories of customers such as architects and engineers. Stocks would have to be adjusted at frequent intervals, not merely in response to total demand but also to meet the requirements of the different categories of customer in a given area. Exactly how to achieve this was a major problem.

The products had previously been lost in catalogues covering hundreds, perhaps thousands, of other items. In some way Letraset would have to ensure that its products were of real significance, in profit terms, to whatever intermediaries were selected. At the same time the exact future role of the catalogue would need to be thought through.

Reliance on selling in to distributors had proved a disaster; some means of selling out, from intermediary to end user, would have to be devised. This in itself would be a form of motivation, but motivation of intermediaries would in any case require special consideration, given the present demoralisation among distributors and dealers.

The new distribution strategy would need to take all these factors into account.

Questions

1. What practical alternatives to the appointment of an agent might reasonably have been considered by the board, even at this early stage in the company's development, when financial resources were still very limited?

2. Even if the appointment of an agent was a correct decision, in what significant ways might the agency agreement have been improved, from Letraset's point of view?

3. Accepting the need to present an attractive prospectus and, therefore, to reach some kind of settlement with Chartpak, what alternative proposals might have been put forward?

4. If, after all, it was decided that a licensing agreement was appropriate, what might have been the particularly important terms of such an agreement, given the rather special circumstances?

5. The appointment of wholesalers (distributors) must have seemed at the time a major step forward in the US distribution arrangements. Why did it prove not to be so?

6. Why, when dealer loading had proved so successful in all other markets, was it almost inevitably destined to end in failure in the USA?

7. In Soper's position, what system of distribution would you have introduced? Go into as much detail as possible. Consider in particular the problems as Soper saw them (detailed under 'Future action').

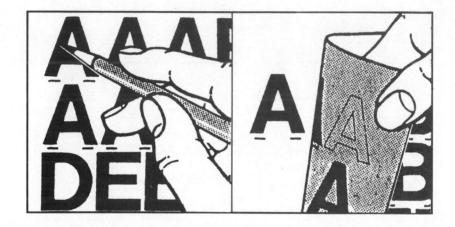

Annex III.1 *The Letraset dry transfer process.*

Remove the backing tissue from lettering sheet, and align the guidelines on the sheet with those on the artwork. Rub lightly over the letter with ballpoint pen or blunt pencil, using sweeping strokes. Carefully lift sheet away. Repeat until word is complete. Cover entire word with protective backing tissue and reburnish for added protection and permanence.

Esselte Letraset picture framing materials: A contrast in distribution strategies – USA, Japan and Germany

The distribution system established by Letraset in Canada and the USA (see preceding case study) was adopted, as far as practicable, in every country that offered a significant market. This system was undoubtedly a major factor in the continued and remarkable success of the instant lettering product. Sales in the 1970s moved inexorably upwards.

Letraset had always recognised, however, that eventually instant lettering would be superseded by new technological developments; diversification was a constant preoccupation. In the mid-1970s a number of acquisitions were made, notably into the toy business, with varying degrees of success. Then, in 1979, Letraset made a major acquisition with its purchase of Stanley Gibbons, the undisputed world leader in philately. Shortly afterwards the market for stamps collapsed, taking Letraset's share price with it. In 1981 the company became a target for a hostile takeover bid, from which it was rescued by a 'white knight' in the shape of Esselte, the Swedish office supplies company. Letraset was re-named Esselte Letraset (EL), though otherwise, apart from the early divestment of Stanley Gibbons and the toy businesses, it continued as a largely separate entity.

The instant lettering business continued to thrive, reaching its peak in 1981. From that date onwards sales began to decline gradually until the mid-1980s and then, especially with the advent of desk-top publishing, at an increasingly alarming rate. (The 1992 instant lettering sales represented only 18 per cent of the peak level of 1981.) Clearly diversification had become a matter of urgency.

One possible diversification route was, of course, into desk-top publishing software, and in 1986 EL took practical steps to move into this market. It soon became clear, however, that technologically Letraset would always remain a follower rather than an innovator in this market, that new software packages and new competitors would always spring up, and that the established distribution channel (computer hardware and software dealers) would prove difficult and unwelcoming, especially to a new entrant into the market. EL soon decided that real diversification success lay elsewhere, though a by-product of this diversification attempt was ultimately a thriving business in the distribution of software developed by other organisations.

USA

A more significant diversification was eventually to result from the purchase in 1974 of a small American company, Bainbridge, based in New York City. For Letraset, the logic of this acquisition was that Bainbridge manufactured illustration board, a thick card used extensively by graphic designers and, therefore, a product compatible with the existing art requisite dealer network. Bainbridge was also involved, however, in the production of mountboard, card used as a surround or backing by picture framers. Mountboard was sold through entirely different channels: major distributors selling to the picture framers. Sales were concentrated heavily in the north-east of the USA.

Letraset decided there was scope at Bainbridge for their marketing talents in terms of product improvement (of mountboard) and geographical extension of sales. The standard board was upgraded in quality, and a wide range of new colours and surface finishes was introduced. New mountboard products were developed, the most important being an upgrade to conservation quality, a completely alkaline board containing no acidic or degrading elements. (See Annex IV. 1 for details of Bainbridge's 1992 product range.)

Letraset decided to extend Bainbridge mountboard distribution to the whole of the USA and Canada. It was accepted that distributors were a necessary link in the distribution chain: mountboards are of low unit value, large (with a perimeter of several feet), heavy and expensive to transport, especially in such a vast country as the USA, while orders from picture framers are almost invariably small.

The result was a success in sales and profit terms. Perhaps more important, however, was that it alerted Letraset, and later EL, to the potential size and profitability of the market for other picture framing materials. EL began actively to seek acquisitions in that field and, in 1984, purchased the Nielsen Molding Co. of Townsend, New Hampshire.

Nielsen had been established to manufacture aluminium picture frame mouldings, aluminium being a new material in picture framing, but one that is particularly versatile, offering the possibility of many different finishes. Nielsen had been first in the field with the aluminium product and had successfully promoted it in the market-place. The company had at first no direct competitors, though it competed, of course, with suppliers of the traditional wood picture frame mouldings, which Nielsen did not at that time supply. (See Annex IV. 2 for some examples of the 1992 range of Nielsen aluminium mouldings.)

To justify its expensive purchase EL would have to improve significantly the sales and profits of an already successful company; distribution was one area which EL hoped would contribute significantly to this improvement. Distribution channels in the USA for picture framing materials were as indicated in Annex IV. 3 (a). Much of the trade was in the hands of the large regional distributors already mentioned. These distributors had, over the years, become well entrenched, doubtless assisted by the weight and bulk of the traditional wood product and the high cost of transport in a country the size of the USA. The distributors also imported significant quantities of wood mouldings on their own account, usually marketing them under their own label.

These regional distributors sold to a total of about 20,000 picture framers in the USA (in comparison, the UK has only about 2,500 framers, though its population is about a quarter of that of the USA). A few of these framers are of a significant size; these include art galleries, museums, department stores selling ready-framed pictures, and contract framers who meet part of the demand from the first three categories. The vast majority of framers, however, as in most countries, are mainly very small operations, often one-man bands or husband and wife teams operating from small retail premises. For entry into picture framing, capital requirements are low, while it is not too difficult to acquire the necessary skills. Picture framing has been described as the last of the cottage industries.

In fact, the real problem for the small picture framer lies in the marketing of his services. Many picture framers secure much of their business through loose sales agreements with local retailers, not only art and photographic shops but often stores in entirely unrelated trades. These retailers display moulding sample boards, mountboard, etc. and accept orders, sometimes on behalf of the framer, but often in their own name, so that the end purchaser often does not realise that the framing is undertaken elsewhere.

At the time of the EL purchase, Nielsen was selling in significant quantity through distributors, but the bulk of its sales of framing products were made direct to picture framers. For these picture framer sales it relied not on a conventional sales force but, as is common practice in the USA, on a network of independent manufacturers' representatives. These representatives acted on behalf of a number on non-competing manufacturers of picture framing materials, endeavouring in this way to offer a full and balanced product range to framers.

The Nielsen management made strong recommendations for the future extension of the direct selling operation, pointing out that their aluminium product was lighter and of a higher unit value than the Bainbridge mountboard. EL, on the other hand, foresaw significant savings in sales and administration costs, especially if Nielsen sales could be handled within the Bainbridge distributor sales organisation. They also took into account the dauntingly large number of very small framers and were undoubtedly mindful of the success of their partnership approach to art requisite dealers in the instant lettering field. After long consideration EL decided to move almost the whole of the Nielsen business increasingly towards distributors; they notified their then direct sales customers accordingly. This meant, of course, that the arrangements with the manufacturers' representatives had to be terminated.

These representatives, having in this way lost a major part of their hitherto complete product range, necessarily looked urgently for a replacement product. In effect, Nielsen competitors had been provided with a ready-made sales force with established connections. As might be expected, however, the distributors were delighted and EL looked forward, in the general atmosphere of goodwill, to developing its partnership approach. In the event, however, distributors remained quite uncommitted to the Nielsen product and positively discouraged direct Nielsen approaches to picture framers. EL came gradually and reluctantly to the conclusion that its decision to reduce direct selling and to develop its business through distributors had been a mistake.

In 1990, to complement its range of aluminium mouldings, EL bought a wood moulding supplier, Nurre Caxton, with distribution bases in Ohio and Florida. Nurre Caxton had a sophisticated sales force selling direct to framers, mainly in the south, the Mid-West and California, by-passing distributors entirely and, of course, competing with the wood moulding ranges of Nielsen and Bainbridge customers. EL made no change in these arrangements. (Examples of the 1992 EL range of wood mouldings are given in Annex IV. 4.)

Nielsen had been first in the field with aluminium mouldings in the USA; it developed and popularised the product. It now, in 1992, faces two major US competitors and several smaller ones. It is at least arguable that Nielsen's decision virtually to abandon direct sales assisted these competitors in gaining market share. Nielsen now have about one-third of the US market.

Japan

Letraset had originally entered the Japanese market with its instant lettering products. A single distributor was appointed for the whole country and, almost to Letraset's surprise, the whole operation was a real and almost immediate success in profit terms. The product range was soon widened to include other graphic arts products and these too proved highly successful. The distributor, highly enthusiastic, pressed for the establishment of a factory in Japan.

Overseas production ran counter to Letraset's normal policy; instant lettering, of negligible weight and high value, is ideally suited to export. In Japan, however, the distributor's overwhelming enthusiasm simply could not be ignored, especially as remarkably generous government grants could be obtained in return for establishment in a designated development area. Ultimately a factory was built in an economically depressed area, a former coal-mining district. Letraset took a 49 per cent stake in a new manufacturing and distribution company, the distributor taking the remaining 51 per cent (at that time it was not legally permissible for a foreign company to take a majority holding in a Japanese company).

Despite unremitting effort from all parties, the venture was a financial disaster and the plant had to close. Letraset's status in Japan was seriously damaged, particularly in the light of the government grants it had received. Letraset's art requisite dealers also suffered in the wake of the closure.

In the meantime, Bainbridge USA had been acquired and some attempts had been made to sell its mountboard products in Japan. Very little progress was made, however, and, in 1984, the mountboard distribution rights were transferred to a Japanese picture framer, Deco-Art, which sold complete frames to department stores. Deco-Art achieved some success in mountboard distribution.

Once EL had fully realised the scope and profit potential for picture framing materials, however, it made the decision to re-enter the Japanese market. Two months later the owner of Deco-Art died; his widow was happy to sell the business to EL.

After the débâcle of the local manufacture of instant lettering, EL felt a greater than usual responsibility towards its art requisite dealers. It pressed hard to persuade them to enter the picture frame business, selling completed frames to the general public. Some 150 of them took up the challenge, providing EL with a ready-made distribution system.

The problem was to supply the final framed picture. The art requisite dealers could not be expected to undertake the picture framing themselves: they did not have the requisite skills and many were unwilling to train in order to acquire them, while in any case their premises, in cities where real estate prices are phenomenally high, were mostly too small to permit even so small-scale a manufacturing operation as picture framing. By this time, however, EL had acquired Nielsen USA. After careful consideration it decided to undertake the picture framing itself, leaving the dealer only with the task of selling the framing service. For this purpose it established a central picture framing factory in Yokohama (*see* Annex IV. 3(b)).

Dealers entered into a formal agency agreement with EL, undertaking to purchase, on their own account, comprehensive moulding and mountboard sample boards from which customers could select their frames. In return for this negligible outlay (around US $1,000) and some investment in their own sales and product training, they received 30 per cent of the value of all orders passed to EL. For its part, EL undertook to deliver, at least in Tokyo and Yokohama, the framed pictures back to the dealer on the day following receipt of the order.

Under this system, pricing the service required especially close attention. Most picture framers, as might be expected with one- or two-man operations, have an attitude to costing which might be described as, at best, cavalier; in particular, their estimates of the value of their own time and their overhead costs are approximations, to say the least. Any such approach on a large scale would clearly be fatal; of necessity, EL devised an elaborate pricing system for use by their authorised agents. This system covers every possible combination of materials, sizes, colours, finishes and manufacturing operation: the type of moulding (wood or aluminium); the moulding cross-section; the type of mountboard and number of boards; the size of the frame; the size of the central hole cut from the mountboard to display the picture; the nature and number of decorative V-grooves required in the mountboard, if any; the method of backing and the backing material; and so on. The full Japanese price list runs to 15 pages, but, on the basis of it, the agent can assist the end customer to select exactly what he wants from all possible alternatives and to know exactly what each alternative will cost him. It organises not merely the prices but the whole customer satisfaction process down, as EL put it, to the last comma.

The appointment of the instant lettering dealers as agents proved to be the turning point in EL picture frame sales in Japan. Business soared, a number of picture framers applied to join the original 150 agents, and EL now has a total of 250 agents.

Demand was such that it soon became necessary to set up two new factories, in Osaka and Fukuoka. These factories, offering nothing but one-off products, all with a next-day delivery guarantee, must, EL believe, be unique in the world.

Germany

The founder of Nielsen USA, who had sold the American company to EL, had also established in the early 1980s in partnership with a German national a company in north Germany, with a view to the manufacture of aluminium picture frame mouldings, then a product new to most of Europe. Success in Germany was immediate and sales subsidiaries were soon established in France and Sweden. In December 1987 EL, encouraged by the success achieved by Nielsen USA despite the distribution channel problem, acquired Nielsen Germany and its subsidiaries.

As a new company, offering a product new to the market and with no direct competitors, Nielsen had seen its main task as the conversion of picture framers to the view that aluminium mouldings were a desirable, even exciting, alternative to the traditional wood mouldings. A direct sales approach seemed an essential part of this process, but in fact, after the product had been on display at a number of exhibitions, sales took off to such an extent that a sales force, for the time being at least, hardly seemed necessary. The new product had caught the tide of fashion.

This happy state of affairs could hardly be expected to continue for long and EL, once it had bought the company, began to look towards strengthening the sales effort. There were in Germany no established specialist distributors of picture framing materials, though for reasons of logistics the earlier management had appointed a distributor in Bavaria. EL bought this distributor in 1990, but otherwise concentrated on building up a sales force selling direct to framers (*see* Annex IV. 3(c)).

The decision to sell direct brought EL up against the usual problem: the economics of personal selling to large numbers of very small companies with a very limited range of products. To widen the range EL bought Teichert, the main German manufacturer of mountboard, which also offered a range of wood mouldings. Bainbridge mountboard was imported from the USA and distributed by Nielsen. The opportunity was taken to add a range of machinery for the precision cutting of mountboard, glass and plastic manufactured by C&H, a US company acquired by EL in 1985.

At the same time EL was extending its original aluminium moulding range in terms of design, colour and surface finish, and developing entirely new products: for example, the gallery hanging system, a simple yet sophisticated way of hanging large numbers of pictures, and an ingenious security screw system which prevents the theft of pictures on display. Nielsen also offered complete ready-made frames for department stores and for display on framers' premises, with a view to sales from impulse purchases or gift buying.

Still with the economics of personal direct selling in mind, EL introduced in Germany and other European countries what they describe as their 'chop service'. Under this service, originally introduced in the USA, mouldings are supplied not in stock lengths but already mitre-cut to the specified frame size, thus relieving the framer of one of his more difficult tasks and, at the same time, considerably reducing wastage. The service is offered with next-day or 48-hour delivery, which in return relieves the framer of the need to carry stock, giving that significant saving in working capital which is always of special importance in small businesses. The price per foot of the chop service is, of course, higher than that for moulding in stock lengths, so that added value is considerably increased. Germany offers much greater scope for the expansion of the chop service than does the USA, where distributors also offer the service, so that EL must be sensitive to the danger of competing with its own customers.

Regular training courses are held for framers: for new entrants to the business the courses provide training in basic techniques and the use of framing equipment; for experienced framers the courses cover new product developments.

In short, the product range has been constantly widened and upgraded, with the interest of the customer, the framer, constantly in mind. A sales force of around a dozen can now be economically justified. That sales force, coupled with a high-quality product and competent product marketing, has more than proved its worth: sales in Germany are now, in 1992, two and a half times higher than they were prior to the takeover by EL. Nielsen still have over 80 per cent of the German market for aluminium mouldings and the only serious competition is from products imported by the local sales subsidiary of an American company.

Conclusion

World-wide, EL has, over some ten years, successfully converted from an instant lettering business in serious decline into one that has 50 per cent of its turnover in picture framing materials; instant lettering now, in 1992, accounts for no more than 6 per cent of turnover.

Reviewing those ten years, EL's Planning and Development Manager, Jerry Waters, attributed the company's success to its high product quality, its marketing skills and, in particular, its close attention to distribution channel strategy and management in every country in which it operates.

'We've made mistakes, of course,' he added, 'most notably in the USA. Our most serious error was perhaps not so much the decision to transfer the Nielsen direct sales business to distributors as to attempt to impose indiscriminately that one single solution for the whole of the country, and for products where the logistics were quite different. We ought to have examined the problems on the ground, region by region and product by product. There will always be areas of the USA where we will happily remain reliant on distributors, but there is no doubt that in other areas the transfer of the Nielsen business was a mistake and it will now be a very long time before we can put matters right.

'Japan was a special case. Our very formal Japanese organisation really takes the US chop service to its logical conclusion, and it has proved highly successful. Can the Japanese experience be repeated elsewhere? I would say no. But perhaps there are lessons to be learnt from Japan that might be of relevance in other countries.

'In Germany, of course, we started from scratch and the whole distribution system went like a dream. If there is such a thing as a model distribution system for our business, then the German system must come pretty close to it. Not that we're satisfied, even there. We're always reviewing our marketing, especially distribution, and I'm sure there are improvements still to be made, particularly at the sharp end.'

THE BAINBRIDGE RANGE

Bainbridge Standard

Strict specification of raw-materials and on going quality control are your assurance that Bainbridge Standard is top quality compared to other mountboards. Bainbridge is made from top quality wood pulp, which guarantees creamy, speck free bevels with the smoothest cut ever experienced.

Our board is produced to an alkaline pH and is then buffered with calcium carbonate to slow the process of natural deterioration.

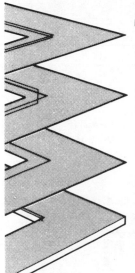

Black by Bainbridge

This is the Mountboard with the black middle and backing, to help you cut a distinctive line around any picture. With Black by Bainbridge, the edge you cut is not only clean and crisp, it is well defined thanks to its deep black core. The black line surrounding the inside of the mount draws the eye directly to the centre of the picture, enhancing overall presentation.

Nothing goes better with Black by Bainbridge than our wide range of distinctly coloured facing papers. Both the core and the facing papers are 100% pigmented to resist fading or bleeding.

HT Colour

The HT Colour Collection takes the Black by Bainbridge range one step further by offering the framer 4 additional core options. The spectacular combination of colour cores and surface papers will guarantee to match and harmonise any type of artwork.

Speciality Mountboards

Foils and pebbled surfaces create a unique and fashionable look that will appeal to your discerning customer. With our three shiny foils and our six double sided pebble boards, creating the unusual and the original will become your speciality, too.

Alphamat (Museum Quality) Mountboard

No-one in the world can offer you a range to compete with Alphamat, a museum quality mountboard in a range of over 100 colours.

ALPHAMAT is completely alkaline in composition, containing no acidic or degrading elements in either middle board, surface paper or backing paper.

A unique and important feature of the Alphamat range is its ability to offer your customers total protection against bleeding and fading of their chosen mount colour, through its use only of pigments for surface colouring.

Annex IV.1 *Part of the Bainbridge mountboard range.*

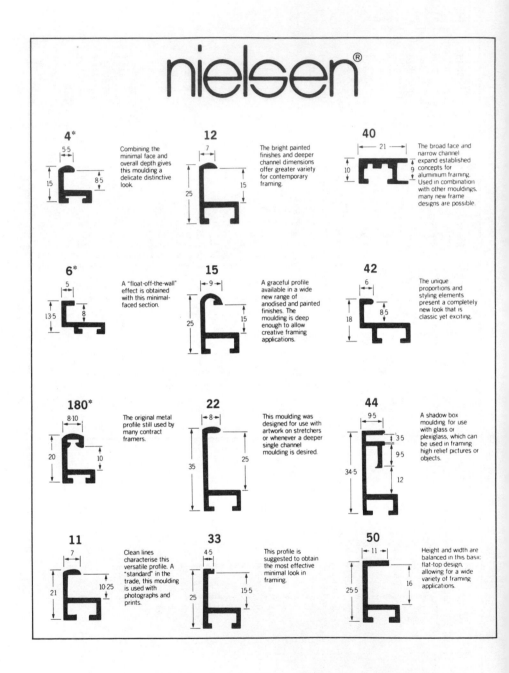

nielsen®

4*

5·5
15
8·5

Combining the minimal face and overall depth gives this moulding a delicate distinctive look.

12

7
25
15

The bright painted finishes and deeper channel dimensions offer greater variety for contemporary framing.

40

21
10
9

The broad face and narrow channel expand established concepts for aluminium framing. Used in combination with other mouldings, many new frame designs are possible.

6*

5
13·5
8

A "float-off-the-wall" effect is obtained with this minimal-faced section.

15

9
25
15

A graceful profile available in a wide new range of anodised and painted finishes. The moulding is deep enough to allow creative framing applications.

42

6
18
8·5

The unique proportions and styling elements present a completely new look that is classic yet exciting.

180*

8·10
20
10

The original metal profile still used by many contract framers.

22

8
35
25

This moulding was designed for use with artwork on stretchers or whenever a deeper single channel moulding is desired.

44

9·5
3·5
9·5
34·5
12

A shadow box moulding for use with glass or plexiglass, which can be used in framing high relief pictures or objects.

11

7
21
10·25

Clean lines characterise this versatile profile. A "standard" in the trade, this moulding is used with photographs and prints.

33

4·5
25
15·5

This profile is suggested to obtain the most effective minimal look in framing.

50

11
25·5
16

Height and width are balanced in this basic flat-top design, allowing for a wide variety of framing applications.

Annex IV.2 *A selection from the Nielsen aluminium profile specifier.*

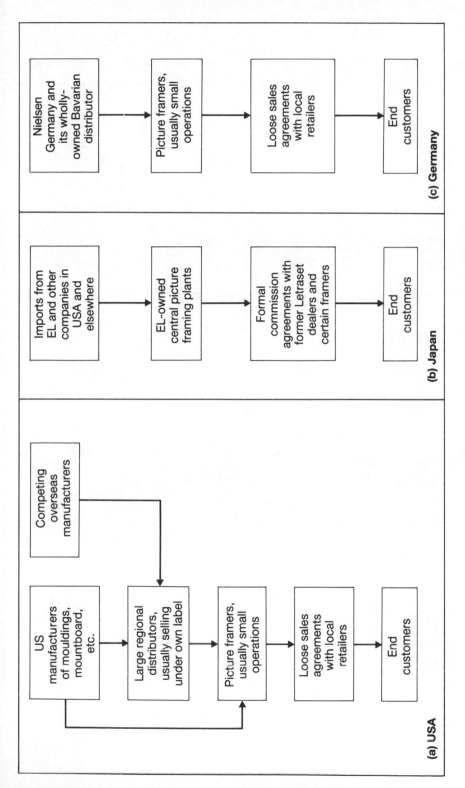

Annex IV.3 *Esselte Letraset Ltd: distribution channels for picture framing materials.*

niels⊖n

The Veneer Collection	**The Oakwoods**
	Collection

Profile 401

Code	Description
	Matt finish
40115	Poplar
40116	Elm
40117	Walnut
40118	Mahogany
	Gloss finish
40145	Burgundy poplar
40146	Natural poplar
40147	Blue poplar
40151	Green poplar
40155	Grey poplar

Oakwoods Profile 82		Oakwoods Profile 86	
220	Black Oak	220	Black Oak
221	White Oak	221	White Oak
222	Red Oak	222	Red Oak
223	Cherry Gold Oak	223	Cherry Gold Oak
224	Dark Oak	224	Dark Oak
225	Gold Dust Oak	225	Gold Dust Oak
226	Medium Oak	226	Medium Oak
227	Natural Oak	227	Natural Oak
228	Blue Grey Oak	228	Blue Grey Oak
229	Pink Oak	229	Pink Oak

A choice of two contemporary profiles, providing a most unusual solution in natural oak framing - equally suited to both modern and traditional pieces.

Profile 402

	Matt finish
40215	Poplar
40216	Elm
40217	Walnut
40218	Mahogany

Profile 403

	Matt finish
40315	Poplar
40316	Elm
40317	Walnut
40318	Mahogany

Nielsen Veneers are a new range of mouldings designed to complement both traditional prints and contemporary art.

Four natural finishes are available in three sizes using the finest poplar, elm, walnut and mahogany and a traditional satin matt lacquer.

A new tradition

Our new range of solid oak mouldings heralds a revival in the fine tradition of wooden frame making. The Oakwoods range features the classic appeal of natural oak, hand finished by craftsmen. Brought to you in a choice of two profiles and ten finishes, this superb range fulfils the current demand for stylish simplicity.

Consistent quality

Unique to Nielsen, this new collection has been painstakingly sourced to ensure guaranteed consistency of finish. Top priority was also given to conservation of the world's forests in our choice of supply, leading us to our final selection of a well-managed and sustainable source.

Annex IV.4 *Part of the Nielsen wood mouldings range: veneers and solid oak.*

Case study V

CompAir Ltd: Entry into the West German market

1. Introductory note

This case study outlines the various steps taken by CompAir Ltd prior to its successful entry into the West German market for air compressors, and compressed-air road tools and industrial hand tools.

The study may simply be read straight through as an account of one company's market-entry operation. Alternatively, the reader may like to pause at each case problem and prepare his own solution before considering the action taken by CompAir. Purely technical data have been largely omitted and certain market data have necessarily been simplified. Nevertheless, the problems outlined in the case study are those actually faced, and the reader has available all the data necessary to arrive at an independent solution. The CompAir decisions are those actually taken in the light of the inevitable financial constraints on research and other expenditure; they are not put forward as the theoretical ideal.

2. The company

CompAir Ltd is a major group of companies which resulted mainly from the merger of the two leading UK companies in the compressed-air field, Broom and Wade Ltd and Holman Bros. Both these companies were already heavily engaged in international operations.

The merger gave rise to a global review of the new group's existing marketing activities and to the examination of a number of possible new market opportunities. One such opportunity, it seemed, was West Germany, where it was decided to undertake a detailed market investigation.

3. The products

The products for which it was thought potential existed in West Germany were:

(a) mobile air compressors of the type used by construction companies and civil engineering contractors, which can be seen on any major building site and at any road repair operation;

(b) road tools, known in the trade as road breakers, but more popularly known as pneumatic drills – such tools are, of course, normally powered by compressed air from mobile air compressors;

(c) high-output stationary air compressors of the kind installed by major manufacturing companies as a central source of power for compressed-air equipment of all kinds;

(d) industrial hand tools, which consist of a compressed-air motor, hand grip and a tool, usually interchangeable, and often consisting of a simple drill, screwdriver or spanner. Such tools are normally powered from the stationary air compressors already described, and are used in assembly line operations.

The four product lines are illustrated in Annex V. 1. All require servicing and repair facilities.

CompAir knew from its experience in other markets that road tools and mobile compressors were frequently sold through distributors, whereas stationary compressors of the size relevant to the survey were bought as major capital items intended for plant expansion or new factories direct from manufacturers. Distribution arrangements for hand tools varied from one market to the next. In West Germany, of course, distribution arrangements would not necessarily follow the general pattern.

4.   Marketing situation

CompAir had no experience of, or information on, the West German market for these products. The board decided to authorise a market survey, and Norman Burden, Director of Group Marketing, sat down to draft out the terms of reference. Well aware of the extensive and diffuse nature of the markets to be investigated, and of how easy it might be, as a result, to incur heavy and often unnecessary expenditure on research information of only marginal value, he decided:

(a) that no information would be sought that would not influence subsequent marketing action;

(b) that, as regards quantitative estimates, particular care would be taken not to demand an unnecessary degree of precision.

5.   Major user industries

It was already known, from previous experience in other markets, that the major user industries included:

(a) for mobile compressors and road tools, the construction industry, mining and quarrying;

(b) for stationary compressors and industrial hand-tools, car and commercial vehicle manufacture;

(c) for stationary compressors only, food processing.

Case problem 1

Prepare summary terms of reference for the market investigation in West Germany. In the case of quantitative estimates consider the required

breakdown by market segment and the required degree of precision. Where you think it appropriate, indicate the reasons for your inclusion (or exclusion) of a particular item of information. The purely technical aspects of the investigation may be ignored.

6. Terms of reference for the market investigation

The terms of reference for the market investigation, as decided by CompAir, are summarised below.

Scope
The survey would cover the four products already discussed. Initially the survey would cover only the major user industries already known, from experience in other markets, to offer real potential. The survey was to cover the whole of West Germany. Initial market entry on a regional basis was not in this case practicable, since some of the products were not only mobile or portable, and, therefore, likely to be moved regularly from one construction site to another, but also required servicing and repair. Servicing facilities at least, therefore, would need to be on a nationwide basis.

Market size
Market size estimates would be required for each of the survey industries, with a cross-breakdown by the relevant survey products, as shown in Annex V. 2. A geographical breakdown of market size would not be necessary, for the reasons already indicated.

Degree of precision
The assessment of market size often presents some difficulty in industrial market research, at least in markets as vast and diffuse as construction and food processing: in such industries it is simply not economically possible to prepare a valid sampling frame (a list of names and addresses of all or-ganisations relevant to the survey) from which a probability sample can be taken. Under these circumstances, insistence on a specific degree of precision can only lead to a vast increase in research expenditure rarely justified by the value of the information obtained. Burden reasoned that at this stage all he required was a clear and definite indication of a minimum market size sufficient to enable CompAir to achieve significant turnover and profit with-out the need to capture an excessively high market share.

Forecasts
Forecasts would be required for each major user industry.

Market shares
Identification of the leading suppliers, both domestic and foreign, to each major user industry was essential, together with some indication of their relative importance. Percentage market share figures would not be required,

as they would be of little value in the preparation of the marketing plan, and would in this market be inordinately expensive to obtain.

Distribution
A detailed analysis of the present accepted distribution channels would be essential.

Prices
Prices would be required in each product group, related to specific competing products. Distributor margins, discounts and credit terms would also need to be investigated.

Promotion
Competitors' promotional activities were to be investigated in as much detail as possible, with particular emphasis on:

(a) the more usual advertising media;
(b) the importance of exhibitions;
(c) the extent to which distributors were relied upon for promotional activity by the manufacturer.

Market entry
Burden decided that, even at the research stage, mere fact-finding was not enough: the research ought also to generate ideas on the critical subject of market entry. With this in mind he would require the research consultants to report on:

(a) possible areas of user dissatisfaction or market need;
(b) possible innovation in distribution (e.g. the extent to which plant hire was established in West Germany as an alternative method of distribution);
(c) the practicability of acquisition of distributors, thus ensuring control of distribution channels;
(d) possible cooperation with compressor manufacturers (licensing, or reciprocal distribution of non-competing product ranges);
(e) possible acquisition of compressor manufacturers.

7.   Desk research

Burden's next step was to carry out a thorough programme of desk research both in the UK and in West Germany. This revealed a published survey giving complete market size figures, with appropriate breakdowns and forecasts. These figures showed an unexpectedly high market potential and growth rate in all the industries selected as being of interest.

The investigation now became largely qualitative. Designing the research programme, however, still presented a number of problems, which Burden discussed with three different firms of research consultants.

Case problem 2

Design the research programme covering the qualitative items of the terms of reference laid down by Burden. As always, the research design should aim, in its overall strategy, at achieving maximum value (in terms of information of value to the marketing plan) for every pound spent on research. More specifically, it should also consider the composition of the sample, sample size and sampling methods, and the extent of use of the (expensive) personal interview. Bear in mind that a good deal of technical information is to be sought from end-users, even though, for simplicity, the details have been omitted from this case study.

8. Research design

Overall strategy
The research was to cover four different and complex product ranges, in four different industries, two of which have already been described as 'vast and diffuse'.

Some of the qualitative information could have been analysed on a quantitative basis, as in consumer research (e.g. *x* per cent of informants in the construction industry were dissatisfied with present servicing and repair arrangements). Burden believed, however, that this would be a facile and over-simplified approach. He regarded it as essential to probe fully the reasons for informants' replies and to obtain full details of their past experiences. Technical problems demanded, in any case, a similar in-depth approach.

In these circumstances, it was clear that a considerable number of personal interviews was required; yet it was difficult to decide *how* many. Burden decided on a two-stage approach:

(a) an initial stage, based entirely on personal interviews;
(b) a second stage, perhaps relying principally on telephone interviewing and postal questionnaires, designed to cover those points left in doubt on completion of the first stage.

In this way initial research expenditure could be kept within reasonable limits while subsequent expenditure could be redirected, in the light of the market information then obtained, where it would be most needed.

Sample
End-user organisations, CompAir's potential customers, would, of course, need to be contacted in all four of the industries relevant to the survey.

End-user organisations alone, however, could not provide a complete picture of the market. It would be essential to interview also: component suppliers (principally the manufacturers of petrol and diesel engines supplied to mobile compressor manufacturers), manufacturers of compressors, road tools and industrial hand-tools (i.e. competitors), and distributors.

In other words, it would be necessary, as with many industrial market research projects, to direct the interviews along the whole chain of demand. The composition of the sample is shown diagrammatically in Annex V. 3.

Sample size

Certain categories of informants were limited in number and all could be interviewed (i.e. a census would be undertaken, not a sampling operation); these included engine manufacturers, competitors, and the car and commercial vehicle industry.

In the case of distributors and the remaining end-user industries, interviewing was to concentrate on the major companies only. (In most industries it will be found that the vast bulk of both purchases and sales are accounted for by a very small number of enterprises.)

The sample size clearly had to cover all major segments of the market adequately, the critical factor being the number of companies of significance in the end-user industries, other than car and commercial vehicle manufacturers. A total of 100 interviews was eventually decided upon. It was recognised that this figure was to some extent arbitrary, but it was certainly a minimum, and it could always be extended at the end of the initial stage.

9.   Research findings

Both the planned stages of the assignment were undertaken. The first stage provided most of the required information; the second stage was limited in scope and is not further considered here. The findings of both stages are summarised below.

All products

It was found in the case of all products that the CompAir range could meet all local technical and legal regulations and was acceptable to all end users, and that CompAir delivered prices in West Germany would be broadly competitive with other suppliers, but would offer no significant price advantage.

Mobile compressors

Four competitors were found to share 75 per cent of the total market as shown in Annex V.4.

All competitors except competitor B sold through independent distributors. Competitor B sold mainly through its own network of sales and service branches but was beginning to develop sales through independent distributors as well.

Distributors could be divided into two main categories: the traditional construction industry distributors dealing in all kinds of construction equipment and plant, and newly developing specialist distributors of compressed air equipment known as 'air houses'. These latter, however, were limited in number and size.

Distributors did not sell on an exclusive representation basis. Most carried two manufacturers' product lines. They expected, and received, very high discounts from manufacturers on large quantity purchases.

Plant hire was virtually unknown. There was some feeling among informants that it was alien to the German character.

Apart from the obvious factor of price, reliability was of the utmost importance, coupled with the prompt supply of replacement parts when breakdowns did occur. All competitors provided a remarkably efficient service, with the exception of competitor C, which had clearly jeopardised its future prospects in the market.

Purchasers usually endeavoured, though not always with success, to standardise on not more than two makes of compressor, and the products currently available in the market were regarded in all cases as completely satisfactory from a technical viewpoint.

A strong preference was expressed for engines of West German manufacture; about half of the informants felt German-made engines were absolutely essential.

Personal selling was heavily relied upon. There was evidence of some direct mail, but little media advertising.

Road tools

It was not possible to be confident on the question of market shares. Nevertheless, leading competitors included the four companies already mentioned as suppliers of mobile compressors, plus two specialist manufacturers of road tools only.

Otherwise, as might be expected, the market followed very much the pattern of the mobile compressor market.

Stationary compressors

Again, it was not possible to establish market shares. Leading manufacturers, however, were competitors A, B and C (all also involved in the manufacture of mobile compressors) and one other specialist manufacturer of stationary compressors only.

Distribution was almost invariably direct from manufacturer to end-user.

Cost, reliability and prompt supply of replacement parts were again critical factors.

Industrial hand-tools

Leading suppliers were competitors B and C (both also involved in the manufacture of mobile compressors) and three specialist manufacturers.

Distribution was both direct and by specialist distributors. These distributors did not operate on an exclusive dealing basis, but usually concentrated on one or two makes only, so as to take maximum advantage of the very high quantity discounts offered by manufacturers.

Case problem 3

In the light of the information given, decide on the most appropriate market entry strategy for CompAir. Consider the two principal alternatives: independent market entry, or some form of cooperation with, or acquisition of, a competitor. In both cases give particular importance to the problem of distribution. Justify your decisions for or against each course of action considered.

10. Market entry strategy

General

The size and growth rate of the market, coupled with the technical acceptability and price-competitiveness of the whole CompAir range, made West Germany, prima facie, a particularly attractive market.

Nevertheless, the overall impression could only be one of a market well catered for. There were some areas of competitor weakness (e.g. in replacement parts) and perhaps some scope for innovation (e.g. in plant hire) but these were not significant. In particular:

(a) although the CompAir products could meet all local technical standards and compared favourably with competing equipment, they offered no major technical advantage;

(b) although reasonably competitive on price, there was little scope for major price reductions, and in any case Burden regarded price wars very definitely as an undesirable last resort;

(c) Burden believed that he could improve on the fairly pedestrian promotional methods of his competitors, but to prove this, as he was subsequently to do, it was first essential to secure nationwide distribution at reasonable cost.

Distribution, it seemed to him, was the key to the market. Even stationary compressors, though necessarily sold direct, would benefit from a local sales force, while local servicing and spares availability, clearly an important factor in the purchasing decision, might almost be regarded as a necessity. For all other products a sales and service network was essential.

Distribution

Distribution could be obtained by:

(a) persuading the existing independent distributors to stock and sell the products;

(b) building up an independent CompAir distribution network similar to that already established by competitor B;

(c) acquisition of some of the existing independent distributors;

(d) some form of cooperation (e.g. licensing, joint venture assembly or manufacture) with a manufacturer already established in the independent distribution chain.

Sales through the existing independent distributors were considered to offer real difficulties since:

(a) distributors were known to attempt to standardise on two makes of compressor;
(b) CompAir could offer the distributor no major product advantage;
(c) as a newcomer, CompAir could not expect to take, at least initially, large-size orders, yet would need to match the quantity discounts currently offered by competitors;
(d) although there might be some possibility of capitalising on market disaffection by endeavouring to replace competitor C in the distribution chain (which, as mentioned, had jeopardised its market position by an inadequate supply of spare parts), this was regarded as a last resort.

Establishment of an independent distribution network was a possibility, as had been proved by competitor B, but:

(a) it would involve heavy investment;
(b) return on investment would be long term, at best;
(c) CompAir believed they were likely to achieve a better rate of return on a manufacturing-based investment.

Acquisition of the traditional construction industry distributors would:

(a) again involve CompAir in heavy investment in distribution facilities;
(b) involve them also in the wider aspects of building material supply, of which they had no experience;
(c) require a succession of takeovers if national distribution was to be achieved since, as mentioned, distributors' influence was limited to specific regions;
(d) involve CompAir in handling at least one competitive product range and, probably, after several distributor takeovers in an unsatisfactory mix of competing products which it would be by no means easy to abandon.

The specialist air houses might have offered a more attractive takeover proposition, but at their then early stages of development they clearly shared some of the disadvantages of establishing an independent network.

Cooperation with a manufacturer
Under these circumstances, Burden decided that some form of cooperation with a local manufacturer was likely to be the most suitable method of market entry. He preferred a joint venture to an outright acquisition, which would involve a much greater financial outlay, but recognised that much depended on finding a willing partner and on the partner's preferences. Either method would offer both immediate distribution and local assembly facilities for the inclusion of German engines in the CompAir mobile compressors.

Burden set down his criteria for the ideal partner company:

(a) it must be small enough to enable CompAir to be the dominant partner in the venture, or to acquire it if necessary;

(b) it must, nevertheless, have a sufficient market share in the mobile compressor and road tool market to have achieved effective distribution on a national basis;

(c) on the other hand, its mobile compressor and road tool manufacturing facilities should not be too extensive, the aim after all, being the export of CompAir's production to West Germany;

(d) its product range should otherwise be complementary rather than competitive with CompAir's and, ideally, it would not manufacture stationary compressors at all;

(e) it must have an unblemished reputation in the market-place.

It will be clear from an examination of even the abridged market data given that competitor D most nearly approached the ideal, while competitor A offered a reasonable alternative.

11. Market entry

Both competitors D and A were approached and the acquisition route was eventually followed.

CompAir (Deutschland) GmbH was established at a newly completed headquarters strategically located alongside the motorway network on the northern outskirts of Cologne. The premises embraced extensive assembly, repair and servicing facilities, a central spare parts warehouse, and marketing and administrative support for a national network of company sales and service engineers and independent distributors.

12. Updating note

CompAir is now, in 1992, a division of Siebe PLC, one of the world's one hundred largest multinational companies. The German operation is an important part of the division's activities.

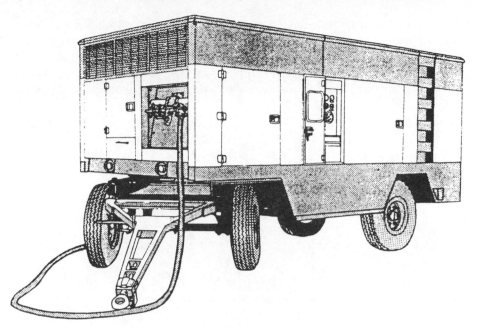

(a) Mobile air compressor

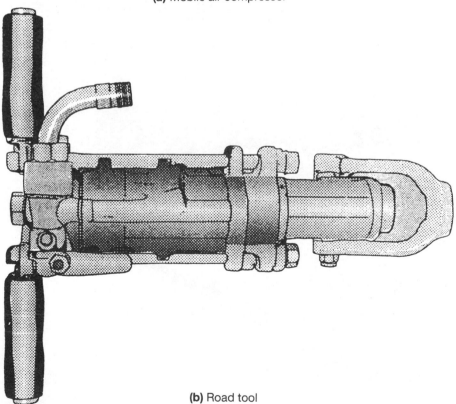

(b) Road tool

Annex V.1 *CompAir's product lines.*

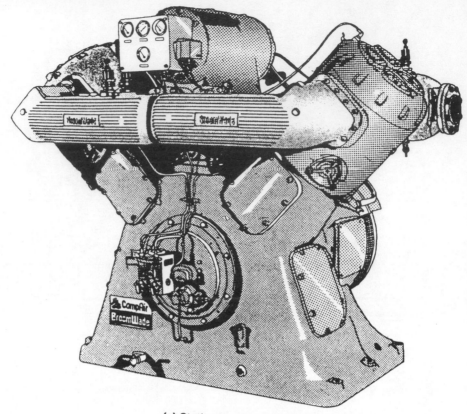

(c) Stationary air compressor

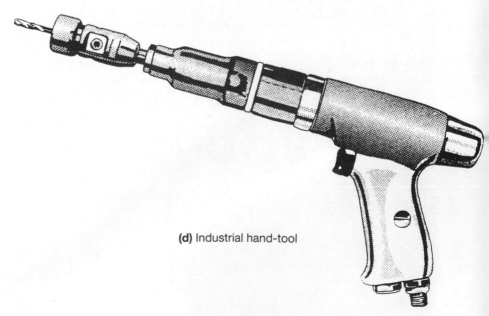

(d) Industrial hand-tool

Annex V.1 *Continued*

PRODUCT / INDUSTRY	Road tools	Mobile compressors	Hand tools	Stationary compressors
Construction			▓	▓
Mining and quarrying			▓	▓
Car and commercial vehicle manufacture	▓	▓		
Food processing	▓	▓	▓	

☐ REQUIRED   ▓ NOT REQUIRED

Annex V.2 *CompAir Ltd research terms of reference: market size breakdown required.*

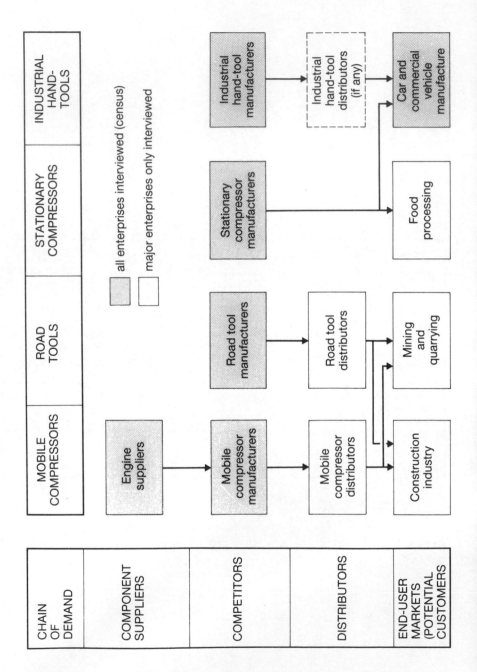

Annex V.3 *CompAir Ltd research design: composition of the sample.*

Competitor	Competitor's manufacturing base	Share of market (%)
A	W. German	23
B	Multinational	20
C	Multinational	17
D	W. German	15
Total		75

Annex V.4 *CompAir's competitors.*

Appendix I

Bibliography

Alexander, Ralph S. *et al.*, *Marketing Definitions: A Glossary of Marketing Terms*, American Marketing Association, 1960.

Ash, B., *Tiger in your Tank*, Cassell, 1969.

Bonoma, Thomas V. and Shapiro, Benson P., *Segmenting the Industrial Market*, Lexington Books, 1983.

Brazell, D. E., *Manufacturing under Licence*, Kenneth Mason, 1968; *Licensing Checklists*, 2nd edition, Kenneth Mason, 1974.

Brooke, Michael Z. and Remmers, H. Lee, *The Strategy of Multinational Enterprise: Organisation and Finance*, Longman, 1970.

Cateora, Philip R., *International Marketing*, Richard D. Irwin, 1983.

Cundiff, Edward W. and Hilger, Marye T., *Marketing in the International Environment*, 2nd edition, Prentice-Hall, 1988.

Czinkota, Michael R., and Ronkainen, Ilkka A., *International Marketing*, 2nd edition, Dryden Press, 1988.

Douglas, Susan P. and Craig, C. Samuel, *International Marketing Research*, Prentice-Hall, 1983.

Engel, James F., Blackwell, Roger D. and Kollat, David T., *Consumer Behaviour*, 3rd edition, Dryden Press, 1978.

Fayerweather, John, *International Marketing*, 2nd edition, Prentice-Hall, 1970.

Ferber, Robert (ed.), *Handbook of Marketing Research*, McGraw Hill, 1974.

Frank, R. E., Massy, W. F. and Wind, Y., *Market Segmentation*, Prentice-Hall, 1972.

International Chamber of Commerce: *Rules of Conciliation and Arbitration*, 1988; *Incoterms*, 1990; *Managing Exchange Rate Risks*, 1991; *Commercial Agency: Guide for the Drawing up of Contracts*, 1991.

ITI Research, *Concentration on Key Markets: A Development Plan for Exports* (the Betro Report), Betro Trust Committee of the Royal Society of Arts, 1977.

Jain, Subhash C., *International Marketing Management*, 3rd edition, PWS-Kent, 1990.

Jeannet, Jean Pierre and Hennessey, Hubert D., *International Marketing Management*, Houghton Mifflin, 1988.

Keegan, Warren J., *Multinational Marketing Management*, 3rd edition, Prentice-Hall, 1984.

Kolde, Endel J., *International Business Enterprise*, 2nd edition, Prentice-Hall, 1973.

Kollat, David T., Blackwell, Roger D. and Robeson, James F., *Strategic Marketing*, Holt, Rinehart & Winston, 1972.

Kotler, P., *Marketing Management: Analysis, Planning and Control*, 7th edition, Prentice-Hall, 1991.

Kramer, Roland L., *International Marketing*, South-Western Publishing, 1970.

McDonald, Malcolm H. B. and Cavusgil, S. T. (eds), *International Marketing Digest*, Heinemann, 1992.

McMillan, C. and Paulden, S., *Export Agents: A Complete Guide to their Selection and Control*, 2nd edition, Gower Press, 1974.

Mallen, B. (ed.), *The Marketing Channel*, John Wiley & Sons, 1975.

Majaro, Simon, *International Marketing. A Strategic Approach to World Markets*, George Allen & Unwin, 1977.

Mason, R. Hal., Miller, Robert R. and Weigel, Dale R., *The Economics of International Business*, John Wiley & Sons, 1975.

Miracle, Gordon E. and Albaum, Gerald S., *International Marketing Management*, Richard D. Irwin, 1970.

Morin, Bernard A. (ed.), *Marketing in a Changing World*, article by James C. Baker, American Marketing Association, 1969.

Murdock, George P., 'The common denominator of cultures', in *The Science of Man in the World Crises* (Linton, R. ed.), Columbia University Press, 1945.

Ohmae, Kenichi, *The Borderless World*, Collins, 1990; *Triad Power*, Collier Macmillan, 1985.

Porter, Michael E., *Competitive Strategy*, Macmillan, 1980.

Root, Franklin R., *Strategic Planning for Export Marketing*, International Textbook Company, 1966.

Royal Mail International, *Marketing without Frontiers, the RMI Guide to International Direct Marketing*, 1992.

Sharman, G. H., *Thinking Managerially – About Exports*, Institute of Export, 1971.

Stern, Louis W. and El-Ansary, Adel I., *Marketing Channels*, 2nd edition, Prentice-Hall, 1982.

Terpstra, Vern and Sarathy, Ravi, *International Marketing*, 5th edition, Dryden Press, 1991.

Young, Stephen, Hamill, James, Wheeler, Colin and Davis, J. Richard, *International Market Entry and Development*, Harvester Wheatsheaf, 1989.

NOTE: *See* also list of acknowledgements on page viii.

Appendix II

Addresses of UK organisations mentioned in the text

Arlington Management Services, Hay Hill, Berkeley Square, London W1X 7LF.

BBC World Service, Export Liaison, Bush House, Strand, London WC2B 4PH.

British Exporters Association, 16 Dartmouth Street, London SW1H 9BL.

BSCC (formerly British-Soviet Chamber of Commerce), 42 Southwark Street, London SE1 1UN.

CAM Foundation, Communication Advertising and Marketing Education Foundation Ltd, Abford House, 15 Wilton Road, London SW1V 1NJ.

The Centre for International Briefing, Farnham Castle, Surrey GU9 0AG.

Chartered Institute of Marketing, Moor Hall, Cookham, Maidenhead, Berks. SL6 9QH.

City Business Library, 1 Brewers Hall Garden, London EC2V 9BX.

Croner Publications, Croner House, London Road, Kingston-upon-Thames, Surrey KT2 6SR.

DTI Overseas Trade Services (Export Marketing Research Scheme), Association of British Chambers of Commerce, 4 Westwood House, Westwood Business Park, Coventry CV4 8HS.

Dun and Bradstreet Ltd, Holmers Farm Way, High Wycombe, Bucks. HP12 4UL.

East European Trade Council, Suite 10, Westminster Palace Gardens, Artillery Row, London SW1P 1RL.

Employment Conditions Abroad Ltd, Anchor House, 15 Britten Street, London SW3 3TY.

Euromonitor, 87–88 Turnmill Street, London EC1M 5QU.

Export Credits Guarantee Dept, 2 Exchange Tower, Harbour Exchange Square, London E14 9GS.

Export Intelligence Service (EIS), PreLink Ltd., 87a Wembley Hill Road, Wembley, Middx. HA9 8BU.

Export Market Information Centre, Ashdown House, 123 Victoria Street, London SW1E 6RB.

Exports to Japan Unit, Overseas Trade Division, Department of Trade and Industry, 1 Victoria Street, London SW1H 0ET.

IIS (International Information Services), Mintel International Group, 18–19 Long Lane, London EC1A 9HE.

International Chamber of Commerce, 14–15 Belgrave Square, London SW1X 8PS.

Institute of Export, 64 Clifton Street, London EC2A 4HB.

Japan External Trade Organisation, Leconfield House, Curzon Street, London W1Y 7FB.

London Chamber of Commerce and Industry, 69 Cannon Street, London EC4N 5AB.

Market Research Society, 15 Northburgh Street, London EC1V 0AH.

NCM Holdings (Nederlandsche Credietverzekering Maatschappij), Crown Buildings, Cathays Park, Cardiff CF1 3PX.

Price Waterhouse, 32 London Bridge Street, London SE1 9SY.

Proplan, The Red House, Clare Park, Amersham, Bucks. HP7 9HW.

Rainbow Commercial Centre Ltd, Bridgewater Way, Windsor, Berks. SL4 1RD.

Royal Mail International, 12–15 Fenton Way, Basildon SS15 4BR.

Science Reference Library and Business Information Service, 25 Southampton Buildings, Chancery Lane, London WC2A 1AW.

Technical Help to Exporters (THE), British Standards Institute, Linford Wood, Milton Keynes MK14 6LE.

Trade Indemnity PLC, 12–34 Great Eastern Street, London EC2A 3AX.

World Aid Section, Projects and Export Policy Division, Department of Trade and Industry, 1 Victoria Street, London SW1H 0ET.

Appendix III
Examination technique

1. Introduction
This appendix is concerned not with examination techniques in general but specifically with examinations in international marketing.

2. Syllabus
The first essential is to obtain your own copy of the examination syllabus, to read it carefully as a basis for the initial planning of your study programme, and to refer to it regularly as your studies proceed. You must be sure that you are covering the syllabus laid down by your particular examining body, and only that syllabus.

Too many students rely, in this respect, on their tutors: it is, after all, the tutors' duty to adhere to the requirements of the syllabus. Even the most conscientious tutor, however, may have to suit his tuition to the pace of his class, and he may never reach areas of the syllabus in which you have a particular interest. In examinations there is no substitute for self-reliance.

3. Past examination papers and reports
Similarly, you should obtain copies of previous (recent) examination papers and study them with care. At the very least you will gain some idea of what to expect.

Some examining bodies publish examiners' reports. These, too, will give you a very good idea of what the examiners expect of you, and will usually indicate some special pitfalls to be avoided.

4. Factual questions
Some examination papers include questions which require merely a factual answer. If you have learnt the facts, then such questions are a gift. You can usually improve your answers, however, by including brief and relevant examples. Ideally these examples would come from your own experience, but they may also be drawn from your own wider reading of newspapers, trade and professional journals and textbooks.

International Marketing, quite deliberately, has included a large number of examples.

5. Questions demanding analytical thought
Marketing is a practical subject: the art of the marketing manager is the application of marketing theory to practical business situations. Any market-

ing examination worth taking will include a number of questions which require the student to apply his knowledge to a specific business problem. In international marketing that problem might typically include references to a particular product, a particular country, or both.

Do not be put off if you are unfamiliar with the product. So many candidates, with widely different business backgrounds, are sitting the examination that no examiner can reasonably expect more than a layman's knowledge of any particular product area. Reference to a specific product will rarely do more than identify the relevant areas of marketing theory. For instance, a reference to research on biscuits would merely indicate consumer, rather than industrial, research techniques.

The position is rather different, however, when specific countries are named. In a paper devoted to international marketing, it is perfectly reasonable to expect candidates to display some familiarity with the special problems associated with at least the countries of major potential. A CIM paper, for instance, included three questions – out of ten – which required a knowledge of marketing within the EC, Eastern Europe and Latin America; in all three cases the examiners' report deplored the candidates' failure to display any real awareness of the specific problems involved in each area. Sometimes, too, questions ask you to illustrate your answers by reference 'to a country of your choice'. Again, your own experience can be an invaluable support, but if that experience is limited, then a careful study of Part four of this book is likely to pay off.

But, for questions of this type, the essential knowledge is no more than the start: you still have to prove your ability to apply that knowledge. It is here that practice will help. Written answers, assessed and commented on by your tutor, are the ideal, but they are inevitably time-consuming. The questions at the end of each chapter of this book may provide a useful supplement or alternative to written work. To gain the greatest benefit from these questions, learn the chapters first (do not merely read through them) and then frame the answers to each question at least mentally, and perhaps by jotting down the salient points. In this way you can develop your powers of analytical thought and at the same time fix the facts more firmly in your mind.

6.   Case studies

Again with the emphasis on the practical application of marketing theory, certain examining bodies, such as the Chartered Institute of Marketing, include a compulsory case study in their international marketing examination. Case study practice in preparation for examinations of this nature will stand you in good stead. Case studies are inevitably, of course, also a test of your wider knowledge of general marketing theory, even when they are set in an international context.

International Marketing includes five case studies. One of these, CompAir Ltd, is in several stages, and is specifically designed to assist the independent student.

Index